By the same author

The Social and Cultural Setting of the 1890s
John Galsworthy the Dramatist
Comedy and Tragedy
Sean O'Casey: A Bibliography of Criticism
A Bibliography of Modern Irish Drama 1899–1970
Dissertations on Anglo-Irish Drama: A Bibliography of Studies
    1870–1970
The Sting and the Twinkle: Conversations with Sean O'Casey (*co-editor
    with John O'Riordan*)

J. M. SYNGE: A BIBLIOGRAPHY OF CRITICISM

J. M. SYNGE

A Bibliography of Criticism

E. H. Mikhail

Professor of English Literature
University of Lethbridge, Canada

Foreword by
Robin Skelton
Professor of English
University of Victoria, British Columbia

ROWMAN AND LITTLEFIELD
TOTOWA, NEW JERSEY

First published in the United States 1975
by Rowman and Littlefield, Totowa, N.J.

First published in the United Kingdom 1975
by The Macmillan Press Ltd

Library of Congress Cataloging in Publication Data

Mikhail, E   H
    J. M. Synge: a bibliography of criticism.

    1.   Synge, John Millington, 1871-1909—Bibliography.
Z8857.8M54   016.822'9'12   73-23006
ISBN 0-87471-513-X

Printed in Great Britain

To my Wife

Contents

Contents

Foreword by Robin Skelton

The amount of information given in this volume is a clear indication of the interest that the work of J. M. Synge has aroused over the years. Even a brief scrutiny of the titles of the various articles and critical works reveals the way in which Synge's work has aroused an extraordinary variety of reactions. Synge, indeed, is a Shakespearean figure in that he, like Shakespeare, had been used in the service of a wide variety of causes. We can find critics who use him to maintain the importance of Irish Nationalism; we can find others who use him as an exemplar of the European Sensibility. He has been viewed as primarily a satirist, as essentially a romantic, as a thoroughgoing realist, and as the most subtle of symbolists. *The Aran Islands* has been lauded as an exact portrayal of an important aspect of Irish life and tradition, and as a deeply personal piece of myth-making. *The Playboy of the Western World* has aroused almost as much controversy as *Hamlet*, and a good deal more political disturbance.

It is not only the work but also the personality of Synge which present problems of this kind. Here again we find differing views. How can we reconcile the tough-minded, harsh-tongued Synge of some of the more 'brutal' poems with the anxious, jealous, neurotic writer of the letters to Molly? How can we reconcile the author of the *Letter to a Hedge Schoolmaster* with the man who adored the Irish language? How can we, even, reconcile the anarchist (or at least socialist) opinions implied by many essays, with those of others which reveal a nostalgia for the days of the 'Big House' and how bring together the anarchism and the elitism?

The problem of seeing Synge clear and of seeing him whole has been intensified by the accidents of history. Until the nineteen-sixties, when the Oxford University Press edition of his work began to come off the presses, we had no texts of half his poems, and only a hint or two about many of his early essays into drama. The Greene and Stevens biography emerged fifty years after the writer's death, and this has been followed by a number of books in which additional biographical information has been given, as well as several collections of letters many of which were unknown to the biographers. As a consequence of this, much relating to Synge remains to be discussed. His political views have only been touched upon gingerly, possibly because it is difficult to fit him into any acceptable party or category. His lifelong (almost) obsession with the Muse-like figure of the inspiring and shaping woman has not yet received due attention. (One should recall here that Petrarch first saw Laura in a green gown, that Synge called one of his earliest lady friends in Paris, La Robe Verte, and translated Petrarch towards the end of his life, and that green is the colour of Ireland.) Much, indeed, remains to ponder over and to comment upon, but no fresh investigation can be begun without a close examination of all that has been said so far.

It is here that this book is of such enormous value. It directs us, with clarity and precision, to all the most significant and symptomatic reactions to the work of Synge. It enables us to begin to see how the criticism of Synge has been distorted by political enthusiasms, by personal prejudice, and by the changing perspectives of history. It does not, of course, give us everything we could possibly need. We are not provided with a check-list of the translations of Synge's work, and are thus deprived of an accurate insight into Synge's significance as a world figure. It does not give us the detailed information that could only be provided by a full-dress bibliography of of Synge's works. These are two matters which fall outside its province, and rightly so. This book is not intended to do our work for us, but to direct us to work that is yet to be done. It is less a conclusive summary than a compulsive summons, and it is to be hoped that when the time for a second edition comes around there will be many more entries reflecting the way in which the first one has directed and assisted us towards the further exploration of an author whose works and personality remain significant, not only to

Foreword

the history of Anglo-Irish literature and drama but also to the
continuing exploration of the human condition.

ROBIN SKELTON

University of Victoria
British Columbia

Preface

In 1971, the J. M. Synge Centennial celebrations showed the wide attention this playwright continues to command. As this bibliography itself demonstrates, studies on Synge are assuming greater proportions with each passing year. The result is an unusually large output of material, which has never been recorded in one full-length authoritative reference work. Most of the existing bibliographies are either incomplete or inaccurate. Some of these inaccuracies, whether in standard bibliographical aids or appended to such works as Maurice Bourgeois' *John Millington Synge and the Irish Theatre*, have been repeated unchecked in subsequent studies of the dramatist.

The present bibliography, which comprises some 2500 items, has been compiled on the lines shown in the Table of Contents. With articles in periodicals and similar short pieces, I have given page-references whenever possible; in the case of books (those, for example dealing with drama in general, where references to Synge are scattered) I have given only the name of the book. Some reviews of books or play productions were worth including in the articles section. The bibliography is intended to be complete up to the end of 1971, although some later studies have been listed.

Acknowledgements are due to the following libraries for their cooperation and assistance: The University of Lethbridge Library; the British Museum Library; the National Library of Ireland; and the Newspaper Library at Colindale. I am also grateful to Miss Bea Ramtej for her immense help.

E. H. MIKHAIL

Lethbridge, Canada

Bibliographies

Abstracts of English Studies, 1958 to present (Boulder, Colo.: National Council of Teachers of English).

Adelman, Irving and Rita Dworkin, 'John Millington Synge, 1871–1909', *Modern Drama; A Checklist of Critical Literature on 20th Century Plays* (Metuchen, N.J.: The Scarecrow Press, 1967) pp. 306–9.

American Doctoral Dissertations, 1966 to present. Compiled for The Association of Research Libraries (Ann Arbor, Mich.: University Microfilms).

Annual Bibliography of English Language and Literature, 1920 to present (London: Modern Humanities Research Association).

Annual Magazine Subject-Index, 1907–49 (Boston: F. W. Faxon). Reprinted as *Cumulated Magazine Subject Index, 1907–1949* (Boston: G. K. Hall, 1964).

Babler, O. F., 'John Millington Synge in Czech Translations', *Notes and Queries*, CXCI (21 Sep 1946) 123–4.

Baker, Blanch M. 'Synge', *Theatre and Allied Arts* (New York: H. W. Wilson, 1952) p. 118.

Bateson, F. W. (ed.), 'John Millington Synge', *The Cambridge Bibliography of English Literature* (Cambridge: Cambridge University Press, 1940) vol. III, pp. 1062–3; *Supplement* (Cambridge: Cambridge University Press, 1957) pp. 704–5.

1

Book Review Index, 1965 to present (Detroit: Gale Research Company).

Bourgeois, Maurice, 'General Bibliography', *John Millington Synge and the Irish Theatre* (London: Constable, 1913; New York: Benjamin Blom, 1965; Haskell House, 1966) pp. 251–314.

Breed, Paul F. and Florence M. Sniderman (eds.), 'John Millington Synge', *Dramatic Criticism* (Detroit: Gale Research Company, 1972) pp. 685–93.

British Humanities Index, 1962 to present (London: The Library Association). Continuation of *Subject Index to Periodicals*.

Brown, Stephen J. (ed.), *A Guide to Books on Ireland* (Dublin: Hodges Figgis; New York and London: Longmans Green, 1912).

Bushrui, S. B., 'A Select Bibliography', *Sunshine and the Moon's Delight; A Centenary Tribute to John Millington Synge 1871–1909* (Gerrard Cross, Bucks.: Colin Smythe; Beirut: The American University, 1972) pp. 317–38.

Coleman, Arthur and Gary R. Tyler, 'John Synge', *Drama Criticism*, vol. I: *A Checklist of Interpretation Since 1940 of English and American Plays* (Denver: Alan Swallow, 1966) pp. 202–5.

Cumulative Book Index, 1928 to present (New York: H. W. Wilson).

Dissertation Abstracts, 1938 to present (Ann Arbor, Mich.: University Microfilms).

Doctoral Dissertations Accepted by American Universities, ed. Arnold H. Trotier and Marian Harman (New York: H. W. Wilson, 1933–55). Continued as *Index to American Doctoral Dissertations*, 1955 to present.

Bibliographies

Dramatic Index, 1909—49 (Boston: F. W. Faxon).

Dysinger, Robert E., 'The John Millington Synge Collection at Colby College', *Colby Library Quarterly*, IV (Feb 1957) 166—72.

'Additions to the John Millington Synge Collection: A Supplementary Check List', *Colby Library Quarterly*, IV (Feb 1957) 192—4.

Eager, Alan R., *A Guide to Irish Bibliographycal Material: Being a Bibliography of Irish Bibliographies and Some Sources of Information* (London: The Library Association, 1964).

Essay and General Literature Index, 1900 to present (New York: H. W. Wilson).

Estill, Adelaide Duncan, 'Bibliography', *The Sources of Synge* (Philadelphia: University of Pennsylvania, 1939; Folcroft, Pa.: The Folcroft Press, 1969) pp. 42—51.

Faxon, F. W., M. E. Bates, and A. C. Sutherland (eds.), *Cumulated Dramatic Index 1909—1949* (Boston: G. K. Hall, 1965).

Gerstenberger, Donna, 'Selected Bibliography', *John Millington Synge* (New York: Twayne Publishers, 1964) pp. 142—52.

Greene, David H. and Edward M. Stephens, 'A List of the Published Writings of J. M. Synge', *J. M. Synge, 1871—1909* (New York: Macmillan, 1959; Collier Books, 1961) pp. 308—10.

Harmon, Maurice, *Modern Irish Literature, 1800—1967: A Reader's Guide* (Dublin: The Dolmen Press, 1967).

An Index to Book Reviews in the Humanities, 1960 to present (Williamston, Mich.: Phillip Thomson).

3

Bibliographies

Index to Little Magazines, 1943 to present (Denver: Alan Swallow).

An Index to One-Act Plays, comp. Hannah Logasa and Winifred Ver Nooy (Boston: F. W. Faxon, 1924); *Supplement 1924–31* (Boston: F. W. Faxon, 1932); *Second Supplement 1932–40* (Boston: F. W. Faxon, 1941); *Third Supplement 1941–8* (Boston: F. W. Faxon, 1950); *Fourth Supplement 1948–57* (Boston: F. W. Faxon, 1958).

Index to Theses Accepted for Higher Degrees in the Universities of Great Britain and Ireland, 1950 to present (London: ASLIB).

International Index to Periodicals, 1907 to present (New York: H. W. Wilson). From vol. XIX (April 1965–March 1966) called *Social Sciences and Humanities Index*.

Litto, Fredric M., 'Synge', *American Dissertations on the Drama and the Theatre* (Kent: Kent State University Press, 1969) p. 315.

MLA Bibliography, 1919 to present (New York: The Modern Language Association of America).

McGirr, Alice Thurston, 'Reading List on John Millington Synge', *Bulletin of Bibliography* VII (April 1913) 114–15.

MacManus, M. J., 'Bibliographies of Irish Authors No. 4: John Millington Synge', *Dublin Magazine*, V, no. 4, New Series (October–December 1930) 47–51. Reprinted in an eight-page pamphlet entitled *A Bibliography of Books Written by John Millington Synge* (1930). Twenty-five copies were printed.

MacNamara, Brinsley (ed.), *Abbey Plays 1899–1948: Including the Productions of The Irish Literary Theatre* (Dublin: At the Sign of The Three Candles, n.d. [1949]).

McNamee, Lawrence F., 'John M. Synge', *Dissertations in*

4

Bibliographies

Bibliographies

English and American Literature: Theses Accepted by American, British and German Universities, 1865–1964 (New York and London: R. R. Bowker, 1968) p. 527; 'John M. Synge', *Supplement One* (New York and London: R. R. Bowker, 1969) p. 210.

MacPhail, Ian, 'John Millington Synge: Some Bibliographical Notes', *The Irish Book* I (Spring 1959) 3–10 [paper read to the Bibliographical Society of Ireland on 23 March 1959].

Mikhail, E. H., 'Sixty Years of Synge Criticism, 1907–1967', *Bulletin of Bibliography and Magazine Notes* (Westwood, Mass.) XXVII, no. 1 (January–March 1970) 11–13; and XXVII, no. 2 (April–June 1970) 53–6.

The New York Times Index.

Nineteenth Century Readers' Guide to Periodical Literature 1890–1899. With Supplementary Indexing 1900–1922 (New York: H. W. Wilson).

O'Hegarty, P. S., 'Bibliographical Notes: The Abbey Theatre Wolfhound Series of Plays', *Dublin Magazine*, XXII (April –June 1947) 41–2.

'Some Notes on the Bibliography of J. M. Synge, Supplemental to Bourgeois and MacManus', *Dublin Magazine*, XVII (January–March 1942) 56–8.

O'Mahony, Mathew, *Guide to Anglo-Irish Plays* (Dublin: Progress House, 1960).

Ottemiller, John H., 'John Millington Synge', *Index to Plays in Collections* (New York and London: The Scarecrow Press, 1964) p. 139. Reprinted as *Ottemiller's Index to Plays in Collections*. Fifth Edition revised and enlarged by John M. and Billie M. Connor (Metuchen, N.J.: The Scarecrow Press, 1971) pp. 158–9.

Palmer, Helen H. and Anne Jane Dyson (comps.), 'John

Millington Synge', *European Drama Criticism* (Hamden, Conn.: The Shoe String Press, 1968) pp. 407–10.

Patterson, Charlotte A. (comp.), *Plays in Periodicals: An Index to English Language Scripts in Twentieth Century Journals* (Boston: G. K. Hall, 1970).

Play Index 1949–1952: An Index to 2616 Plays in 1138 Volumes, comp. Dorothy Herbert West and Dorothy Margaret Peake (New York: H. W. Wilson, 1953) p. 176; *Play Index 1953–1960: An Index to 4592 Plays in 1735 Volumes,* ed. Estelle A. Fidell and Dorothy Margaret Peake (New York: H. W. Wilson, 1963) p. 296; *Play Index 1961–1967: An Index to 4793 Plays,* ed. Estelle A. Fidell (New York: H. W. Wilson, 1968) pp. 339–40.

Pollard, M. and Ian MacPhail, *John Millington Synge (1871–1909): A Catalogue of an Exhibition Held at Trinity College Library, Dublin, on the Occasion of the Fiftieth Anniversary of His Death* (Dublin: Dolmen Press for the Friends of the Library of Trinity College Dublin, 1959).

Price, Alan, 'Bibliography', *Synge and Anglo-Irish Drama* (London: Methuen, 1961) pp. 229–31.

Readers' Guide to Periodical Literature, 1900 to present (New York: H. W. Wilson).

The Royal Irish Academy: Committee for the Study of Anglo-Irish Language and Literature, *Work in Progress,* 1969 to present.

Salem, James M., 'John Millington Synge', *A Guide to Critical Reviews,* pt. III: *British and Continental Drama from Ibsen to Pinter* (Metuchen, N. J.: The Scarecrow Press, 1968) pp. 244–6.

Santaniello, A. E., 'Synge', *Theatre Books in Print; An Annotated Guide to the Literature of the Theatre, the Technical*

Bibliographies

Arts of the Theatre, Motion Pictures, Television and Radio (New York: The Drama Book Shop, 1966) p. 83.

Skelton, Robin, 'Bibliography', *J. M. Synge*, Irish Writers Series (Lewisburg: Bucknell University Press, 1972) pp. 86–9.

'Chronology and Bibliography', *The Writings of J. M. Synge* (London: Thames and Hudson, 1971) pp. 177–84.

Subject Index to Periodicals, 1915–1961 (London: The Library Association). Continued as *British Humanities Index*, 1962 to present.

The Times Index (London).

Trinity College Dublin, 'A Checklist of First Editions of Works by John Millington Synge and George William Russell', *T. C. D. Annual Bulletin* (1956) 4–9.

Year's Work in English Studies, 1919 to present (London: The English Association).

Zydler, Tomasz, 'John Millington Synge and the Irish Theatre', *Kwartalnik Neofilologiczny*, XVIII (Warsaw, 1971) 383–96.

Books by J. M. Synge
and their Reviews

In the Shadow of the Glen (New York: John Quinn, 1904).

The Shadow of the Glen and Riders to the Sea (London: Elkin Mathews, 1905).

The Well of the Saints (London: A. H. Bullen, 1905).

The Aran Islands (Dublin: Maunsel; London: Elkin Mathews, 1907). Reviewed in *Tribune* (London, 6 May 1907) 2; in *The Times Literary Supplement* (London, 28 Jun 1907) 202; by R. W. L. in *Black and White* (London, 11 May 1907) 658; in *Athenaeum* (London, 22 Jun 1907) 754–5; in *The Clarion* (London, 19 Jul 1907) 2; in *Bookman*, XLI, no. 243, Christmas Supplement (London, Dec 1911) 82–3; in *Belfast News-Letter* (27 Jun 1907) 5; in *Irish Times* (Dublin, 7 Jun 1907) 9; and in *Public Opinion* (London, 21 Jun 1907) 774.

The Playboy of the Western World (Dublin: Maunsel, 1907; Boston: J. W. Luce, 1911). Reviewed in *Evening Standard and St. James's Gazette* (London, 30 Apr 1907) 5; in *Bookman*, XXXII (London, Aug 1907) 181; in *Daily Chronicle* (London, 13 Sep 1907) 3; in *Athenaeum* (London, 5 Oct 1907) 415–16; in *The Times Literary Supplement* (London, 15 Jun 1911) 231; in *Morning Post* (London, 13 May 1907) 2; in *Belfast News-Letter* (27 Jun 1907) 5; in *Northern Whig* (Belfast, 4 May 1907) 10; by Holbrook Jackson in *New Age* (London, 2 May 1907) 7; in *Outlook* (London, 8 Jun 1907) 770–1; in *Tribune* (London, 21 May 1907) 2; in *Universe* (London, 19 Apr 1907) 15; and in *New York Times Book Review* (1 Oct 1911) 584.

Books by J. M. Synge and Their Reviews

The Tinker's Wedding (Dublin: Maunsel, 1908; Boston: J. W. Luce, 1911). Reviewed in *Bookman*, XXXIII (London, Mar 1908) 260; and in *Independent* (N.Y., 13 Apr 1911) 792–3.

Poems and Translations (Dundrum: The Cuala Press; New York: John Quinn, 1909). Reviewed in *Daily Chronicle* (London, 26 Jul 1909) 3; by James Douglas in *Star* (London, 24 Jul 1909) 2; by Francis Bickley in *Bookman*, XXXVI (London, Aug 1909), 224; in *Star* (London, 24 Jul 1909) 2; in *Athenaeum*, no. 4268 (London, 14 Aug 1909) 178; by Geraldine E. Hodgson in *Contemporary Review*, XCVIII (London, Sep 1910) 323–40; by Francis Hackett in *Chicago Evening Post* (2 Jul 1909) 1; and in *Evening Post* (N.Y., 13 Aug 1909) 4.

Deirdre of the Sorrows (Churchtown, Dundrum: Cuala Press, 1910). Reviewed in *Glasgow News* (7 Jul 1910) 4.

The Works of John M. Synge, 4 vols. (Dublin: Maunsel, 1910).
  Vol. I *The Shadow of the Glen, Riders to the Sea, The Tinker's Wedding, The Well of the Saints*
    II *The Playboy of the Western World, Deirdre of the Sorrows, Poems, Translations from Petrarch, Translations from Villon and Others*
    III *The Aran Islands*
    IV *In Wicklow, In West Kerry, In the Congested Districts, Under Ether*
Reviewed in *The Times Literary Supplement* (London, 23 Feb 1911) 1–2; by Edmund Gosse in *Morning Post* (London, 26 Jan 1911) 2; by R. A. Scott-James in *Daily News* (London, 1 Feb 1911) 3; in *Daily Express* (Dublin, 20 Apr 1911) 8; in *Pall Mall Gazette* (London, 16 Jan 1911) 4; in *Westminster Gazette* (London, 4 Feb 1911) 4; in *Manchester Guardian* (19 Jan 1911) 4; by James Douglas in *Star* (London, 18 Feb 1911) 2; by W. P. Ryan in *Daily Chronicle* (London, 4 Feb 1911) 6; in *Evening Standard* (London, 24 Jan 1911); in *Birmingham Daily Post* (1 Feb 1911) 4; in *Glasgow News* (2 Feb 1911) 2; in *Glasgow Herald* (16 Feb 1911) 12; in *Aberdeen Press* (6 Feb 1911) 3; in *Athenaeum* (London, 18 Feb 1911) 182–3; by Darrell

Figgis in *Bookman*, XL (London, Apr 1911) 30–3; in
Saturday Review (London, 28 Jan 1911) 114–15; in
Nation, VIII, no. 26 (London, 25 Mar 1911) 1043–4; in
Spectator (London, 1 Apr 1911) 482–3; in *Sphere*
(London, 22 Apr 1911) 96; by Charles Tennyson in
Quarterly Review, CCXV, no. 428 (London, Jul 1911) 227–
34; by Herbert Hughes in *New Age*, VIII, no. 24 (London,
13 Apr 1911) 562–3; by Lady Gordon in *Ladies' Field*,
LIII, no. 680 (London, 25 Mar 1911) 176–7; in *Country
Life*, XXIX, no. 733 (London, 21 Jan 1911) 102–3; in
Church Quarterly Review, LXXII (London, Jul 1911) 406–
13; by Ernest H. Pittwood in *Holborn Review*, IV, New
Series (London, Jul 1913) 489–501; in *Irish Times* (Dublin,
23 Jan 1911) 7; in *Freeman's Journal* (Dublin, 23 Jan 1911)
8; by Elia W. Peattie in *Chicago Daily Tribune* (21 Jan 1911)
11; by Stuart P. Sherman in *Nation*, XCV, no. 2478 (N.Y.,
26 Dec 1912) 608–11; in *Evening Post* (N.Y., 11 Jan 1913)
6; in *Current Literature*, LIII (N.Y., Jul–Dec 1912) 695; by
Henry Seidel Canby in *Yale Review*, II, New Series (Jul
1913) 767–72; in *Living Age*, CCLXIX (Boston, 15 Apr
1911) 163–6; and CCLXXI (7 Oct 1911) 15–24; by H. L.
Mencken in *Smart Set* (N.Y., Oct 1912) 147–52; and by
James A. Roy in *Anglia*, XXXVII (1913) 129–45.

*Some Unpublished Letters and Documents of J. M. Synge
Formerly in the Possession of Mr. Lawrence Wilson*
(Montreal: The Redpath Press, 1959).

*The Autobiography of J. M. Synge; Constructed from the
Manuscripts by Alan Price, with Fourteen Photographs by
J. M. Synge and the Photography of His Time by P. J.
Pocock* (Dublin: The Dolmen Press; London: Oxford
University Press, 1965). Reviewed in *The Times* (London,
16 Sep 1965) 14; by Denis Donoghue in *New Statesman*,
LXXII (London, 16 Sep 1966) 399; by T. R. Henn in *Modern
Language Review*, LXII (London, Apr 1967) 325; by A. G.
Owen in *Library Journal*, XCII (N.Y., 1 Jun 1967) 2151; and
by René Fréchet in *Études anglaises*, XXI (Paris, 1968) 319–20.

Collected Works, vol. I: *Poems*, ed. Robin Skelton (London

and New York: Oxford University Press, 1962). Reviewed
in *The Times* (London, 5 Oct 1962) 17; in *The Times
Literary Supplement* (London, 26 Oct 1962) 824; by
Geoffrey Grigson in *New Statesman*, LXIV (London, 19
Oct 1962) 528–9; in *The Times Weekly Review* (London,
11 Oct 1962) 13; by T. R. Henn in *Modern Language
Review*, LVIII (London, Jul 1963) 420; by John Montague
in *Spectator* (London, 7 Dec 1962) 898; by Derek Parker
in *Poetry Review*, LIV (London, Summer 1963) 185; by
Howard Sergeant in *English*, XIV (London, Spring 1963)
164; and by F. T. Wood in *English Studies*, XLIII
(Amsterdam, Jun 1963) 232.

Collected Works, vol. II: *Prose*, ed. Alan Price (London and
New York: Oxford University Press, 1966). Reviewed in
The Times (London, 21 Jul 1966) 16; in *The Times Literary
Supplement* (London, 22 Dec 1966) 1190; by Denis
Donoghue in *New Statesman*, LXXII (London, 16 Sep 1966)
399–400; by Anthony Burgess in *Spectator* (London, 22
Jul 1966) 124; by William Trevor in *Listener*, LXXVI
(London, 11 Aug 1966) 210; and by William E. Hart in
Studies, LV (1966) 443–6.

Collected Works, vols. III and IV: *Plays*, ed. Ann Saddlemyer
(London and New York: Oxford University Press, 1968).
Reviewed by Irving Wardle in *The Times* (London, 15 Jun
1968) 20; in *The Times Literary Supplement* (London,
8 Aug 1968) 852; by P. Anderson in *Spectator* (London,
9 Aug 1968) 196; by R. Gaskell in *Critical Quarterly*, XI
(London, Winter 1969) 383; by Jeanne Flood in *Eire-
Ireland*, III (St. Paul, Minn., Winter 1968) 143–4; by René
Fréchet in *Études anglaises*, XXI (Paris, 1968) 320–3; and
by W. Angus in *Queen's Quarterly*, LXXVI (Kingston, Ont.,
Winter 1969) 724.

*Some Letters of John M. Synge to Lady Gregory and W. B.
Yeats*, selected by Ann Saddlemyer (Dublin: Cuala Press,
1971).

Letters to Molly: John Millington Synge to Maire O'Neill

1906–1909, ed. Ann Saddlemyer (Cambridge, Mass.: Harvard University Press; London: Oxford University Press, 1971). Reviewed in *The Times Literary Supplement* (London, 17 Mar 1972) 306.

The Synge Manuscripts in the Library of Trinity College Dublin (Dublin: The Dolmen Press; London: Oxford University Press, 1971). Reviewed in *The Times Literary Supplement* (London, 2 Jul 1971) 749–50; and by Laurence Lerner in *Encounter*, XXXVIII, no. 1 (London, Jan 1972) 62–7.

Some Sonnets from 'Laura in Death' after the Italian of Francesco Petrarch (Dublin: The Dolmen Press; London: Oxford University Press, 1971). Reviewed in *The Times Literary Supplement* (London, 2 Jul 1971) 749–50; and by Laurence Lerner in *Encounter*, XXXVIII, no. 1 (London, Jan 1972) 62–7.

Synge to Lady Gregory and Yeats, ed. Ann Saddlemyer (Dublin: Cuala Press, 1971).

My Wallet of Photographs: The Collected Photographs of J. M. Synge, arranged and introduced by Lilo Stephens (Dublin: The Dolmen Press; London: Oxford University Press, 1971). Reviewed in *The Times Literary Supplement* (London, 2 Jul 1971) 749–50; and by Laurence Lerner in *Encounter*, XXXVIII, no. 1 (London, Jan 1972) 62–7.

Criticism on J. M. Synge

(a) BOOKS

The Abbey Row. Not Edited by W. B. Yeats (Dublin, 1907). [Written mainly by Page Dickinson with the help of Joseph Hone and Frank Sparrow].

'The Abbey Theatre', *The Ireland of Today. Reprinted, with Some Additions, from the London Times* (London: John Murray, 1913; Boston: Small Maynard, 1915), pt III, ch. V, pp. 131–7.

Abbey Theatre 1904–1966 (Dublin: The National Theatre Society, 1966).

Agate, James, 'The Irish Players', *Buzz, Buzz! Essays of the Theatres* (London: W. Collins, 1917; New York: Benjamin Blom, 1969) pp. 150–60.

The Amazing Theatre (London: George G. Harrap, 1939) pp. 218–9 [on *The Playboy of the Western World*].

Alexander, Jean, 'Synge's Play of Choice: *The Shadow of the Glen*', *Sunshine and the Moon's Delight*, ed. S. B. Bushrui (Gerrards Cross, Bucks.: Colin Smythe, 1972) pp. 21–31.

Allison, Alexander, *et al* (eds.), 'John Synge: *Riders to the Sea*', *Masterpieces of the Drama*, 2nd ed. (New York: Macmillan, 1966) pp. 505–18 [text and commentary].

Altenbernd, Lynn and Leslie L. Lewis (eds.), 'John Millington Synge: *Riders to the Sea*', *Introduction to Literature: Plays*

(New York: Macmillan, 1963) pp. 288–94 [text and commentary].

Andrews, Charlton, *The Drama Today* (Philadelphia and London: J. B. Lippincott, 1913) pp. 161–4.

Archer, William, *Play-Making; A Manual of Craftsmanship* (London: Chapman and Hall; Boston: Small, Maynard, 1912; New York: Dover Publications, 1960).

Armstrong, W. A., 'The Irish Dramatic Movement' and *The Playboy of the Western World*', *Classic Irish Drama* (Harmondsworth: Penguin Books, 1964) pp. 7–15 and 65–7 [text and commentary].

Aufhauser, Annemarie, *Sind die Dramen von John Millington Synge durch französische Vorbilder beeinflusst?* (Würzburg: Buchdruckerei Richard Mayr, 1935).

Aughtry, Charles Edward (ed.), 'Folk Drama. John Millington Synge: *The Playboy of the Western World*', *Landmarks in Modern Drama from Ibsen to Ionesco* (Boston: Houghton Mifflin, 1963) pp. 417–63 [text and commentary].

Ball, John (ed.), 'John Millington Synge: *In the Shadow of the Glen*', *From Beowulf to Modern British Writers* (New York: Odyssey Press, 1959) pp. 1195–201 [text and commentary].

Barnes, John R., *et al* (eds.), *Prose and Poetry of the World* (Syracuse, N.Y.: Singer, 1941).

Barnet, Sylvan, Morton Berman, and William Burto (eds.), 'The Irish Theater: An Introduction' and 'John Millington Synge: *Deirdre of the Sorrows*', *The Genius of the Irish Theater* (New York: The New American Library, 1960) pp. 7–11 and 151–4 [text and commentary].

(eds.), 'John Millington Synge: *Riders to the Sea*', *An Introduction to Literature*, 4th ed. (Boston: Little, Brown, 1971) pp. 541–4 [text and commentary].

Bateman, Reginald, 'Synge – A Fragment', *Reginald Bateman, Teacher and Soldier; A Memorial Volume of Selections from His Lectures and Other Writings* (London: H. Sotheran, 1922) pp. 85–91.

Beach, Joseph Warren, 'The Drama in Ireland', *English Literature of the Nineteenth and the Early Twentieth Century*, vol. IV of *A History of English Literature*, ed. Hardin Craig (New York: Collier Books; London: Collier-Macmillan, 1962) pp. 221–6.

Beckerman, Bernard, *Dynamics of Drama; Theory and Method of Analysis* (New York: Alfred A. Knopf, 1970) pp. 64–77, 138–9, 170–1, 235–6 [on *Riders to the Sea*].

Beerbohm, Max, 'Some Irish Plays and Players', *Around Theatres* (London: Rupert Hart-Davis; New York: British Book Centre, 1953) pp. 314–9 [on *Riders to the Sea* and *In the Shadow of the Glen*].

Bellinger, Martha Fletcher, *A Short History of the Drama* (New York: Henry Holt, 1927) pp. 344–5.

Benet, William Rose, 'John Millington Synge', *The Reader's Encyclopedia* (New York: Thomas Y. Crowell, 1965) p. 981.

Bennet, C. R. and Lorne Pierce, *The Canada Book of Prose and Verse*, Bk 6 (Toronto: Macmillan, 1936).

Bentley, Eric, 'Heroic Wantonness', *In Search of Theater* (New York: Random House, 1953) pp. 307–21. Reprinted from *Poetry*, LXXIX, no. 4 (Chicago, Jan 1952) 216–32.

Bickley, Francis, *J. M. Synge and the Irish Dramatic Movement* (London: Constable; Boston: Houghton Mifflin, 1912). Reviewed in *Evening Standard and St. James's Gazette* (London, 3 and 12 Oct 1912) 11 and 9; in *Manchester Guardian* (8 Oct 1912) 4; in *Daily Dispatch* (Manchester, 7 Oct 1912) 3; in *Athenaeum* (London, 5 Oct 1912) 387; by Ernest H. Pittwood in *Holborn Review*, IV (London,

Jul 1913) 489–501; in *New Witness*, I, no. 9 (London, 2
Jan 1913) 282–3; in *Hearth and Home*, XLIV (London, 12
Dec 1912) 310; in *The Tablet* (London, 2 Nov 1912) 687–8;
in *Rhythm* (London, Mar 1913) 486; in *Southport Guardian*
(23 Oct 1912) 11; in *Irish Book Lover*, IV, no. 4 (London
and Dublin, Nov 1912) 70; in *Cork Constitution* (16 Oct
1912); in *Irish News and Belfast Morning News* (5 Oct
1912) 7; by Harry Seidel Canby in *Yale Review*, II (Jul
1913) 767–72; by James W. Tupper in *Dial*, LIX (Chicago,
16 Mar 1913) 233–5; in *Independent*, LXXIII (N.Y., 7 Nov
1912) 1071–3; and in *Transvaal Leader* (Johannesburg,
17 Dec 1912) 10.

Blankenship, Russell *et al* (eds.), '*Riders to the Sea.* John
Millington Synge', *Contemporary Literature* (Chicago:
Charles Scribner's, 1938) pp. 581–91 [text and
commentary].

Bliss, Alan, 'A Synge Glossary', *Sunshine and the Moon's
Delight*, ed. S. B. Bushrui (Gerrards Cross, Bucks.: Colin
Smythe, 1972) pp. 297–316.

Block, Haskell M. and Robert G. Shedd (eds.), 'John
Millington Synge: *Riders to the Sea* and *The Playboy of the
Western World*', *Masters of Modern Drama* (New York:
Random House, 1962) pp. 397–426 [texts and
commentaries].

Blunt, Jerry, 'Irish', *Stage Dialects* (San Francisco: Chandler
Publishing Company, 1967) pp. 75–81.

Blythe, Ernest, *The Abbey Theatre* (Dublin: The National
Theatre Society [1965]).

Bonazza, Blaze O. and Emil Roy (eds.), '*Riders to the Sea*:
Synge', *Studies in Drama*, 2nd ed. (New York: Harper &
Row, 1968) pp. 7–18 [text and commentary].

Bourgeois, Maurice, *John Millington Synge and the Irish
Theatre* (London: Constable, 1913; New York: Benjamin

Blom, 1965; Haskell House, 1966). Reviewed in *British Review*, V (London, Feb 1914) 317; and by James W. Tupper in *Dial*, LVI (Chicago, 1 Mar 1914) 177–9.

Bourniquel, Camille, *Ireland* (London: Vista Books; New York: Viking Press, 1960) pp. 159–62.

Boyd, Ernest A., 'J. M. Synge', *Ireland's Literary Renaissance* (New York: Alfred A. Knopf, 1912; John Lane, 1916) pp. 316–35.

'Impulse to Folk Drama: J. M. Synge and Padraic Colum', *The Contemporary Drama of Ireland* (Dublin: Talbot Press London: T. Fisher Unwin, 1918) pp. 88–120.

Bradbrook, M. C., *English Dramatic Form* (London: Chatto & Windus; New York: Barnes & Noble, 1965).

Brahms, Caryl, 'The Playboy of the Western World. Synge (The Piccadilly Theatre)', *The Rest of the Evening's My Own* (London: W. H. Allen, 1964) pp. 160–1.

Brawley, Benjamin, 'John Millington Synge', *A Short History of the English Drama* (London: George G. Harrap; New York: Harcourt, Brace, 1921) pp. 233–4.

Briggs, Thomas Henry, *et al* (eds.), *English Literature* (Boston: Houghton Mifflin, 1934).

Brockett, Oscar G., 'The Irish Renaissance', *History of the Theatre* (Boston: Allyn and Bacon, 1968) pp. 576–8.

Brook, Donald, 'Irish Creation and Provincial Awakening', *The Romance of the English Theatre* (London: Rockliff, 1952) pp. 167–8.

Brooke, Stopford Augustus and Thomas William Rolleston (eds.), *A Treasury of Irish Poetry in the English Tongue*, rev. and enl. ed. (New York: Macmillan, 1932) pp. 596–8.

Brooks, Cleanth and Robert B. Heilman (eds.), *'Riders to the Sea'*, *Understanding Drama; Twelve Plays* (New York: Henry Holt, 1945) appendix A, pp. 26–7.

Brugsma, Rebecca Pauline Christine, *The Beginnings of the Irish Revival*, pt I (Groningen and Batavia: P. Noordhoff [1933]) pp. 94–7.

Bryant, Sophie, 'The Gael in Literature', *The Genius of the Gael; A Study in Celtic Psychology and Its Manifestations* (London: T. Fisher Unwin, 1913) pp. 188–93.

Bullard, Catharine (ed.), *'Riders to the Sea*. John Millington Synge', *One-Act Plays for Junior High School* (New York: Henry Holt, 1937) pp. 201–18 [text only].

Bushrui, S. B., *Shiʾun Min Synge* (Beirut: Rihani, 1971) [in Arabic].

(ed.), *Sunshine and the Moon's Delight; A Centenary Tribute to John Millington Synge 1871–1909*. With a Foreword by A. Norman Jeffares (Gerrards Cross, Bucks.: Colin Smythe; Beirut: The American University, 1972).

Byrne, Dawson, *'The Playboy of the Western World'*, *The Story of Ireland's National Theatre: The Abbey Theatre, Dublin* (Dublin: Talbot Press, 1929) ch. V, pp. 56–64.

Cahalan, Thomas and Paul A. Doyle, *Modern British and Irish Drama*, Hymarx Outline Series, no. 123 (Boston: Student Outlines, 1961) pp. 63–71.

Calderwood, James L. and Harold E. Toliver (eds.), 'Synge: *Riders to the Sea*', *Forms of Tragedy* (Englewood Cliffs, N.J.: Prentice-Hall, 1972) pp. 211–21 [text and biographical note].

Canfield, Curtis (ed.), 'Plays of the Peasant Character: Tragedy', *Plays of the Irish Renaissance 1880–1930*

(New York: Ives Washburn, 1929) pp. 155–70 [commentary and text of *Riders to the Sea*].

Cannan, Gilbert, *The Joy of the Theatre* (London: B. T. Batsford, 1913).

Carpenter, Bruce, 'Riders to the Sea', *The Way of the Drama; A Study of Dramatic Forms and Moods* (New York: Prentice-Hall, 1929) pp. 64–5.

(ed.), '*Riders to the Sea* by John Synge' [text] and 'Modern Classic Tragedy', *A Book of Dramas* (New York: Prentice-Hall, 1949) pp. xiv–xv and 255–68.

Carroll, Sydney W., '*The Playboy of the Western World*', *Some Dramatic Opinions* (London: F. V. Whitehead, 1923; Port Washington, N.Y.: Kennikat Press, 1968) pp. 69–73.

Cartmell, Van H. (ed.), '*The Playboy of the Western World*' and 'Riders to the Sea', *Plot Outlines of 100 Famous Plays* (Garden City, N.Y.: Doubleday, 1945; Dolphin Books, 1962) pp. 247–54.

Cerf, Bennett A. and Van H. Cartmell (comps.), '*The Playboy of the Western World* by John M. Synge', *Sixteen Famous European Plays* (Garden City, N.Y.: Garden City Publishing Co., 1943) pp. 941–84, xx [text and commentary].

(eds.), '*Riders to the Sea.* J. M. Synge', *Thirty Famous One-Act Plays* (New York: The Modern Library, 1943) pp. 231–8, 606 [text and biographical note].

(eds.), '*In the Shadow of the Glen* – J. M. Synge', *24 Favorite One-Act Plays* (Garden City, N.Y.: Doubleday, 1963) pp. 467–83 [text only].

Chandler, Frank Wadleigh, 'Irish Plays of Mysticism and Folk History' and 'Irish Plays of the Peasantry', *Aspects of Modern Drama* (New York: Macmillan, 1914) pp. 233–56 and 257–76.

Chew, Samuel C. and Richard D. Altick, 'Synge', *The Nine-teenth Century and After, 1789–1939*, vol. IV of *A Literary History of England*, ed. Albert C. Baugh (New York: Appleton-Century-Crofts, 1967) pp. 1513–4.

Chislett, William, Jr., 'The Irish Note in J. M. Synge's Transla-tions', *Moderns and Near-Moderns* (New York: The Crafton Press, 1928) pp. 157–9.

Clark, Barrett H., 'John Millington Synge', *The British and American Drama of Today* (New York: Holt, 1915; Scribner's, 1930; AMS Press, 1971) pp. 188–97.

'John M. Synge', *A Study of the Modern Drama* (New York and London: Appleton-Century, 1936) pp. 336–44.

(ed.), '*Riders to the Sea*. J. M. Synge', *Representative One-Act Plays by British and Irish Authors* (Boston: Little, Brown, 1928) pp. 391–408 [text and commentary].

and George Freedley (eds.), 'Irish Drama', *A History of Modern Drama* (New York and London: Appleton-Century, 1947) pp. 217–22.

Clark, David R., 'Synge's "Perpetual Last Day": Remarks on *Riders to the Sea*', *Sunshine and the Moon's Delight*, ed. S. B. Bushrui (Gerrards Cross, Bucks.: Colin Smythe, 1972) pp. 41–51.

(ed.), *John Millington Synge: Riders to the Sea*, the Merrill Library Casebook Series (Columbus, Ohio: Charles E. Merrill, 1970).

Clark, William Smith (ed.), 'Introduction to *The Playboy of the Western World*', *Chief Patterns of World Drama; Aeschylus to Anderson* (Boston: Houghton Mifflin, 1946) pp. 887–91 [text and commentary].

Clayes, Stanley A. (ed.), '*Riders to the Sea* by John Millington Synge', *Drama and Discussion* (New York: Appleton-

Century-Crofts, 1967) pp. 231–9 [text and commentary by William E. Hart].

Cleeve, Brian (comp.), *Dictionary of Irish Writers, First Series: Fiction* (Cork: The Mercier Press, 1966) pp. 131–2.

Coffman, George R., '*Riders to the Sea* by John M. Synge', *A Book of Modern Plays* (Chicago: Scott, Foresman, 1925) pp. 219–39 [text and commentary].

Cohen, Helen Louise (ed.), 'The Irish National Theatre' and '*Riders to the Sea* by John Millington Synge', *One-Act Plays by Modern Authors*, enl. ed. (New York: Harcourt, Brace, 1934) pp. 19–24 and 197–212 [text and commentary].

Cohn, Ruby and Bernard Dukore (eds.), '*The Playboy of the Western World*: John Millington Synge', *Twentieth Century Drama: England, Ireland, the United States* (New York: Random House, 1966) pp. 91–145 [text and commentary].

Cole, Toby (ed.), *Playwrights on Playwriting* (New York: Hill and Wang, 1961) pp. 201–3 [contains Synge's 'Prefaces' to *The Playboy of the Western World* and *The Tinker's Wedding*].

Collins, A. S., 'J. M. Synge', *English Literature of the Twentieth Century* (London: University Tutorial Press, 1951; 4th ed., 1960) pp. 290–4.

Colum, Mary, *Life and the Dream* (Garden City, N.Y.: Doubleday, 1947) pp. 136–40.

Colum, Padraic, *My Irish Year* (London: Mills & Boon; New York: James Pott, 1912) pp. 93–4.

The Road Round Ireland (New York: Macmillan, 1926) pp. 352–73.

Combs, George Hamilton, 'Moore, Synge and Yeats', *The*

Amazing Moderns (St. Louis: The Bethany Press, 1933)
pp. 220–47.

Connolly, Francis X. (ed.), 'John Millington Synge: *Riders to
the Sea*', *Literature: The Channel of Culture* (New York:
Harcourt, Brace, 1948) pp. 556–61 [text only].

Corkery, Daniel, *Synge and Anglo-Irish Literature; A Study*
(Dublin and Cork: Cork University Press; London and New
York: Longmans, Green, 1931; New York: Russell and
Russell, 1965). Reviewed by Austin Clarke in *New
Statesman and Nation*, II (London, 29 Aug 1931) 258–9;
by P. S. O'Hegarty in *Dublin Magazine*, VII, no. 1 (Jan–Mar
1932) 51–6; by Sean O'Faolain in *Criterion*, XI (London,
Oct 1931) 140–2; by Hugh De Blacam in *Spectator*
(London, 18 Jul 1931) 89; and in *The Times Literary
Supplement* (London, 23 Jul 1931) 578.

Corrigan, Robert W. (ed.), *The Modern Theatre* (New York:
Macmillan, 1964). [contains biographical note, p. 878;
Synge's Preface to *The Playboy of the Western World*, p.
899; Synge's Preface to *The Tinker's Wedding*, p. 900; text
of *The Playboy of the Western World*, pp. 901–925; and
text of *Riders to the Sea*, pp. 926–31].

(ed.), *Masterpieces of the Modern Irish Theatre* (New York:
Collier Books, 1967). [contains 'Preface: The Irish Dramatic
Flair' and texts of *The Playboy of the Western World* and
Riders to the Sea].

and James L. Rosenberg (eds.), 'J. M. Synge: *Riders to the
Sea*,' *The Art of the Theatre; A Critical Anthology of Drama*
(San Francisco: Chandler Publishing Company, 1964), pp.
455–67 [text only].

and Glenn M. Loney (eds.), '*The Playboy of the Western
World*: John Millington Synge', *Comedy: A Critical
Anthology* (Boston: Houghton Mifflin, 1971) pp. 431–77
[text and commentary].

Cousin, John W., 'John Millington Synge', *A Short Biographical Dictionary of English Literature* (London: Dent; New York: Dutton, 1910) p. 370.

Cowell, Raymond, 'Synge', *Twelve Modern Dramatists* (Oxford: Pergamon Press, 1967) pp. 57—65 [contains extract from *The Playboy of the Western World*].

Cox, R. David and Shirley S. (eds.), '*Riders to the Sea*. John M. Synge', *Themes in the One-Act Play* (New York: McGraw-Hill, 1971) pp. 266—75 [text and commentary].

Coxhead, Elizabeth, 'Collaboration — Hyde and Synge', *Lady Gregory; A Literary Portrait* (London: Macmillan, 1961) pp. 119—29. 2nd rev. and enl. ed. (London: Secker and Warburg, 1966) pp. 108—21.

J. M. Synge and Lady Gregory, writers and their Works No. 149 (London: Longmans, Green, 1962).

Daughters of Erin; Five Women of the Irish Renascence (London: Secker & Warburg, 1965) pp. 177—94.

'Synge and Lady Gregory', *Sunshine and the Moon's Delight*, ed. S. B. Bushrui (Gerrards Cross, Bucks.: Colin Smythe, 1972) pp. 153—8.

Crace, Gay, 'John Millington Synge', *Twentieth Century Writing; A Reader's Guide to Contemporary Literature*, ed. Kenneth Richardson (London: Newnes, 1969) pp. 596—7.

Cross, E. A. and Helen Fern Daringer (eds.), '*Riders to the Sea*. John M. Synge' and 'The Irish Literary Revival', *Heritage of British Literature* (New York: Macmillan, 1954) pp, 355—62 and 667—8.

Cubeta, Paul M. (ed.), 'J. M. Synge: *The Playboy of the Western World*', *Modern Plays for Analysis*, rev. ed. (New York: The Dryden Press, 1955) pp. 259—328 [text and commentary].

Cunliffe, J. W., 'The Irish Movement', *English Literature during the Last Half Century* (New York: Macmillan, 1925; Freeport, N. Y.: Books for Libraries Press, 1971) pp. 257–63.

'The Irish Drama and J. M. Synge', *Modern English Playwrights; A Short History of the English Drama from 1825* (New York and London: Harper, 1927; Port Washington, N.Y.: Kennikat Press, 1969) pp. 131–42.

'John Millington Synge', *English Literature in the Twentieth Century* (New York: Macmillan, 1933) pp. 105–13.

Daiches, David, *A Critical History of English Literature*, vol. II (London: Secker and Warburg, 1963) pp. 1109–10.

et al (eds.), 'J. M. Synge: *Riders to the Sea*', *English Literature* (Boston: Houghton Mifflin, 1968) pp. 714–21 [text and commentary].

Davenport, William H., Lowry C. Wimberly, and Harry Shaw (eds.), 'John M. Synge: *Riders to the Sea*', *Dominant Types in British and American Literature*, vol. I: *Poetry and Drama* (New York: Harper, 1949) pp. 539–44 [text and commentary].

Day, Martin, 'John Millington Synge', *History of English Literature 1837 to the Present* (Garden City, N.Y.: Doubleday, 1964) pp. 252–4.

Dickinson, Page L., *The Dublin of Yesterday* (London: Methuen, 1929).

Dickinson, Thomas H., 'J. M. Synge', *An Outline of Contemporary Drama* (New York: Houghton Mifflin, 1927; Biblo and Tannen, 1969) pp. 227–8.

(ed.), '*Riders to the Sea* by John Millington Synge', *Chief Contemporary Dramatists*. First Series (Boston: Houghton Mifflin, 1943) pp. 217-26, 662, 668-9 [text and commentaries].

Books

Dietrich, Margaret, *Das modern Drama: Strömungen, Gest-
alten, Motive* (Stuttgart: Alfred Kröner, 1961).

Dodson, Daniel (ed.), 'The Playboy of the Western World:
John Millington Synge', *Twelve Modern Plays* (Belmont,
Calif.: Wadsworth Publishing Company, 1970) pp. 219—49
[text and commentary].

Dooley, Roger B., 'John Millington Synge', *Modern British
and Irish Drama*, Monarch Review Notes and Study Guide
no. 624 (New York: Thor Publications, 1964) pp. 92—5.

Driver, Tom F., *Romantic Quest and Modern Query; A History
of the Modern Theater* (New York: Dell, 1970) pp. 136—40.

Dukes, Ashley, *The Scene is Changed* (London: Macmillan,
1942).

'J. M. Synge', *The Youngest Drama; Studies of Fifty Dramatists* (Chicago: Charles H. Sergel, 1924; Folcroft, Pa.: The
Folcroft Press, 1969) pp. 50—1.

Duncan, Douglas, 'Synge and Jonson', *Sunshine and the Moon's
Delight*, ed. S. B. Bushrui (Gerrards Cross, Bucks.: Colin
Smythe, 1972) pp. 205—18.

Durham, Willard Higley and John W. Dodds (eds.), 'John
Millington Synge: *The Playboy of the Western World*',
British and American Plays 1830—1945 (New York: Oxford
University Press, 1947) pp. 229—59 [text and commentary].

Dyboski, Roman, 'Dramat: John Millington Synge (1871—
1909)', *Sto Lat Literatury Angielskiej* (Warsaw: 'Pax', 1957)
pp. 825—36.

Eaton, Walter Prichard, *Plays and Players; Leaves from a
Critic's Scrapbook* (Cincinnati: Stewart & Kidd, 1916) pp.
149, 296, 313.

' "Local" Drama and the Irish Revival—Synge and O'Casey',

27

The Drama in English (New York: Scribner's, 1930) pp. 287–91.

Eliot, T. S., *Poetry and Drama* (London: Faber & Faber, 1951) pp. 19–20 [on *The Playboy of the Western World*].

Ellehauge, Martin, 'J. M. Synge', *Striking Figures among Modern British Dramatists* (Copenhagen: Levin & Munksgaard, 1931; Folcroft Library Editions, 1971) pp. 16–29.

Ellis-Fermor, Una, 'John Millington Synge', *The Irish Dramatic Movement* (London: Methuen, 1948; 2nd rev. ed. 1954) pp. 163–86.

'Synge', *The Oxford Companion to the Theatre*, ed. Phyllis Hartnoll (London: Oxford University Press, 1967) p. 931.

Elton, Oliver, *Modern Studies* (London: Edward Arnold, 1907) pp. 308–12.

Empson, William, *Seven Types of Ambiguity* (London: Chatto & Windus, 1956) pp. 4–5, 38–42 [on *Deirdre of the Sorrows*].

Erskine, John, *The Delight of Great Books* (New York: Columbia University Press, 1916) pp. 310–13.

Ervine, St. John G., *The Organised Theatre; A Plea in Civics* (London: Allen & Unwin, 1924).

Some Impressions of My Elders (London: Allen & Unwin, 1923) pp. 188–92. Reprinted from *North American Review*, CCXI (N.Y., May 1920) 669–81.

How to Write a Play (London: Allen & Unwin, 1928) pp. 20–2.

Erzgräber, Willi, 'John Millington Synge: *The Playboy of the Western World*', *Das moderne englische Drama*, ed. Horst Oppel (Berlin: Erich Schmidt, 1963) pp. 87–108.

Books

Estill, Adelaide Duncan, *The Sources of Synge* (Philadelphia:
University of Pennsylvania Press, 1939; Folcroft, Pa.: The
Folcroft Press, 1969). [Ph.D. dissertation, University of
Pennsylvania, 1937]. Reviewed by La Tourette Stockwell
in *Journal of English and Germanic Philology*, XXXIX
(Urbana, Illinois, Jul 1940) 436—7.

Evans, Sir Ifor, *A Short History of English Drama* (London:
Penguin Books, 1948); 2nd rev. and enl. ed. (Boston:
Houghton Mifflin, 1965) pp. 179—80.

Fallon, Gabriel, *The Abbey and the Actor* (Dublin: The
National Theatre Society, 1969).

Farren, Robert, 'Synge', *The Course of Irish Verse in English*
(London: Sheed & Ward, 1948) pp. 123—8.

Fay, Gerard, *The Abbey Theatre: Cradle of Genius* (Dublin:
Clonmore & Reynolds; London: Hollis & Carter; New York:
Macmillan, 1958).

Fay, W. G. and Catherine Carswell, *The Fays of the Abbey
Theatre* (New York: Harcourt, Brace; London: Rich &
Cowan, 1935).

Fehr, Bernhard, 'Das Drama der keltischen Renaissance:
Synge und Colum', *Die englische Literatur des 19 und 20
Jahrhunderts* (Berlin—Neubabelsberg: Akademische Verlags-
gesellschaft Athenaion, 1923) pp. 503—4.

Figgis, Darrell, 'J. M. Synge' and 'The Art of J. M. Synge',
Studies and Appreciations (London: J. M. Dent; New York:
Dutton, 1912) pp. 23—33 and 34—59. Reprinted from
Bookman (London, Apr 1911) 30—3; and *Fortnightly
Review*, XC, New Series (London, Dec 1911) 1056—68,
respectively.

Fisher, Chas H. and G. Sil-Vara, 'Preface', *Der Held des
Westerlands* [*The Playboy of the Western World*] (Munich:
Georg Muller, 1912).

Ford, Ford Madox, *The Critical Attitude* (London: Duckworth, 1911; Freeport, N.Y.: Books for Libraries Press, 1967) pp. 82–4 [on *The Playboy of the Western World*].

Fraser, G. S., 'The Irish Dramatic Revival', *The Modern Writer and His World* (Harmondsworth: Penguin Books, 1953) pp. 204–11.

Freedley, George and John A. Reeves, 'The Irish National Theatre', *A History of the Theatre*. 3rd ed. (New York: Crown Publishers, 1968) pp. 481–94.

Frenzel, Herbert, *John Millington Synge's Work As A Contribution to Irish Folk-Lore and to the Psychology of Primitive Tribes* (Duren-Rhld., 1932; Folcroft, Pa.: The Folcroft Press, 1969) [dissertation submitted to the University of Bonn].

Freyer, Grattan, 'The Irish Contribution', *The Modern Age*, vol. VII of *The Pelican Guide to English Literature*, ed. Boris Ford (Harmondsworth: Penguin Books, 1961) pp. 196–208.

Galsworthy, John, 'Meditation on Finality', *The Inn of Tranquillity; Studies and Essays* (London: Heinemann, 1912; New York: Scribner's, 1914; St. Clair Shores, Mich.: Scholarly Press, 1970) p. 207 [on *The Playboy of the Western World*]. Reprinted from *The English Review*, XI (London, Jul 1912) 537–41.

Gassner, John, 'John Millington Synge and the Irish Muse', *Masters of the Drama* (New York: Random House, 1940; Dover Publications, 1954) pp. 542–74.

'John Millington Synge: Synthesis in Folk Drama' and '*The Playboy of the Western World*, 1946', *The Theatre in Our Times; A Survey of the Men, Materials and Movements in the Modern Theatre* (New York: Crown Publishers, 1954) pp. 217–24 and 537–41 respectively.

Gassner, John (ed.), 'John Millington Synge: *Riders to the Sea*', *A Treasury of the Theatre from Henrik Ibsen to Eugene Ionesco* (New York: Simon & Schuster, 1966) pp. 626–32 [text and commentary].

Directions in Modern Theatre and Drama (New York: Holt, Rinehart & Winston, 1967) pp. 99–100.

Dramatic Soundings; Evaluations and Retractions Culled from 30 Years of Dramatic Criticism, ed. Glenn Loney (New York: Crown Publishers, 1968).

and Ralph G. Allen, *Theatre and Drama in the Making* (Boston: Houghton Mifflin, 1964).

George, W. L., *Dramatic Actualities* (London: Sidgwick & Jackson, 1914).

Gerstenberger, Donna, *John Millington Synge* (New York: Twayne Publishers, 1964).

'Yeats and Synge: "A Young Man's Ghost"', *W. B. Yeats, 1865–1965: Centenary Essays on the Art of W. B. Yeats*, ed. D. E. S. Maxwell and S. B. Bushrui (Ibadan: Ibadan University Press, 1965) pp. 79–87.

'Analysis of *Riders to the Sea*', *An Introduction to Drama and Criticism*, ed. Emil Hurtik and Robert Yarber (Waltham, Mass.: Xerox College Publishing, 1971) pp. 321–6.

Gogarty, Oliver St. John, *As I Was Going Down Sackville Street* (London: Rich & Cowan; New York: Reynal & Hitchcock, 1937; London: Sphere Books, 1968).

Goldstone, Richard H. and Abraham H. Lass (eds.), '*Riders to the Sea*: John Millington Synge', *The Mentor Book of Short Plays* (New York: The New American Library; London: The New English Library, 1969) pp. 311–26 [text and commentary].

Graham-Lujan, James, '*Riders to the Sea, Blood Wedding and Mother Courage*', *Drama & Discussion*, ed. Stanley A. Clayes (New York: Appleton-Century-Crofts, 1967) pp. 328—9.

Graves, A. P., 'Anglo-Irish Literature', *The Cambridge History of English Literature*, vol. XIV, ed. A. W. Ward and A. R. Waller (Cambridge: Cambridge University Press, 1964), pp. 329—30.

Grebanier, Bernard D., 'Synge', *English Literature*, vol. II: *The Nineteenth Century to the Present* (Woodbury, N.Y.: Barrons Educational Series, 1948) pp. 746—7.

et al (eds.), 'John Millington Synge: *The Playboy of the Western World*', *English Literature and Its Backgrounds*. rev. ed., vol. II (New York: Holt, Rinehart & Winston, 1949) pp. 1056—82 [text and commentary].

and Seymour Reiter (eds.), 'John Millington Synge: *The Playboy of the Western World*', *Introduction to Imaginative Literature* (New York: Thomas Y. Crowell, 1960) pp. 848—72 [annotated text].

Green, Elizabeth Lay, 'The Irish Dramatic Movement: Yeats, Lady Gregory and Synge', *A Study Course in Modern Drama* (Chapel Hill, N.C.: University of North Carolina Press, 1921) pp. 41—3.

Greene, David H. and Edward M. Stephens, *J. M. Synge, 1871— 1909* (New York: Macmillan, 1959; Collier Books, 1961). Reviewed in *The Times* (London, 4 Jun 1959) p. 15; in *New York Times Book Review* (19 Apr 1959) p. 5; by Walter Starkie in *Saturday Review*, XLII (N.Y., 18 Apr 1959) 19—20; by R. A. Fraser in *Nation*, CXC (N.Y., 20 Feb 1960) 171—3; by M. Cosman in *Commonweal*, LXX (N.Y., 17 Jul 1959) 380—2; in *Newsweek*, LIII (20 Apr 1959) 119; by Robert Crosby in *Quarterly Journal of Speech*, XLV, no. 3 (Oct 1959) 337—8; by Ellen Douglass Leyburn in *Modern Drama*, III (May 1960) 93—5; by Louis MacNeice in *London Magazine*, VII (Aug 1960) 70—3; by

Monk Gibbon in *Studies*, XLVIII (Dublin, Autumn 1959) 359–61; by George Brandon Saul in *Arizona Quarterly*, XV (Tuscon, Winter 1959) 373–4; by John Hewitt in *Listener* (London, 8 Oct 1959) p. 590; by Donat O'Donnell in *Spectator* (London, 14 Aug 1959) p. 201; and in *The Times Literary Supplement* (19 Jun 1959) p. 370.

Gregory, Lady [Isabella Augusta], *Our Irish Theatre; A Chapter of Autobiography* (London and New York: G. P. Putnam's, 1913; New York: Capricorn Books, 1965).

Guernsey, Otis L., Jr., 'Milwaukee Repertory Theater: *The Playboy of the Western World*', *The Best Plays of 1964–1965* (New York: Dodd, Mead, 1965) p. 61.

Guerrero Zamora, Juan, 'John Millington Synge', *Historia del teatro contemporaneo*, III (Barcelona: Juan Flors, 1962) pp. 28–33.

Gwynn, Stephen, *Irish Literature and Drama in the English Language; A Short History* (London: Thomas Nelson, 1936; Folcroft, Pa.: The Folcroft Press, Inc., 1969) pp. 161–4, 178–80.

Hackett, Francis, 'John Synge', *Horizons; A Book of Criticism* (New York: B. W. Huebsch, 1918) pp. 189–97 [on *Poems and Translations*].

Halpin, Rev. L. F. *et al*, *Adventures in English* (N.Y.: Harcourt, 1954).

Hamilton, Clayton, 'The Irish National Theatre', *Studies in Stagecraft* (New York: Henry Holt; London: Grant Richards, 1914) pp. 138–44.

Seen on the Stage (New York: Henry Holt, 1920) pp. 226, 229.

Hampden, John (ed.), '*Riders to the Sea*. J. M. Synge', *Nine*

Modern Plays (London: Thomas Nelson, 1926) pp. 179—93, 214—16 [text and commentary].

(sel.), 'Riders to the Sea: J. M. Synge', *Twenty-Four One-Act Plays*, Everyman's Library (London: Dent, 1954) pp. 13—24 [text only].

Harmon, Maurice (ed.), *Synge Centenary Papers* (Dublin: The Dolmen Press, 1971).

Hart, Francis R., 'John Millington Synge', *Merit Students Encyclopedia*, vol. XVII (New York: Crowell-Collier Educational Corporation, 1971) p. 573.

Hart, William E. (ed.), *J. M. Synge: The Playboy of the Western World and Riders to the Sea*, Crofts Classics (New York: Appleton-Century-Crofts, 1966).

Hatcher, Harlan (ed.), 'J. M. Synge: *The Playboy of the Western World*', *Modern British Dramas* (New York: Harcourt Brace, 1941) pp. 211—51 [text and commentary].

Havighurst, Walter *et al* (eds.), 'J. M. Synge: *Riders to the Sea*', *Selection; A Reader for College Writing* (New York: The Dryden Press, 1955) pp. 600—6 [text and commentary].

Heilman, Robert B., *Tragedy and Melodrama; Versions of Experience* (Seattle and London: University of Washington Press, 1968) pp. 38—40.

Henderson, W. A. (comp.), *The Playboy of the Western World, by J. M. Synge. A Play that Shocked. A Compendium of Comments, Criticisms, Calumnies, Carpings, Caricatures, Cavillings, Clamours, Congratulations.* (Privately printed.)

Henn, T. R., 'Yeats and Synge', *The Lonely Tower: Studies in the Poetry of W. B. Yeats* (London: Methuen, 1950) pp. 72—87.

'The Irish Tragedy', *The Harvest of Tragedy* (London:

Methuen, 1956; University Paperbacks, 1966) pp. 197–205.

(ed.), *J. M. Synge: The Playboy of the Western World* (London: Methuen, 1960). Reviewed briefly by T. J. B. Spencer in *Modern Language Review*, LVI, no. 4 (London, Oct 1960) 635.

(ed.), *J. M. Synge: Riders to the Sea and In the Shadow of the Glen* (London: Methuen, 1961).

(ed.), 'Introduction', *The Plays and Poems of J. M. Synge* (London: Methuen, 1963). Reviewed in *The Times* (London, 12 Dec 1963) p. 14; in *The Times Literary Supplement* (London, 6 Feb 1964) p. 101; by W. R. Rodgers in *Listener*, LXX (London, 5 Dec 1963) 951–2; by Ronald Gaskell in *Critical Quarterly*, VI (London, Winter 1964) 381–2; by Richard Ellmann in *New Statesman*, LXVII (London, 20 Mar 1964) 461; and by A. R. Robertson in *Tablet*, CCXVII (London, 1 Feb 1964) 130.

'*Riders to the Sea*: A Note', *Sunshine and the Moon's Delight*, ed. S. B. Bushrui (Gerrards Cross, Bucks.: Colin Smythe, 1972) pp. 33–9.

Hensel, Georg, 'Synge: die irische Realität, fröhlich', *Spielplan: Schauspielführer, von der Antike bis zur Gegenwart*, II (Berlin: Propylaen, 1966) pp. 792–796.

Hillebrand, Harold Newcomb, *Writing the One-Act Play: A Manual for Beginners* (New York: F. S. Crofts, 1925).

Hind, C. Lewis, 'J. M. Synge', *More Authors and I* (London: John Lane; New York: Dodd, Mead, 1922) pp. 279–84.

Hinkson, Katherine Tynan, *Twenty-Five Years; Reminiscences* (London: Smith, Elder, 1913).

Hoare, Dorothy Mackenzie, *The Works of Morris and of Yeats in Relation to Early Saga Literature* (Cambridge: Cambridge University Press, 1937) pp. 105–10.

Hogan, Robert, *After the Irish Renaissance; A Critical History of the Irish Drama Since 'The Plough and the Stars'* (Minneapolis: University of Minnesota Press, 1967; London: Macmillan, 1968).

'Synge's Influence in Modern Irish Drama', *Sunshine and the Moon's Delight*, ed. S. B. Bushrui (Gerrards Cross, Bucks.: Colin Smythe, 1972) pp. 231–44.

Holloway, Joseph, *Joseph Holloway's Abbey Theatre: A Selection from His Unpublished Journal 'Impressions of a Dublin Playgoer'*, ed. Robert Hogan and Michael J. O'Neill. With a Preface by Harry T. Moore (Carbondale and Edwardsville: Southern Illinois University Press; London and Amsterdam: Feffer & Simons, 1967).

Joseph Holloway's Irish Theatre, 1926–1944, 3 vols., ed. Robert Hogan and Michael J. O'Neill (Dixon, Calif.: Proscenium Press, 1968–70).

Hornstein, Lillian Herlands (ed.), 'John Millington Synge', *The Reader's Companion to World Literature* (New York: Holt, Rinehart & Winston; Mentor Books, 1956) pp. 434–5.

Hortmann, Wilhelm, *Englische Literatur im 20. Jahrhundert* (Berne: A. Francke, 1965) pp. 30–3.

Howarth, Herbert, *The Irish Writers, 1880–1940: Literature under Parnell's Star* (London: Rockliff, 1958; New York: Hill & Wang, 1959) pp. 212–44.

Howe, P. P., 'Miss Horniman: The Abbey Theatre, Dublin', *The Repertory Theatre; A Record and A Criticism* (London: Martin Secker, 1910) pp. 42–51.

J. M. Synge; A Critical Study (London: Martin Secker; New York: Mitchell Kennerley, 1912; Folcroft, Pa.: The Folcroft

Press, 1969). Reviewed in *The Times Literary Supplement*
(London, 29 Aug 1912) p. 338; in *Daily Mail* (London, 12
Jul 1912) p. 2; in *Pall Mall Gazette* (London, 24 Jun 1912)
p. 5; by C. E. Montague in *Manchester Guardian* (24 Jun
1912) p. 5; by Robert Lynd in *Daily News and Leader*
(London, 14 Jun 1912) p. 8; by John Palmer in *Saturday
Review* (London, 13 Jul 1912) pp. 42—3; in *English Review*,
XII (London, Sep 1912) 326—7; by Darrell Figgis in
Bookman, XLIII (London, Oct 1912) 58—59; in *Athenaeum*
(London, 29 Jun 1912) pp. 726—7; in *New Witness*, I, no. 9
(London, 2 Jan 1913) 282—3; in *Oxford Chronicle* (5 Jul
1912) p. 7; in *American Review of Reviews* (Dec 1912)
p. 750; in *North American Review* (N.Y., Oct 1912) pp.
571—2; in *Current Literature*, LIII (N.Y., Jul—Dec 1912)
695; by Henry Seidel Canby in *Yale Review*, II (Jul 1913)
767—72; by Stuart P. Sherman in *Nation*, XCV (N.Y., 26
Dec 1912) 608—11; in *Evening Post* (N.Y., 11 Jan 1913)
p. 6; by James W. Tupper in *Dial*, LIX (Chicago, 16 Mar
1913) 233—5; in *Independent*, LXXIII (N.Y., 7 Nov 1912)
1071—3; and by James A. Roy in *Anglia*, XXXVII (1913)
129—45.

Hubbell, Jay B. and John O. Beaty, 'John Millington Synge:
Riders to the Sea', *An Introduction to Drama* (New York:
Macmillan, 1929) pp. 777—83 and 522—4 [text and
commentary].

Hudson, Lynton, *The Twentieth-Century Drama* (London:
George G. Harrap, 1946) pp. 41—4.

Hughes, Leo, 'John Millington Synge', *The World Book
Encyclopedia*, vol. XVII (Chicago: Field Enterprises
Educational Corporation, 1966) p. 852.

Huneker, James, 'John M. Synge', *The Pathos of Distance; A
Book of a Thousand and One Moments* (London: T. Werner
Laurie; New York: Charles Scribner's, 1913; repr. 1922)
pp. 228—35.

Inglis, Rewey Belle and Josephine Spear (eds.), 'John

Millington Synge: *Riders to the Sea*', *Adventures in English Literature* (New York: Harcourt, Brace, 1958) pp. 770–7 [text and commentary].

Irish Plays. Toured under the direction of Alfred Wareing, Summer 1906 (Dublin, 1906) pp. 8–10 [pamphlet].

Jackson, Holbrook, 'John M. Synge', *All Manner of Folk; Interpretations and Studies* (New York: Mitchell Kennerley; London: Grant Richards, 1912) pp. 61–77.

Jacquot, Jean (ed.), *Le theatre moderne; hommes et tendances* (Paris: Editions du centre national de la recherche scientifique, 1965) pp. 325–30.

James, Thelma G. *et al* (eds.), 'Riders to the Sea — John Millington Synge', *World Neighbors; A Book of Readings of Many Countries* (New York: Harper, 1950) pp. 391–8 [text and commentary].

Jameson, Storm, 'J. M. Synge', *Modern Drama in Europe* (London: Collins; New York: Harcourt, Brace, 1920) pp. 212–6.

'John Millington Synge', *McGraw-Hill Encyclopedia of World Drama* (New York: McGraw-Hill, 1972), vol. 4, pp. 258–65.

Johnston, Denis, *John Millington Synge*, Columbia Essays on Modern Writers no. 12 (New York and London: Columbia University Press, 1965). Reviewed by Norman Suckling in *Notes and Queries*, XIII, New Series (1966) 438–9.

Jordan, John, 'The Irish Theatre: Retrospect and Premonition', *Contemporary Theatre*, ed. John Russell Brown and Bernard Harris, Stratford-upon-Avon Studies 4 (London: Edward Arnold, 1962) pp. 165–8.

Joyce, James, 'Programme Notes for the English Players', *The Critical Writings of James Joyce*, ed. Ellsworth Mason and

Richard Ellmann (London: Faber & Faber, 1959) pp. 249–
50 [on *Riders to the Sea*].

Kain, Richard M., *Dublin in the Age of William Butler Yeats and James Joyce* (Norman, Okla.: University of Oklahoma Press, 1962; repr. 1967).

'The Playboy Riots', *Sunshine and the Moon's Delight*, ed. S. B. Bushrui (Gerrards Cross, Bucks.: Colin Smythe, 1972) pp. 173–88.

Kavanagh, Peter, *The Irish Theatre; Being A History of the Drama in Ireland from the Earliest Period to the Present Day* (Tralee: Kerryman, 1946).

The Story of the Abbey Theatre, From Its Origins in 1899 to the Present (New York: Devin-Adair, 1950).

Kelly, Blanche Mary, 'Stage Directions', *The Voice of the Irish* (New York: Sheed & Ward, 1952) 264–8.

Kennedy, J. M., *English Literature, 1880–1905* (London: Stephen Swift, 1912) pp. 281, 309.

Kennelly, Brendan, 'John Millington Synge', *Encyclopedia Britannica*, vol. XXI (London, 1970) p. 567.

Kenny, P. D., 'That Dreadful Play', *Specimens of English Dramatic Criticism XVII–XX Centuries*, ed. A. C. Ward (London: Oxford University Press, 1945) pp. 254–9 [on *The Playboy of the Western World*].

Kernan, Alvin B., '*Riders to the Sea* by John Millington Synge', *Character and Conflict; An Introduction to Drama*. 2nd ed. (New York: Harcourt, Brace & World, 1969) pp. 557–69 [text and commentary].

Kernodle, George R., 'Poetic Drama of Ireland and Spain', *Invitation to the Theatre* (New York: Harcourt, Brace, 1967) pp. 229–31.

Kerr, Moira and John Bennett (eds.), 'The Irish Theatre' and *'Riders to the Sea* by J. M. Synge', *Theatre*, vol. II: *The Twentieth Century* (Toronto: The Copp Clark Publishing Company, 1967) pp. 6–7 and 57–67 [text], respectively.

Kilroy, James, *The Playboy Riots* (Dublin: The Dolmen Press; London: Oxford University Press, 1971). Reviewed in *The Times Literary Supplement* (London, 2 Jul 1971) pp. 749–50.

Kleinstück, Johannes, *W. B. Yeats oder: Der Dichter in der modernen Welt* (Hamburg: Leibniz-Verlag, 1963) pp. 54–6.

'Synge in Germany', *Sunshine and the Moon's Delight*, ed. S. B. Bushrui (Gerrards Cross, Bucks.: Colin Smythe, 1972) pp. 271–7.

Knickerbocker, Edwin Van B. (ed.), *'Riders to the Sea.* John M. Synge', *Short Plays*. Rev. (New York: Henry Holt, 1949) pp. 161–75 [text and commentary].

Knight, G. Wilson, *The Golden Labyrinth; A Study of British Drama* (London: Phoenix House, 1962; University Paperbacks, 1965) pp. 322–5.

Kraft, Irma, 'Ireland – The Rebellious', *Plays, Players, Playhouses: International Drama of Today* (New York: Dobsevage, 1928) pp. 144–51.

Krause, David, 'John Millington Synge', *The Reader's Encyclopedia of World Drama*, ed. John Gassner and Edward Quinn (New York: Thomas Y. Crowell, 1969; London: Methuen, 1970) pp. 833–4.

Krieger, Hans, *John Millington Synge, ein dichter der 'Keltischen renaissance'* (Marburg: N. G. Elwert'-sche Verlagsbuchandlung, 1916).

Kronenberger, Louis, 'Synge', *The Thread of Laughter: Chapters on English Stage Comedy from Jonson to*

Maugham (New York: Alfred A. Knopf, 1952; Hill & Wang, 1970) pp. 279–88.

(ed.), 'John Millington Synge: *The Playboy of the Western World*', *Cavalcade of Comedy* (New York: Simon & Schuster, 1953) pp. 438–60 [text and commentary].

(ed.), *The Best Plays of 1956–1957* (New York: Dodd, Mead, 1957) p. 55.

Krutch, Joseph Wood, 'Synge and the Irish Protest', *'Modernism' in Modern Drama; A Definition and An Estimate* (Ithaca, N.Y.: Cornell University Press, 1953; Cornell Paperbacks, 1966) pp. 88–103.

Kunitz, Stanley J. and Howard Haycraft (eds.), 'John Millington Synge', *Twentieth Century Authors; A Biographical Dictionary of Modern Literature* (New York: H. W. Wilson, 1942) pp. 1378–80.

Lalou, René, 'Synge et le théâtre', *Panorama de la littérature anglaise contemporaine* (Paris: Editions KRA, 1926) pp. 189-95.

Lamm, Martin, 'Irish Drama', *Modern Drama*, trans. Karin Elliott (Oxford: Blackwell, 1952; New York: Philosophical Library, 1953) pp. 293–314.

Law, Hugh Alexander, 'Dramatists', *Anglo-Irish Literature*, with a foreword by A. E. (London: Longmans, Green, 1926) pp. 250–71.

Leblanc, Gerard, 'Synge in France', *Sunshine and the Moon's Delight*, ed. S. B. Bushrui (Gerrards Cross, Bucks.: Colin Smythe, 1972) pp. 265–70.

Legouis, Emile and Louis Cazamian, *A History of English Literature* (London: J. M. Dent, 1965) pp. 1286–7.

Lennartz, Franz, *Auslandische Dichter und Schriftsteller* (Stuttgart: Alfred Kröner, [1955]).

Leonard, Sterling Andrus, *'Riders to the Sea*. John Millington Synge', *The Atlantic Book of Modern Plays* (Boston: Little, Brown, 1935) pp. 197–210 [text] and 361–2 [commentary].

Letts, W. M., 'For Sixpence', *Songs from Leinster* (London: Smith, Elder, 1913) p. 40 [a poem written from the point of view of the sixpenny audience at the Abbey Theatre when W. G. Fay was acting there in *The Playboy*].

'Synge's Grave', *Songs from Leinster* (London: Smith, Elder, 1913) p. 42 [a poem]. Reprinted from *Westminster Gazette* (London, 20 Dec 1912).

Lewisohn, Ludwig, *The Modern Drama* (New York: B. W. Huebsch; London: Martin Secker, 1916; New York: The Viking Press, 1931) pp. 273–4.

Lieder, Paul Robert *et al* (eds.), 'John Millington Synge: *The Playboy of the Western World*', *British Poetry and Prose*, rev. ed., vol. II (Boston: Houghton Mifflin, 1938) pp. 970–1 [commentary] and pp. 971–99 [text].

Locke, Louis Glenn, William M. Gibson and George Arms (eds.), 'J. M. Synge: *In The Shadow of the Glen*', *Introduction to Literature*, 3rd ed. (N.Y.: Rinehart, 1957).

Loomis, Roger Sherman *et al*, *'Riders to the Sea*. John Millington Synge', *Modern English Readings* (New York: Rinehart, 1958) pp. 715–24 [text only].

Lucas, F. L., 'John Millington Synge', *The Drama of Chekhov, Synge, Yeats and Pirandello* (London: Cassell, 1963; 2nd ed., 1965) pp. 149–237. Reviewed in *The Times* (London, 21 Nov 1963) p. 19.

Lunari, Gigi, 'Lady Gregory e Synge', *Il movimento drammatico irlandese (1899–1922)*, Documenti di teatro 13 (Bologne: Cappelli, 1960) pp. 85–107.

Books

Lynch, Arthur, *My Life Story* (London: John Long, 1924)
pp. 121, 148–50.

Lynd, Robert, 'Literature and Music', *Home Life in Ireland*
(London: Mills & Boon, 1909) pp. 305 *et seq.*

'The Fame of J. M. Synge', *Old and New Masters* (London:
T. Fisher Unwin; New York: Scribner's, 1919; Freeport,
N.Y.: Books for Libraries, 1970) pp. 94–7.

Ireland a Nation (London: Grant Richards, 1919; New
York: Dodd, Mead, 1920).

McCallum, James Dow (ed.), *The College Omnibus* (New
York: Harcourt, Brace, 1933) 629–38 [text and
commentary].

McCann, Sean (ed.), *The Story of the Abbey Theatre*. A Four
Square Book (London: The New English Library, 1967).

MacDonagh, Thomas, *Literature in Ireland: Studies in Irish
and Anglo-Irish* (Dublin: Talbot Press; New York: Frederick
A. Stokes, 1916; Port Washington, N.Y. and London:
Kennikat Press, 1970) pp. 16, 48–9.

MacGowan, Kenneth and William Melnitz, 'Ireland's Rich
Drama', *The Living Stage; A History of the World Theater*
(Englewood Cliffs, N.J.: Prentice-Hall, 1955) pp. 421–4.

McHugh, Roger, 'John Millington Synge', *Cassell's Encyclopedia of Literature*, ed. S. H. Steinberg, vol. II (London,
1953) pp. 1531–2.

MacKenna, Stephen, *Journal and Letters*, ed. with a Memoir
by E. R. Dodds and a Preface by Padraic Colum (London:
Constable, 1936).

MacLiammóir, Micheál, *All for Hecuba; An Irish Theatrical
Autobiography* (London: Methuen, 1946; Dublin: Progress
House, 1961).

43

Theatre in Ireland (Dublin: Published for the Cultural Relations Committee of Ireland at The Three Candles, 1950; Printed with Sequel, 1964) p. 15.

(ed.), 'Introduction', *J. M. Synge's Plays, Poems, and Prose*, Everyman's Library (London: J. M. Dent, 1958).

Magill, Frank N. (ed.), *Masterpieces of World Literature* (New York: Harper & Row, 1960).

(ed.), *Cyclopedia of Literary Characters* (New York: Harper & Row, 1963).

Mair, G. H., *Modern English Literature from Chaucer to the Present Day* (London: Williams & Norgate, 1911; New York: Holt, 1914) pp. 247 *et seq.* Reprinted from *Manchester Guardian*.

Maleh, Ghassan, 'Synge in the Arab World', *Sunshine and the Moon's Delight* (Gerrards Cross, Bucks.: Colin Smythe, 1972) pp. 245–52.

Maline, Julian L. and James Berkley (eds.), 'John Millington Synge: *Riders to the Sea*', *Dramatic Literature*, Patterns of Literature, vol. III (New York: L. W. Singer Company, 1967) pp. 165–180 [text and commentary].

Malone, Andrew E., 'The Folk Dramatists: John Millington Synge', *The Irish Drama* (London: Constable; New York: Charles Scribner's, 1929; Benjamin Blom, 1965) ch. VIII, pp. 147–56.

'The Early History of the Abbey Theatre', *The Irish Theatre; Lectures Delivered During the Abbey Theatre Festival Held in Dublin in August 1938*, ed. Lennox Robinson (London: Macmillan, 1939; New York: Haskell House Publishers, 1971) pp. 1–28.

Malye, Jean, *La littérature irlandaise contemporaine* (Paris:
E. Sansot, 1913) pp. 41, 50–1.

Mandel, Oscar, *A Definition of Tragedy* (New York: New
York University Press, 1961).

Mantle, Burns (ed.), *The Best Plays of 1909–19* (New York:
Dodd, Mead, 1919).

(ed.), 'The Playboy of the Western World', The Best Plays
of 1920–21 (New York: Dodd, Mead, 1921) pp. 441–2.

(ed.), 'The Playboy of the Western World', The Best Plays
of 1929–30, pp. 473–4.

(ed.), *The Best Plays of 1934–35* (New York: Dodd, Mead,
1935) pp. 408–

(ed.), *The Best Plays of 1937–38* (New York: Dodd, Mead,
1938) pp. 376–463.

(ed.), 'Off Broadway', The Best Plays of 1938–39 (New
York: Dodd, Mead, 1939) p. 484 [on *The Well of the
Saints*].

(ed.), 'The Playboy of the Western World', The Best Plays
of 1946–47 (New York: Dodd, Mead, 1947) p. 430.

Marcus, Phillip L., *Yeats and the Beginnings of the Irish
Renaissance* (Ithaca & London: Cornell University Press,
1970).

Marriott, J. W., *Modern Drama* (London: Thomas Nelson,
[1934]) pp. 194–7.

Martin, Augustine, 'The Playboy of the Western World:
Christy Mahon and the Apotheosis of Loneliness', *Sunshine
and the Moon's Delight*, ed. S. B. Bushrui (Gerrards Cross,
Bucks.: Colin Smythe, 1972) pp. 61–73.

Masefield, John, 'John Millington Synge', *The Dictionary of National Biography*, 2nd Supplement, vol. III (London: Smith, Elder, 1912) pp. 468–71.

John M. Synge; A Few Personal Recollections with Biographical Notes (Dundrum, Dublin: Cuala Press; New York: Macmillan, 1915; Letchworth: Garden City Press, 1916). Reprinted in *Recent Prose* (London: Heinemann, 1924; New York: Macmillan, 1933) pp. 163–87. Reviewed in *Independent*, LXXXIII (N.Y., 27 Sep 1915) 433–4; in *Sewanee Review*, XXIV (Jan 1916) 120–3; and in *Dial*, LX (Chicago, 16 March 1916) 285.

'Matlaw, Myron, 'Synge', *Modern World Drama; An Encyclopedia* (New York: Dutton; London: Secker & Warburg, 1972).

Matthews, Brander, 'Irish Plays and Irish Playwrights', *The Principles of Playmaking and Other Discussions of the Drama* (New York: Charles Scribner's, 1919) pp. 196–213.

Meisel, Martin, 'John Millington Synge', *The World Book Encyclopedia*, vol. XVII (Chicago: Field Enterprises Educational Corporation, 1971) p. 852.

Melchinger, Siegfried, *Drama swischen Shaw und Brecht* (Bremen: Carl Schünemann, 1957) pp. 388–9.

'John Millington Synge', *The Concise Encyclopedia of Modern Drama* (London: Vision Press, 1970) p. 255.

and Henning Rischbieter (eds.), 'John Millington Synge', *Welttheater: Bühnen, Autoren, Inszenierungen* (Wien: Buchgemeinschaft Donauland, 1962) pp. 429–30.

Mercier, Vivian, *The Irish Comic Tradition* (London and New York: Oxford University Press, 1962; paperback, 1969).

'*The Tinker's Wedding*', *Sunshine and the Moon's Delight*, ed. S. B. Bushrui (Gerrards Cross, Bucks.: Colin Smythe, 1972) pp. 75—89.

and David H. Greene (eds.), 'Introduction', *1000 Years of Irish Prose* (N.Y.: Devin-Adair, 1952; Grosset & Dunlap, 1961). [Contains 'Preface' to *The Playboy of the Western World*; excerpts from *The Aran Islands*; and *In the Shadow of the Glen*].

Miller, Anna Irene, 'The National Theatre of Ireland', *The Independent Theatre in Europe, 1887 to the Present* (New York: R. Long & R. R. Smith, 1931; Benjamin Blom, 1966) pp. 255—310.

Miller, Nellie Burget, 'Synge: The Drama of Contemporary Peasant Life', *The Living Drama: Historical Development and Modern Movements Visualized* (New York & London: Century, 1924) pp. 337—41.

Millet, Fred B., 'The Irish Drama', *Contemporary British Literature: A Critical Survey and 232 Author-Bibliographies*, 3rd rev. and enl. ed., ed. John M. Manly and Edith Rickert (New York: Harcourt, Brace, 1944) pp. 59—62.

'John Millington Synge: *Riders to the Sea*', *Reading Drama; A Method of Analysis With Selections for Study* (New York: Harper, 1950; Freeport, N.Y.: Books for Libraries Press, 1970) pp. 91—104.

Monahan, Michael, 'Yeats and Synge', *Nova Hibernia; Irish Poets and Dramatists of Today and Yesterday* (New York: Mitchell Kennerley, 1914) pp. 13—37.

Montague, C. E., 'The Literary Play', *Essays and Studies by Members of the English Association*, vol. II, collected by H. C. Beeching (Oxford: Clarendon Press, 1911) pp. 81, 85.

'The Plays of J. M. Synge', *Dramatic Values* (London: Methuen; New York: Macmillan, 1911; London: Chatto & Windus, 1931) pp. 1—15.

Moody, William Vaughn and Robert Morss Lovett, 'J. M.
   Synge', *A History of English Literature*, 8th ed. by Fred B.
   Millett (New York: Charles Scribner's, 1964) pp. 398–9.

Moore, George, *Hail and Farewell*, vol. III (London: William
   Heinemann; New York: Appleton, 1911–14; repr. 1925).

Moore, John R., '*Deirdre* and the Sorrows of Mortality',
   Sunshine and the Moon's Delight, ed. S. B. Bushrui
   (Gerrards Cross, Bucks.: Colin Smythe, 1972) pp. 91–105.

Morcos, Louis and Ali Er-Rai (eds.), 'Introduction' and 'John
   Millington Synge: *Riders to the Sea*', *Modern International
   Plays*, Lotus Books (Cairo: Anglo Egyptian Bookshop,
   1957) pp. v–xvi and 29–48 [text only].

More, Paul Elmer, 'Fiona MacLeod', *The Drift of Romanticism*,
   Shelburne Essays, 8th series (Boston and New York:
   Houghton Mifflin, 1913) pp. 135–6.

Morgan, A. E., 'Synge', *Tendencies of Modern English Drama*
   (London: Constable; New York: Charles Scribner's, 1924)
   pp. 158–73.

Morris, Alton Chester *et al* (eds.), 'J. M. Synge: *The Playboy
   of the Western World*', *College English: The First Year*,
   5th ed. (N.Y.: Harcourt, Brace & World, [1968]) pp. 607–
   36 [text and commentary].

   (eds.), 'J. M. Synge: *The Playboy of the Western World*',
   Imaginative Literature: Fiction, Drama, Poetry (N.Y.:
   Harcourt, Brace & World, [1968]) pp. 247–76 [text and
   commentary].

Morris, Lloyd R., 'The Drama', *The Celtic Dawn; A Survey of
   the Renascence in Ireland 1889–1916* (New York:
   Macmillan, 1917; Cooper Square Publishers, Inc., 1970)
   pp. 124–34.

Moses, Montrose J. (ed.), '*Riders to the Sea*. John Millington

Synge', *Representative British Dramas; Victorian and Modern* (Boston: Little, Brown, 1931) pp. 787—89.

Munro, John, 'J. M. Synge and the Drama of the Late Nineteenth Century', *Sunshine and the Moon's Delight*, ed. S. B. Bushrui (Gerrards Cross, Bucks.: Colin Smythe, 1972) pp. 219—30.

Nathan, George Jean, 'Foreword', *Five Great Modern Irish Plays*, The Modern Library (New York: Random House, 1941) [texts of *The Playboy of the Western World* and *Riders to the Sea*].

Theatre Book of the Year, 1946—1947 (New York: Knopf, 1947) pp. 136—9 [on *The Playboy of the Western World*].

Nevinson, H. W., 'Irish Plays of 1904', *Books and Personalities* (London and N.Y.: John Lane, 1905) pp. 248—9 [on *Riders to the Sea* and *In the Shadow of the Glen*].

Nicoll, Allardyce, 'J. M. Synge and the Irish School of Imaginative Dramatists' and 'J. M. Synge and the Irish School', *British Drama; An Historical Survey from the Beginnings to the Present Time* (London: George G. Harrap, 1925; 4th rev. ed., 1947) pp. 410—17 and 432—5.

'The Extension of the Realistic', *World Drama from Aeschylus to Anouilh* (London: George G. Harrap, 1949) pp. 690—5.

The Theory of Drama (London: George G. Harrap; New York: Crowell, 1931; New York: Benjamin Blom, 1966).

'Synge', *Chambers's Encyclopedia*, new rev. ed., vol. XIII (Oxford: Pergamon Press, 1966) p. 396.

Nic Shiubhlaigh, Maire, *The Splendid Years: Recollections of Maire Nic Shiubhlaigh, as Told to Edward Kenny* (Dublin: James Duffy, 1955).

O'Brien, Conor Cruise, *Writers and Politics*, Pantheon Books (New York: Random House, 1965) pp. 110, 121–2.

O'Brien, Edward J., 'Introduction', *Riders to the Sea by J. M. Synge* (Boston: John W. Luce, 1911).

'Introduction', *The Aran Islands* (Boston: J. W. Luce, 1911).

'Preface', *The Works of John M. Synge* (Boston: J. W. Luce, 1912).

O'Casey, Sean, 'Song of a Shift', *Drums under the Window* (London: Macmillan, 1954). Reprinted in *Autobiographies*, vol. I (London: Macmillan, 1963) pp. 506–20.

'John Millington Synge', *Blasts and Benedictions*, ed. Ronald Ayling (London: Macmillan; New York: St. Martin's Press, 1967) pp. 35–41 [first appearance in English of the article published in *Britansky Soyuznik* (Moscow, Jun 1946)].

O'Connor, Frank, 'Synge', *The Irish Theatre: Lectures Delivered During the Abbey Theatre Festival Held in Dublin in August 1938*, ed. Lennox Robinson (London: Macmillan, 1939; New York: Haskell House, 1971) pp. 29–52.

'All the Olympians', *The Backward Look; A Survey of Irish Literature* (London: Macmillan, 1967) pp. 183–93. Reprinted as *A Short History of Irish Literature; The Backward Look* (New York: Capricorn Books, 1967) pp. 183–93. Reprinted from *Saturday Review*, XLIX, no. 50 (N.Y., 10 Dec 1966) 30–32, 99.

O'Conor, Norreys Jephson, *Changing Ireland: Literary Backgrounds of the Irish Free State, 1889–1922* (Cambridge, Mass.: Harvard University Press; London: Humphrey Milford, 1924).

O'Donoghue, D. J., 'John Millington Synge', *The Poets of*

Ireland: A Biographical and Bibliographical Dictionary of Irish Writers of English Verse (Dublin: Hodges Figgis; London: Henry Frowde, Oxford University Press, 1912) p. 448.

O'Driscoll, Robert (ed.), *Theatre and Nationalism in Twentieth-Century Ireland* (Toronto: University of Toronto Press, 1971).

'Yeats's Conception of Synge', *Sunshine and the Moon's Delight*, ed. S. B. Bushrui (Gerrards Cross, Bucks.: Colin Smythe, 1972) pp. 159–71.

O'Hagan, Thomas, 'The Irish Dramatic Movement', *Essays on Catholic Life* (Baltimore: John Murphy, 1916; Freeport, N.Y.: Books for Libraries, 1965) pp. 57–73.

O'hAodha, Mícheál, *The Abbey – Then and Now* (Dublin: The Abbey Theatre, 1969).

Oliver, D. E., *The English Stage: Its Origins and Modern Developments* (London: John Ouseley, 2nd ed., 1912) pp. 118 *et seq.*

O'Marchaigh, Caoimhin, *The Playboy of the Western World* (Dublin: Educational Co., 1972).

Onofrio, Lilia d', 'John M. Synge, dramaturgo irlandes contemporaneo', *Neuovo ensavos de critica literaria* (Buenos Aires: 'El Ateneo', 1942) pp. 69–79.

Oshima, Shotaro, 'Synge in Japan', *Sunshine and the Moon's Delight*, ed. S. B. Bushrui (Gerrards Cross, Bucks.: Colin Smythe, 1972) pp. 253–63.

Page, Curtis C., *Drama: Synge's Riders to the Sea*, Casebooks for Objective Writing, gen. ed. Charlton Laird (Boston: Ginn, 1966).

Palmer, John, *The Future of the Theatre* (London: G. Bell and Sons, 1913).

Paul-Dubois, L., 'Le théâtre irlandais', *L'Irlande contemporaine et la question irlandaise* (Paris: Librarie academique Perrin, 1907) pp. 407–10. English translation by T. M. Kettle, 'The Irish Theatre', *Contemporary Ireland* (Dublin: Maunsel, 1911) pp. 423–6.

Peacock, Ronald, 'Synge', *The Poet in the Theatre* (London: Routledge and Kegan Paul; New York: Harcourt, Brace, 1946; Hill and Wang, 1960) pp. 105–16.

Pellizzi, Camillo, *English Drama: The Last Great Phase*, trans. by Rowan Williams (London: Macmillan, 1935), ch. VI, pp. 212–18.

Perry, Henry Ten Eyck, *Masters of Dramatic Comedy and Their Social Themes* (Cambridge, Mass.: Harvard University Press, 1939; Port Washington, N.Y.: Kennikat Press, 1968) pp. 364–6.

Phelps, W. L., *The Advance of English Poetry in the Twentieth Century* (New York: Dodd, Mead, 1918) pp. 171–7.

Pinto, Vivian de Sola, 'Yeats and Synge', *Crisis in English Poetry 1880–1940* (London: Hutchinson University Library, 1961) pp. 88–111.

Plunkett, Grace, *Twelve Nights at the Abbey Theatre; A Book of Drawings* (Dublin: At the Sign of the Three Candles, 1929).

Pocock, P. J., 'Synge and the Photography of His Time', *The Autobiography of Synge*, ed. Alan Price (Dublin: The Dolmen Press; London: Oxford University Press, 1965).

Popkin, Henry (ed.), *John Millington Synge: The Playboy of the Western World and Riders to the Sea* (New York: Avon Books, 1967).

Power, Patrick C., *A Literary History of Ireland* (Cork: Mercier Press, 1969) p. 163.

Price, Alan, *Synge and Anglo-Irish Drama* (London: Methuen, 1961). Reviewed by John Russell Brown in *Modern Language Review*, LVII (London, Jul 1962) 434–5; by Philip Edwards in *Review of English Studies*, XIII (Aug 1962) 320–2; and by Herbert Huscher in *Anglia*, LXXX (Tübingen, 1962) 226–31.

(ed.), *The Autobiography of J. M. Synge* (Dublin: The Dolmen Press, 1965).

(ed.), *Emerald Apex* (London & Glasgow: Blackie, 1966).

Riders to the Sea. The Playboy of the Western World (J. M. Synge) Notes on English Literature series (Oxford: Basil Blackwell, 1969).

'A Survey of Recent Work on J. M. Synge', *Sunshine and the Moon's Delight*, ed. S. B. Bushrui (Gerrards Cross, Bucks.: Colin Smythe, 1972) pp. 279–95.

Prior, Moody E., *The Language of Tragedy* (New York: Columbia University Press, 1947; Bloomington and London: Indiana University Press, 1966).

Pritchett, V. S., 'The End of the Gael', *In My Good Books* (London: Chatto & Windus, 1942) pp. 155–60.

Reade, Arthur Robert, *Main Currents in Modern Literature* (London: Nicholson & Watson, 1935) pp. 50–55.

Reid, Benjamin L., *The Man from New York: John Quinn and His Friends* (New York: Oxford University Press, 1968).

Reinert, Otto (ed.), 'J. M. Synge: *The Playboy of the Western World*', *Drama; An Introductory Anthology*. Alternate ed. (Boston: Little, Brown, 1961) pp. 650–701 [text and commentary]. Reprinted in *Modern Drama*. Alternate ed. (Boston: Little, Brown, 1961) pp. 282–333.

'John Millington Synge: *Riders to the Sea*', *Classic Through

Modern Drama; An Introductory Anthology (Boston:
Little, Brown, 1970) pp. 579—94 [text and commentary].

Reynolds, Ernest, 'Yeats, Synge, and the Irish School',
Modern English Drama; A Survey of the Theatre from 1900
(London: George G. Harrap, 1949; Norman: University of
Oklahoma Press, 1951) pp. 86—95, 162—3.

Rhys, Ernest (ed.), 'Introduction', *J. M. Synge: Plays, Poems
and Prose*. Everyman's Library (London: J. M. Dent, 1941).
Reviewed by V. S. Pritchett in *New Statesman and Nation*,
XXI, no. 530 (London, 19 Apr 1941) 413.

Riva, S., *La Tradizione Celtica e la Moderna Letteratura
Irlandese: J. M. Synge* (Roma: Religio, 1937).

Rivoallan, Anatole, 'J. M. Synge', *Litterature irlandaise
contemporaine* (Paris: Hachette, 1939) pp. 21—31.

Robinson, Lennox, *Curtain Up: An Autobiography* (London:
Michael Joseph, 1942).

Ireland's Abbey Theatre; A History 1899—1951 (London:
Sidgwick & Jackson, 1951; Port Washington, N.Y.:
Kennikat Press, 1968).

Rodgers, W. R., 'J. M. Synge', *Irish Literary Portraits* (London:
B.B.C., 1972) pp. 94—115.

Ronsley, Joseph, *Yeats's Autobiography; Life as Symbolic
Pattern* (Cambridge, Mass.: Harvard University Press, 1968)
pp. 123—28.

Rowe, Kenneth Thorpe, 'Analysis of a Great Play', *Write That
Play* (New York: Funk & Wagnalls, 1939; repr., 1968) pp.
90—122 [on *Riders to the Sea*].

Roy, Emil, 'J. M. Synge', *British Drama Since Shaw* (Carbondale
and Edwardsville: Southern Illinois University Press; London
& Amsterdam: Feffer & Simons, 1972) pp. 54—67.

Ruberti, Guido, *Storia del teatro contemporaneo: L'evoluzione del teatro europeo dalle origini ai tempi nostri*, vol. III (Bologne: Licinio Cappelli, 1928) pp. 892—4.

Rubinstein, H. F. and J. C. Trewin, 'J. M. Synge: *The Playboy of the Western World*', *The Drama Bedside Book* (London: Victor Gollancz, 1966) pp. 196—9 [extract from Act III and commentary].

Rust, Adolph, *Beiträge zu einer Geschichte der neu-keltischen Renaissance* (Bückeburg: Grimme, 1922) pp. 27—31, 81—7.

Ryan, W. P., 'Ireland at the Play', *The Pope's Green Island* (London: Nisbet; Boston: Small, Maynard, 1912) pp. 299—307.

Rynne, Catherine, 'The Playwrights', *The Story of the Abbey Theatre*, ed. Sean McCann (London: The New English Library, 1967).

Saddlemyer, Ann (ed.), 'Synge to MacKenna: The Mature Years', *Irish Renaissance*, ed. Robin Skelton and David R. Clark (Dublin: Dolmen Press, 1959).

' "A Share in the Dignity of the World": J. M. Synge's Aesthetic Theory', *The World of W. B. Yeats*, ed. Robin Skelton and Ann Saddlemyer (Victoria: Adelphi Bookshop for the University of Victoria; Dublin: Dolmen Press; Seattle: University of Washington Press, 1965).

J. M. Synge and Modern Comedy (Dublin: Dolmen Press, 1968) [A lecture given at the Eighth International Yeats Summer School, Sligo, Ireland, 18 Aug 1967].

'Art, Nature, and "The Prepared Personality": A Reading of *The Aran Islands* and Related Writings', *Sunshine and the Moon's Delight*, ed. S. B. Bushrui (Gerrards Cross, Bucks.: Colin Smythe, 1972) pp. 107—20.

Sahal, N., *Sixty Years of Realistic Irish Drama (1900—1960)* (Bombay: Macmillan, 1971) pp. 15—23.

Salem, James M., 'John Millington Synge', *Drury's Guide to Best Play*, 2nd ed. (Metuchen, N.J.: The Scarecrow Press, 1969) p. 388.

Salerno, Henry F. (ed.), 'John Millington Synge: *The Playboy of the Western World*', *English Drama in Transition 1880–1920* (New York: Pegasus, 1968) pp. 415–62 [text and commentary].

Salvat, Ricard, *Teatre contemporani*, vol. I (Barcelona: Ediciones 62, 1966) pp. 281–3.

Samachson, Dorothy and Joseph, 'Dublin, 1907', *The Dramatic Story of the Theatre* (London and N.Y.: Abehard-Schuman, 1955) pp. 128–31.

Sampson, George, *The Concise Cambridge History of English Literature* (Cambridge: Cambridge University Press, 1961) pp. 902–3.

Sanders, Thomas E. (ed.), 'John Millington Synge: *Riders to the Sea*', *The Discovery of Drama* (Glenview, Ill.: Scott, Foresman, 1968) pp. 497–516 [text and commentary].

Saul, George Brandon (ed.), 'Introduction', *Age of Yeats: The Golden Age of Irish Literature*, Laurel Masterpieces of World Literature (New York: Dell, 1964).

Schweikert, H. C. *et al* (eds.), 'John Millington Synge: *Riders to the Sea*', *Adventures in English Literature* (New York: Harcourt, Brace, 1931) pp. 856–68 [text and commentary].

Scott-James, R. A., 'J. M. Synge', *Personality in Literature* (London: Martin Secker, 1913) pp. 222–5. Reprinted from *Daily News* (London, 1 Feb 1911) p. 3.

Fifty Years of English Literature 1900–1950. With a Postscript—1951 to 1955 (London: Longmans, 1956) pp. 91–3.

Setterquist, Jan, *Ibsen and the Beginning of Anglo-Irish Drama*,

vol.I: *John Millington Synge*, Upsala Irish Studies, no. 2
(Upsala: Bokhandeln; Dublin: Hodges, Figgis; Copenhagen:
Munksgaard; Cambridge, Mass.: Harvard University Press,
1951). Reviewed by Roger McHugh in *Studies; An Irish
Quarterly Review*, XLI, no. 163–4 (Dublin, Sep–Dec 1952)
335–7; by A. J. Farmer in *Revue de littérature comparée*,
XXVII (Paris, Jul–Sep 1953) 369–70; by J. J. Hogan in
Studia Neophilologica, XXIV, no. 3 (Upsala, 1952) 209–11;
by A. Norman Jeffares in *Neuphilologische Mitteilungen*,
LIV, nos. 7–8 (Helsinki, 1953) 371–3; and by B. G.
MacCarthy in *Modern Language Review*, XLIX (January
1954) 73–5.

Shank, Theodore J., 'John Millington Synge', *A Digest of 500
Plays; Plot Outlines and Production Notes* (New York: Collier
Books; London: Collier-Macmillan, 1966) pp. 417–18.

Sharp, R. Farquharson, 'The Dublin Theatres', *A Short
History of the English Stage* (London and New York:
Walter Scott, 1909) p. 317.

Shaw, G. B., *A Note on the Irish Theatre by Theodore
Roosevelt and an 'Interview' on the Irish Players in America
by George Bernard Shaw* (New York: Mitchell Kennerley,
1912). [Roosevelt's contribution to this booklet is a reprint
of his 'Introduction' to 'The Irish Players' in *The Outlook*,
IC (N.Y., 16 Dec 1911) 915].

Sherman, Stuart P., 'The Exoticism of John Synge', *On
Contemporary Literature* (New York: Henry Holt, 1917)
pp. 190–210.

Shipley, Joseph T., 'John M. Synge', *Guide to Great Plays*
(Washington, D.C.: Public Affairs Press, 1956) pp. 761–4.

Short, Ernest, *Theatrical Cavalcade* (London: Eyre &
Spottiswoode, 1942) pp. 205–8.

Sixty Years of Theatre (London: Eyre & Spottiswoode,
1951) pp. 374–6 [same article].

Sidnell, M. J., '*The Well of the Saints* and the Light of this World', *Sunshine and the Moon's Delight* (Gerrards Cross, Bucks.: Colin Smythe, 1972) pp. 53—9.

Simons, Heer Leo, 'Introduction', *De Heiligenbron: Tooneelspel in drie Bedrijven, alleen-Jeautoriseerde Vertaling van L. Simons*, Tooneelbibliotheek order Leiding van L. Simons vitgegeven door de maatschappij voor Goede en Goedkeepe Lectuur (Amsterdam, 1912). Reviewed by Conal O'Riordan in *Irish Review*, II, no. 22 (Dublin, Dec 1912) 557—8.

Het Drama en Het Tooneel in Hun Ontwilleling, V Nederlandsche Bibliotheek, Encyclopaedie in Monografieen (Amsterdam, 1932).

Skelton, Robin (ed.), *J. M. Synge: Translations* (Dublin: The Dolmen Press, 1961) [from the original MSS.]. Reviewed in *The Times Literary Supplement* (London, 2 Feb 1962) p. 74; and in *Virginia Quarterly Review*, XXVIII (Charlottesville, Va., Winter 1962) XXII.

(ed.), 'Introduction', *J. M. Synge: Four Plays and The Aran Islands*, World's Classics no. 585 (London and New York: Oxford University Press, 1962). Reviewed by Geoffrey Grigson in *New Statesman*, LXIV (London, 19 Oct 1962) 528; by Philip Hengist in *Punch*, CCXLII (London, 2 May 1962) 697; in *The Times Literary Supplement* (London, 16 Mar 1962) p. 190; and by Geoffrey Reeves in *New Theatre Magazine*, III, no. 4 (Bristol, Jul—Sep 1962) 37—8.

(ed.), *Riders to the Sea* (Dublin: The Dolmen Press; London: Oxford University Press, 1969). [An edition of 750 copies of the Houghton Library typescript of the play]. Reviewed in *The Times Literary Supplement* (London, 26 Feb 1970) p. 221; and by Austin Clarke in *Irish Times* (Dublin, 1 Nov 1969) p. 10.

Remembering Synge; A Poem in Homage for the Centenary of His Birth, 16 April 1971 (Dublin: The Dolmen Press;

London: Oxford University Press, 1971). Reviewed in *The Times Literary Supplement* (London, 2 Jul 1971) pp. 749–50; and by Laurence Lerner in *Encounter*, XXXVIII, no. 1 (London, Jan 1972) 62–7.

J. M. Synge and His World (London: Thames and Hudson; Indianapolis: Bobbs–Merill; New York: Viking, 1971). Reviewed in *The Times Literary Supplement* (London, 2 Jul 1971) pp. 749–50; by Laurence Lerner in *Encounter*, XXXVIII, no. 1 (London, Jan 1972) 62–7; and by David H. Greene in *Nation*, CCXIII (N.Y., 30 Aug 1971) 150–2.

The Writings of J. M. Synge (London: Thames and Hudson, 1971). Reviewed in *The Times Literary Supplement* (London, 2 Jul 1971) pp. 749–50; by Laurence Lerner in *Encounter*, XXXVIII, no. 1 (London, Jan 1972) 62–7; and by David H. Greene in *Nation*, CCXIII (N.Y., 30 Aug 1971) 150–2.

Synge Petrarch (Dublin: The Dolmen Press, 1971).

J. M. Synge, Irish Writers Series (Lewisburg: Bucknell University Press, 1972).

Slater, Derek, '*The Playboy of the Western World*', *Plays in Action* (Oxford: Pergamon Press, 1964) pp. 134–43.

Sobel, Bernard (ed.), 'Edward John Millington Synge', *The New Theatre Handbook and Digest of Plays* (New York: Crown Publishers, 1959) p. 632.

Solomont, Susan, *The Comic Effect of 'Playboy of the Western World'* (Bangor, Maine: Signalman Press, 1962).

Sprinchorn, Evert (ed.), 'John Millington Synge', *20th-Century Plays in Synopsis* (New York: Thomas Y. Crowell, 1965) pp. 412–16.

Stamm, Rudolf (ed.), '*Riders to the Sea* by J. M. Synge', *Three Anglo-Irish Plays*, Bibliotheca Anglicana, vol. V (Berne: A. Francke, 1943) pp. 3–33 [text and commentary].

Geschichte des englischen Theaters (Berne: A. Francke, 1951) p. 407.

Starkie, Enid, *From Gautier to Eliot: The Influence of France on English Literature, 1851–1939* (London: Hutchinson, 1960) pp. 125–6.

Starkie, Walter, '*The Playboy* Riots', *Scholars and Gypsies* (London: John Murray, 1963).

Steffensen, James L., Jr. (ed.), 'From *The Playboy of the Western World* by J. M. Synge', *Great Scenes from the World Theater* (New York: Avon Books, 1965) pp. 551–6 [extract from Act II and commentary].

Steinberg, M. W. (ed.), 'John M. Synge: *Riders to the Sea* and *The Playboy of the Western World*', *Aspects of Modern Drama* (New York: Holt, Rinehart & Winston, 1960) pp. 445–501 [texts and commentary].

Steinmann, Martin and Gerald Willen (eds.), 'John Millington Synge: *Riders to the Sea*', *Literature for Writing; An Anthology of Major British and American Authors* (Belmont, Calif.: Wadsworth, 1967) pp. 403–10 [text and commentary].

Stephens, James, 'Reminiscences of J. M. Synge', *James, Seumas & Jacques* (London: Macmillan, 1964) pp. 54–60.

Strong, L. A. G., *John Millington Synge* (London: George Allen & Unwin, 1941). Reviewed in *The Times Literary Supplement* (London, 14 Feb 1942) p. 79.

'John Millington Synge', *Personal Remarks* (London: P. Nevill; New York: Leveright, 1953). Reprinted from *The Bookman*, LXXIII (N.Y., Apr 1931) 125–36.

Styan, J. L., *The Elements of Drama* (Cambridge: Cambridge University Press, 1960).

'Synge and O'Casey', *The Dark Comedy; The Development of Modern Comic Tragedy* (Cambridge: Cambridge University Press, 1962; 2nd ed., 1968) pp. 130–3.

The Dramatic Experience; A Guide to the Reading of Plays (Cambridge: Cambridge University Press, 1965).

Sultan, Stanley, 'A Joycean Look at the Playboy of the Western World', *The Celtic Master; Being Contributions to the First James Joyce Symposium in Dublin*, ed. Maurice Harmon (Dublin: Dolmen Press, 1969) pp. 45–55.

Sweetkind, Morris (ed.), '*Riders to the Sea* by John M. Synge', *Ten Great One Act Plays* (New York: Bantam Books, 1968) pp. 85–99 [text and commentary].

Synge, John Millington, 'Prefaces' to *The Playboy of the Western World* and *The Tinker's Wedding*. Reprinted in *Playwrights on Playwrighting*, ed. Toby Cole, with an Introduction by John Gassner (New York: Hill & Wang, 1961) pp. 201–3.

Synge, Lanto M., 'The Autobiography of J. M. Synge', *Sunshine and the Moon's Delight*, ed. S. B. Bushrui (Gerrards Cross, Bucks.: Colin Smythe, 1972) pp. 121–40.

Synge, Rev. Samuel, *Letters to My Daughter: Memories of John Millington Synge* (Dublin: Talbot Press, 1931). Reviewed in *The Times* (London, 1 Mar 1932) p. 10; and in *The Times Literary Supplement* (London, 10 Mar 1932) p. 171.

'Synge', *The Encyclopedia Americana*, International Edition, vol. XXVI (N.Y., 1970) pp. 174–5.

'Synge', *The New Funk & Wagnalls Encyclopedia*, vol. XXXII (New York: Unicorn Publishers, 1951) p. 117–72.

'Synge', *Webster's Biographical Dictionary* (Springfield, Mass.: G. & C. Merriam Co., 1966) p. 1439.

Taniguchi, Jiro, *A Grammatical Analysis of Artistic Representation of Irish English, with a Brief Discussion of Sounds and Spelling* (Tokyo: Shinozaki Shorin, [1955]).

Taylor, Estella Ruth, *The Modern Irish Writers: Cross Currents of Criticism* (Lawrence, Kansas: University of Kansas Press, 1954; New York: Greenwood Press, 1969).

Téry, Simone, 'J. M. Synge', *L'île des bardes* (Paris: Ernest Flammarion, 1925) pp. 140–66.

Thorndike, Ashley H., *English Comedy* (New York: Macmillan, 1929; Cooper Square Publishers, 1965) pp. 582–4.

Thorning, Just, *J. M. Synge: En moderne irsk Dramatiker* (Copenhagen: V. Rio, 1921). Reviewed by S. B. Liljegren in *Englische Studien*, LVIII (Leipzig, 1924) 294–6.

Tilgher, Adriano, 'Il teatro di John Millington Synge', *Studi sul teatro contemporaneo* (Rome: Libreria di Scienze e Lettere, 1923) pp. 225–8.

Tindall, William York, *Forces in Modern British Literature 1885–1956* (New York: Alfred A. Knopf, 1947; Vintage Books, 1956) pp. 68–9.

Tobin, James Edward, *et al*, 'John Millington Synge: *Riders to the Sea*', *College Book of English Literature* (New York: American Book Co., 1949) pp. 1053–9 [text and commentary].

Tracy, Robert (ed.), 'Introduction', *The Aran Islands and Other Writings by John M. Synge* (New York: Vintage Books, 1962).

Trewin, J. C., *The Theatre Since 1900* (London: Andrew Dakers, 1951).

Dramatists of Today (London and N.Y.: Staples Press, 1953).

Tucker, S. Marion and Alan S. Downer (eds.), '*Riders to the Sea* by J. M. Synge', *Twenty-Five Modern Plays* (New York: Harper & Row, 1953) pp. 293–302 [text and commentary].

Tynan, Kenneth, '*The Playboy of the Western World*, by J. M. Synge, at the Piccadilly', *Tynan Right & Left* (London: Longmans, 1967) pp. 39–41.

Ulanov, Barry (ed.), 'John Millington Synge: *The Well of the Saints*', *Makers of the Modern Theater* (New York: McGraw-Hill, 1961) pp. 233–58 [text and commentary].

Van Doren, Carl and Mark, 'Synge 1871–1909', *American and British Literature Since 1890*, rev. and enl. ed. (New York: Appleton-Century, 1939) pp. 328–34.

Van Laan, Thomas F., *The Idiom of Drama* (Ithaca and London: Cornell University Press, 1970) pp. 37–8, 275–80 [on *Riders to the Sea*].

Vernon, Frank, *The Twentieth Century Theatre* (London: George G. Harrap; Boston & N.Y.: Houghton Mifflin, 1924].

Völker, Klaus, *Irisches Theater, I: Yeats [und] Synge*, Friedrichs Dramatiker des Welttheaters, XXIX (Velber/b. Hannover: Friedrich, 1967).

Walbrook, H. M., '*The Playboy of the Western World*', *Nights at the Play* (London: W. J. Ham-Smith, 1911) pp. 107–10.

Walley, Harold R., 'Folk Drama: *The Playboy of the Western World* by John Millington Synge', *The Book of the Play; An Introduction to Drama* (New York: Charles Scribner's, 1950) pp. 443–81 [text and commentary].

Ward, A. C., 'The Irish Theatre', *Twentieth-Century English Literature 1901–1960* (London: Methuen, 1964) pp. 110–17.

(ed.), '*The Playboy of the Western World*', *Specimens of*

English Dramatic Criticism XVII–XX Centuries, The World's Classics (London and New York: Oxford University Press, 1945) pp. 248–59.

Warner, Francis, 'A Note on the Poems of J. M. Synge', *Sunshine and the Moon's Delight*, ed. S. B. Bushrui (Gerrards Cross, Bucks.: Colin Smythe, 1972) pp. 141–52.

Warnock, Robert (ed.), '*Riders to the Sea* by John Millington Synge', *Representative Modern Plays: British* (Chicago: Scott, Foresman, 1953) pp. 338–56 [text and commentary].

(ed.), '*Riders to the Sea* by John Millington Synge', *Representative Modern Plays: Ibsen to Tennessee Williams* (Chicago: Scott, Foresman, 1964) pp. 286–300 [text and commentary].

Watson, E. Bradlee and Benfield Pressey (eds.), '*Riders to the Sea* by John Millington Synge', *Contemporary Drama: European, English and Irish, American Plays* (New York: Charles Scribner's, 1931) pp. 241–7.

Watt, Homer A. and James B. Munn (eds.), 'John M. Synge: *Riders to the Sea*', *Ideas and Forms in English and American Literature* (Chicago: Scott, Foresman, 1925) pp. 726–32.

Wayne, Philip (ed.), '*The Shadow of the Glen*: J. M. Synge', *Modern One-Act Plays* (London and New York: Longmans, 1935) pp. 1–23 and 193–4 [text and commentary].

Weatherly, Edward H., *et al* (eds.), 'John Millington Synge: *Riders to the Sea*', *The English Heritage*, vol. II (Boston: Ginn, 1945) pp. 569–75 [text and commentary].

Weiss, Samuel A., 'John Millington Synge: *The Playboy of the Western World*', *Drama in the Modern World: Plays and Essays* (Boston: D. C. Heath, 1964) pp. 175–211 [text and commentary].

Weygandt, Cornelius, 'John Millington Synge', *Irish Plays and Playwrights* (London: Constable; Boston: Houghton Mifflin; Port Washington, N.Y.: Kennikat Press, 1966) ch. VIII, pp. 160–97. Reviewed in *Manchester Guardian* (14 Mar 1913) p. 7; in *Evening Standard and St. James's Gazette* (London, 22 Feb 1913) p. 11; in *Athenaeum* (London, 1 Mar 1913) p. 260; in *Outlook*, XXXI (London, 12 Apr 1913) 513; by Frank Swinnerton in *Blue Review*, I, no. 3 (London, Jul 1913) 195–6; in *Literary World* (London, 5 Jun 1913) pp. 182–3; in *Irish Book-Lover*, IV, no. 9 (London and Dublin, Apr 1913) 157–8; and by Warren Barton Blake in *Independent*, LXXIV (N.Y., 6 Mar 1913) 515–19.

Whitaker, Thomas R. (ed.), *Twentieth Century Interpretations of The Playboy of the Western World* (Englewood Cliffs, N.J.: Prentice-Hall, 1969).

Whiting, B. J., *et al* (eds.), 'J. M. Synge: *The Playboy of the Western World*', *The College Survey of English Literature*, vol. II (N.Y. and Chicago: Harcourt, Brace, 1942) pp. 1022–46 [text and commentary].

Whiting, Frank M., 'Ireland', *An Introduction to the Theatre* (New York: Harper & Row, 1969) pp. 98–100.

Whitman, Charles Huntington, '*Riders to the Sea* by John Millington Synge', *Seven Contemporary Plays* (Boston: Houghton Mifflin, 1931) pp. 431–45 and 550–2 [text and commentary].

(ed.), '*Riders to the Sea*. John Millington Synge', *Representative Modern Dramas* (N.Y.: Macmillan, 1936) pp. 771–82 [text and commentary].

Whitman, Robert F., *The Play-Reader's Handbook* (Indianapolis: The Bobbs–Merrill Company, 1966) pp. 66–7 [on *Riders to the Sea*].

Wilde, Percival, *The Craftsmanship of the One-Act Play* (Boston: Little, Brown, 1926).

Williams, Harold, 'John Millington Synge', *Modern English Writers; Being A Study of Imaginative Literature, 1890–1914* (London: Sidgwick & Jackson, 1925; Port Washington, N.Y.: Kennikat Press, 1970) pp. 206–17.

Williams, Raymond, 'J. M. Synge', *Drama from Ibsen to Eliot* (London: Chatto & Windus, 1954) pp. 154–74. Reprinted in *Drama from Ibsen to Brecht* (London: Chatto & Windus, 1968) pp. 129–40.

Williams, R. Vaughan, *Riders to the Sea* (London: Oxford University Press; New York: Carl Fischer; Paris: Le Magasin Musical Pierre Schneider; Amsterdam: Brockmans & Van Poppel; Lausanne: Foetisch Freres S.A., 1937). [musical setting].

Williamson, Audrey, 'Irish Stew and Russian Salad', *Theatre of Two Decades* (London: Rockliff, 1951) pp. 185–6 [on *The Playboy of the Western World*].

Wilson, Lawrence (ed.), *J. M. Synge: Some Letters and Documents* (Privately printed, 1959). [An edition of 250 copies].

Wood, E. R. (ed.), 'Introduction', *Riders to the Sea and The Playboy of the Western World by J. M. Synge* (London: Heinemann, 1961). Reviewed in *The Times Literary Supplement* (London, 8 Nov 1961) p. 536.

Woods, George B., *et al* (eds.), 'John Millington Synge: *Riders to the Sea*', *The Literature of England*. 3rd ed., vol. II (Chicago: Scott, Foresman, 1948) pp. 1002–9 [text and commentary].

Yeats, John Butler, 'Synge and the Irish', *Essays, Irish and American* (Dublin: The Talbot Press; London: T. Fisher Unwin; New York: Macmillan, 1918) pp. 51–61.

'Mr. Synge and His Plays', prefixed to *The Well of the Saints* (London: A. H. Bullen, 1905). Reprinted in *Collected Works*, vol. VIII (Stratford-on-Avon: A. H. Bullen, The

Shakespeare Head Press, 1908); in *The Cutting of an Agate*
(London: Macmillan, 1912; New York: Macmillan, 1913)
pp. 36—48; in *Essays* (London: Macmillan, 1924) pp. 369—
78; and in *Essays and Introductions* (New York: Macmillan,
1961) pp. 298—305.

J. M. Synge and the Ireland of His Time (Churchtown,
Dundrum: The Cuala Press; New York: Mitchell Kennerley,
1911). Originally appeared in *Forum*, XLVI (N.Y., Aug
1911) 179—200. Reprinted in *The Cutting of an Agate*
(London and N.Y.: Macmillan, 1912) pp. 146—95; in
Essays (London and N.Y.: Macmillan, 1924) pp. 385—424;
and in *Essays and Introductions* (London and N.Y.:
Macmillan, 1961) pp. 311—40. Reviewed by 'Bernard Lintot'
in *T.P.'s Weekly* (London, 18 Aug 1911) p. 201; in
Athenaeum (London, 26 Aug 1911) pp. 240—1; in *Academy*,
LXXXI (London, 14 Oct 1911) 485—6; and by Walter
Mennloch in *Irish Review* (Dublin, Sep 1911) p. 325; and
in *Independent*, LXXIII (N.Y., 7 Nov 1912) 1071—3.

'The Tragic Theatre', *The Cutting of an Agate* (London and
N.Y.: Macmillan, 1912) pp. 196—207.

'Preface to the First Edition of John M. Synge's *Poems and
Translations*', *The Cutting of an Agate* (New York:
Macmillan, 1912) pp. 139—45. Reprinted in *Essays*
(London: Macmillan, 1924) pp. 379—84; and in *Essays and
Introductions* (London: Macmillan, 1961) pp. 306—10.

'A People's Theatre; A Letter to Lady Gregory', *The Theory
of the Modern Stage; An Introduction to Modern Theatre
and Drama*, ed. Eric Bentley (Harmondsworth: Penguin
Books, 1968) pp. 327—38. Reprinted from *Dial*, LXVIII,
no. 4 (N.Y., Apr 1920) 458—68.

'On Taking *The Playboy* to London', *Plays and Controversies* (London: Macmillan, 1923).

'The Irish Dramatic Movement', *Collected Works*, vol. IV
(Stratford-on-Avon: A. H. Bullen, The Shakespeare Head

Press, 1908). Reprinted in *Plays and Controversies* (London: Macmillan, 1923); and in *Explorations* (London: Macmillan, 1962). [reprints from *Samhain* and *The Arrow*].

The Death of Synge and Other Passages from an Old Diary (Dublin: Cuala Press, 1928). Reprinted in *Dramatis Personae* (N.Y.: Macmillan, 1936); in *The Anthology of William Butler Yeats* (N.Y.: Macmillan, 1938); and in *Autobiographies* (London: Macmillan, 1955). Reviewed by Sean O'Faolain in *The Irish Statesman*, XI, no. 4 (Dublin, 29 Sep 1928) 71–2.

Autobiographies (London: Macmillan, 1955).

(ed.), *Beltaine, May 1899–April 1900* (London: Frank Cass, 1970).

(ed.), *Samhain, October 1901–November 1908* (London: Frank Cass, 1970).

Young, Ella, 'The Playboy', *Flowering Dusk, Things Remembered Accurately and Inaccurately* (New York: Longmans, Green, 1945) pp. 95–96.

(b) PERIODICALS

A., M., 'After the Play', *New Republic*, XVIII (N.Y., 1 Mar 1919) 153 [Synge and Lord Dunsany compared].

'The Abbey Theatre', *Irish Times* (Dublin, 25 Mar 1909) p. 8.

'The Abbey Theatre: Its Origins and Accomplishments', *The Times* (London, 17 Mar 1913) p. 15.

'Acting of the Irish Players', *American Review of Reviews*, XLV (N.Y., Mar 1912) 357.

Adams, J. Donald, 'The Irish Dramatic Movement', *Harvard Monthly*, LIII (Cambridge, Mass., Nov 1911) 44—8.

'All Ireland', *United Irishman*, XIII, no. 311 (Dublin, 11 Feb 1905) 1.

Allen, Beverly S., 'John Synge: A Problem of His Genius', *Colonnade*, XI, no. 1 (N.Y., Jan 1916) 5—15.

Alspach, R. K., 'Synge's *Well of the Saints*', *The Times Literary Supplement* (London, 28 Dec 1935) p. 899 [Letter to the Editor].

'Amherst Acquires Original Manuscript of Synge's *Playboy of the Western World*', *New York Times* (18 May 1930) section 2, p. 2.

Archer, William, 'Three Poets Departed', *Morning Leader* (London, 15 May 1909) p. 4 [obituary of Swinburne, Davidson, and Synge].

'The Art of the Artless', *Nation*, VII, no. 10 (London, 4 Jun 1910) 346—7.

Arnold, Sidney, 'The Abbey Theatre', *Arts and Philosophy*, I (London, Summer 1950) 25—30.

'The "Ascendancy" Writer', *The Times Literary Supplement* (London, 2 Jul 1971) pp. 749–50.

Atkinson, F. M., 'A Literary Causerie', *Dana*, I (Dublin, May 1904–Apr 1905) 313 [announcement of *The Well of the Saints* as vol. I of the Abbey Theatre Series].

Ayling, Ronald, 'Synge's First Love: Some South African Aspects', *Modern Drama*, VII, no. 4 (Laurence, Kansas, Feb 1964) 450–60 [recollections of Synge by Cherry Matheson].

Babler, O. F., 'John Millington Synge in Czech Translations', *Notes and Queries*, CXCI, no. 6 (21 Sep 1946) 123–4.

Barnes, T. R., 'Yeats, Synge, Ibsen and Strindberg', *Scrutiny*, V (Cambridge, Dec 1936) 257–62.

Barnett, Pat, 'The Nature of Synge's Dialogue', *English Literature in Transition*, X, no. 3 (1967) 119–29.

Baughan, E. A., 'The Irish Players', *Daily News and Leader* (London, 14 Jul 1913) p. 6.

Bauman, Richard, 'John Millington Synge and Irish Folklore', *Southern Folklore Quarterly*, XXVII, no. 4 (Gainsville, Fla., Dec 1963) 267–79.

Bennett, Charles A., 'The Plays of John M. Synge', *Yale Review*, I, New Series, no. 2 (New Haven, Conn., Jan 1912) 192–205.

Bentley, Eric, 'Irish Theatre: Splendeurs et Misères', *Poetry*, LXXIX, no. 4 (Chicago, Jan 1952) 216–32. Reprinted in *In Search of Theater* (N.Y.: Vintage Books, 1953) pp. 307–21.

Bessai, Diane E., 'Little Hound in Mayo: Synge's Playboy and the Comic Tradition in Irish Literature', *Dalhousie Review*, XLVIII, no. 3 (Autumn 1968) 372–83.

Bewley, Charles, 'The Irish National Theatre', *Dublin Review*,

Periodicals

CLII, no. 304 (London, Jan 1913) 132–44. Reprinted in
Living Age, CCLXXVI (Boston, 15 Feb 1913) 410–18.

Bickley, Francis, 'The Art of J. M. Synge', *Nation*, V, no. 1
(London, 3 Apr 1909) 17–19.

'Synge and the Drama', *New Quarterly*, III, no. 9 (London,
Feb 1910) 73–84.

'Deirdre', *Irish Review*, II, no. 17 (Dublin, Jul 1912) 252–4.

'The Window in the Bye Street', *Bookman*, XLII (London,
Aug 1912) 211–12 [suggestive parallel with *Riders to the
Sea*].

'Biography on Playwright Set', *New York Times* (7 Aug 1955)
p. 28 [by David H. Greene].

Birmingham, George A. [Rev. J. O. Hannay], 'The Literary
Movement in Ireland', *Fortnightly Review*, LXXXII, New
Series (London and N.Y., Dec 1907) 947–57.

Blake, Warren Barton, 'John Synge and His Plays', *Dial*, L
(Chicago, 16 Jan 1911) 37–41.

'An Irish Playwright', *Independent* (N.Y., 13 Apr 1911) pp.
792–3.

'A Great Irish Playwright: John M. Synge', *Theatre Magazine*,
XIII (N.Y., Jun 1911) 204–5.

'Irish Plays and Players', *Independent*, LXXIV (N.Y., 6 Mar
1913) 515–19.

Blissett, William, 'Synge's *Playboy*', *Adam International
Review*, nos. 239–40 (London, 1954) pp. 17–20.

Bloxam, R. N., 'The Source of a Plot', *The Times Literary
Supplement* (London, 29 Jul 1921) p. 484 [letter to the
Editor on *The Shadow of the Glen*].

Borel, Jacques, 'Sur *le baladin du monde occidental*', *Critique* (Paris, Jan 1966) 54—9.

Bourgeois, Maurice, 'J. M. Synge's Life in France and His Relations to French Literature', *Freeman's Journal* (Dublin, 23 Jan 1912) p. 3.

'Synge and Loti', *Westminster Review*, CLXXIX (London, May 1913) 532—6.

Boyd, Ernest A., 'The Irish National Theatre', *Irish Times* (Dublin, 27 Dec 1912) p. 5. See reply by Ellen Duncan (28 Dec 1912) p. 9 [letter to the Editor].

'The Abbey Theatre', *Irish Review*, II, no. 24 (Dublin, Feb 1913) 628—34.

'Le théâtre irlandais', *Revue de Paris*, V (Sep 1913) 191—205.

Brann, Henry A., 'The Modern Literary Conscience', *America*, VI (N.Y., 21 Oct 1911) 30—1.

Brighouse, Harold, 'The Source of a Plot', *The Times Literary Supplement* (London, 15 Jul 1921) p. 453 [letter to the Editor on *The Shadow of the Glen*].

Brooks, Sydney, 'The Irish Peasant as a Dramatic Issue', *Harper's Weekly*, LI (N.Y., 9 Mar 1907) 344.

Brophy, G. M., 'J. M. Synge and the Revival of the Irish Drama', *Everyman*, I, no. 1 (London, 18 Oct 1912) 8.

Brophy, Liam, 'The "Shocking" Synge', *Word* (Donamon, Co. Roscommon, Mar 1959) pp. 6—8.

Brown, Alan L., 'John Millington Synge', *London Quarterly and Holborn Review*, CLXXV, no. 1 (Jan 1950) 44—9.

Brulé, A., 'John M. Synge: *Plays*', *Revue anglo-américaine*, IX (Paris, 1931—2) 61—3.

'Buono, Che' [William Bulfin]. 'Synge as a Playwright', *Sinn Fein*, I, New Series (Dublin, 2 Apr 1910) 3.

Bushrui, S. B. (ed.), 'John Millington Synge (1871–1909); A Centenary Tribute', *Daily Star* (Beirut, 28 Nov 1971) pp. 7–8.

Capin, Jean and Esther Alcalay, 'Ce théâtre au milieu d'un peuple', *Cahiers Renaud-Barrault*, XXXVII (Feb 1962) 42–51.

Carmody, Terence F., 'A Centennial Note: J. M. Synge', *Independent Shavian*, IX (1971) 27–36.

Carnevali, Emanuel, 'Synge's Playboy of the Western World: Variation', *Dial*, LXVI, no. 787 (Chicago, 5 Apr 1919) 340 [poem].

Carter, Huntly, 'The New Idea of Dramatic Action', *New Age*, IX, no. 12 (London, 20 Jul 1911) 271–2.

Casey, Helen, 'Synge's Use of the Anglo-Irish Idiom', *English Journal*, XXVII (Honolulu, Hawaii, 1939) 773–6.

Cazamian, Madeleine L., 'Le théâtre de J. M. Synge', *La revue du mois*, XII (Paris, 10 Oct 1911) 456–68.

'*The Aran Islands*, by J. M. Synge', *Revue anglo-américaine*, IV, no. 5 (Paris, Jun 1927) 458–9.

Chiba, K., 'Irish Literature and the Modern Literary Trend in Our Country', *Study of English*, XX, no. 4 (Tokyo, Jul 1927) 10–15.

Chica Salas, Susana, 'Synge y García Lorca: Approximación de dos mundos poéticos', *Revista Hispánica Moderna*, XXVII, no. 2 (N.Y., Apr 1961) 128–37.

Clark, Barrett H., '*The Playboy* in Paris', *Colonnade*, XI, no. 1 (The Andiron Club, New York, Jan 1916) 23–6.

Clark, James M., 'The Irish Literary Movement', *Englische Studien*, IL (Leipzig, Jul 1915) 50—98.

Cohen, Helen Louise, 'The Irish National Theatre', *Scholastic*, XXIV (Pittsburgh, 17 Mar 1934) 7—8.

Collins, R. L., 'The Distinction of *Riders to the Sea*', *University of Kansas City Review*, XIII, no. 4 (Summer 1948) 278—84.

Colum, Mary, 'Shaw and Synge', *Forum and Century*, XCIV (N.Y., Dec 1935) 357—8.

Colum, Padraic, 'The Poetry of James Stephens', *Nation*, V, no. 24 (London, 11 Sep 1909) 857—8 [comparison with Synge].

'The Irish Literary Movement', *Forum*, LIII (N.Y. and London, Jan 1915) 133—48.

'Youngest Ireland', *Seven Arts Magazine*, II, no. 11 (N.Y., Sep 1917) 608—23.

'Memories of John M. Synge', *Literary Review*, I, no. 39 (N.Y., 4 Jun 1921) 1—2.

'Tendencies in Irish Art', *Survey-Graphic* (Dec 1921) pp. 341—5.

'The Abbey Theatre Comes of Age', *Theatre Arts Monthly*, X, no. 9 (N.Y., Sep 1926) 580—4.

'Ibsen in Irish Writing', *Irish Writing*, no. 7 (Cork, Feb 1949) pp. 66—70.

Combs, William W., 'J. M. Synge's *Riders to the Sea*: A Reading and Some Generalizations', *Papers of the Michigan Academy of Science, Arts and Letters*, L (1965) pp. 599—607.

Conacher, W. M., 'The Irish Literary Movement', *Queen's Quarterly*, XLV (Spring 1938) 56—65.

Periodicals

Connell, F. Norreys, 'John Millington Synge', *English Review*, II (London, Jun 1909) 609–13.

Cooper, Bryan, 'The Drama in Ireland', *Irish Review*, III (Dublin, May 1913) 140–3.

Corkery, Daniel, 'The Drama of J. M. Synge', *Cork Free Press* (11 Nov 1910) p. 7.

Cousteau, Jacques, 'Synge, vagabond solitaire et passionné', *Cahiers Renault-Barrault*, XXXVII (Feb 1962) 37–41.

'Current Affairs', *Leader* (Dublin, 3 Apr 1909) p. 164 [on the death of Synge].

Currie, Ryder Hector and Martin Bryan, '*Riders to the Sea*: Reappraised', *Texas Quarterly*, XI, no. 4 (Winter 1968) 139–46.

'A Cursory View of Anathema', *Golden Book*, XX (N.Y., Aug 1934) 167.

Cusack, Cyril, 'A Player's Reflections on *Playboy*', *Modern Drama*, IV, no. 3 (Dec 1961) 300–5.

D., E. K., 'The Irish Theatre Society', *Dial*, LI, no. 612 (Chicago, 16 Dec 1911) 521 [letter to the Editor].

Davie, Donald A., 'The Poetic Diction of John M. Synge', *Dublin Magazine*, XXVII, New Series (Jan–Mar 1952) 32–8.

Day-Lewis, Sean, 'Synge's Song', *Drama*, no. 90 (London, Autumn 1968) 35–8.

Deane, Seamus, 'Synge's Poetic Use of Language', *Mosaic*, V, no. 1 (1971) 27–36.

'Death of Mr. J. M. Synge', *Evening Telegraph* (Dublin, 24 Mar 1909) p. 3.

'Death of Mr. J. M. Synge', *Freeman's Journal* (Dublin, 25 Mar 1909) p.7.

'Death of Mr. J. M. Synge', *Cork Examiner* (25 Mar 1909) p. 6.

'Death of Mr. J. M. Synge', *Daily Express* (Dublin, 25 Mar 1909) p.4.

'The Death of Mr. J. M. Synge', *Manchester Guardian* (25 Mar 1909) p.6.

'Death of Mr. J. M. Synge: Clever Irish Playwright Dies in Dublin Hospital', *Irish News and Belfast Morning News* (25 Mar 1909) p.8.

'Death of Mr. J. M. Synge; A Distinguished Irish Dramatist', *Northern Whig* (Belfast, 25 Mar 1909) p.9.

'Death of Mr. J. M. Synge, Famous Irish Playwright', *Evening Herald* (Dublin, 24 Mar 1909) pp.1–2.

'Death of Well-Known Dramatist', *Daily Chronicle* (London, 25 Mar 1909) p.1.

Desmond, Shaw, 'The Irish Renaissance', *Outlook*, CXXXVIII (N.Y., 15 Oct 1924) 247–9.

'De Valera as Play Censor', *Manchester Guardian Weekly*, XXX, no.15 (13 Apr 1934) 296.

Donoghue, Denis, ' "Too Immoral for Dublin": Synge's *The Tinker's Wedding*', *Irish Writing*, no.30 (Cork, Mar 1955) 56–62.

'Synge: *Riders to the Sea*; A Study', *University Review*, I (Dublin, Summer 1955) 52–8.

'Flowers and Timber: A Note on Synge's Poems', *Threshold*, I, no.3 (Belfast, Autumn 1957) 40–7.

Douglas, James, 'The Poems of John M. Synge', *Star* (London, 24 Jul 1909) p. 2.

'Mr. Montague's *Dramatic Values*', *Star* (London, 11 Feb 1911) p. 2.

'The Works of Synge', *Star* (London, 18 Feb 1911) p. 2.

'The Drama of Synge', *Liverpool Echo* (2 Jul 1910) p. 7.

'Dramatic Gossip', *Athenaeum* (London, 27 Mar 1909) 388 [obituary].

'A Drifting Silent Man; the Genius of J. M. Synge', *Daily Mail* (London, 12 Jul 1912) p. 2.

Dukes, Ashley, 'Modern Dramatists: Wedekind', *New Age*, VII, no. 23 (London, 6 Oct 1910) 544–5.

'The Irish Scene: Dublin Plays and Playhouses', *Theatre Arts Monthly*, XIV, no. 5 (N.Y., May 1930) 378–84.

'Fashions in Comedy', *Theatre Arts*, XXVIII, no. 10 (N.Y., Oct 1943) 584–90.

Dunsany, Lord, 'Romance and the Modern Stage', *National Review*, LVII (London, Jul 1911) 827–35.

E., O., 'National Theatre Society', *Manchester Guardian* (10 Apr 1907) p. 12.

Eaton, W. P., 'Some Plays Worth While', *American Magazine* (N.Y., Feb 1912) pp. 491–2.

'The Literary Drama', *American Magazine* (N.Y., Mar 1912) p. 625.

Eckley, Grace, 'Truth at the Bottom of a Well: Synge's *The Well of the Saints*', *Modern Drama*, XVI, no. 2 (Sep 1973) 193–8.

'Editorial', *Irish Times* (Dublin, 25 Mar 1909) p.6.

'Editorial Notes', *Forum*, XLVII (N.Y. and London, Feb 1912) 253.

Ernright, D. J., 'A Note on Irish Literature and the Irish Trad-ition', *Scrutiny*, X (Cambridge, Jan 1942) 247–55.

Ervine, St. John, 'The Irish Dramatist and the Irish People', *Forum*, LI (N.Y.; Jun 1914) 940–8.

'Some Impressions of My Elders: Bernard Shaw and J. M. Synge', *North American Review*, CCXI (N.Y., May 1920) 669–81. Reprinted in *Some Impressions of My Elders* (London: George Allen & Unwin, 1923) pp.188–92.

Everson, Ida G., 'Young Lennox Robinson and the Abbey Theatre's First American Tour (1911–1912)', *Modern Drama*, IX, no.1 (May 1966) 74–89.

'Lennox Robinson and Synge's *Playboy* (1911–1930); Two Decades of American Cultural Growth', *New England Quarterly*, XLIV (Brunswick, Maine, Mar 1971) 3–21.

Fackler, Herbert V., 'J. M. Synge's *Deirdre of the Sorrows*: Beauty Only', *Modern Drama*, XI, no.4 (Feb 1969) 404–9.

Fallon, Gabriel, 'The Ageing Abbey', *Irish Monthly*, LXVI, no.778 (Dublin, Apr 1938) 265–72; and no.779 (May 1938) 339–44.

'Tribute to the Fays', *Irish Monthly*, LXXIII (Dublin, Jan 1945) 18–24.

Farjeon, Herbert, 'The Birth of the Playboy', *Theatre Arts Monthly*, XVI, no.3 (N.Y., Mar 1932) 228–36.

Farrell, James T., 'The Irish Cultural Renaissance in the Last Century', *Irish Writing*, no.25 (Cork, Dec 1953) 50–3.

Farris, Jon R., 'The Nature of the Tragic Experience in *Deirdre of the Sorrows*', *Modern Drama*, XVI, no. 2 (Sep 1971) 243–51.

Fausset, Hugh I'A., 'Synge and Tragedy', *Fortnightly Review*, CXV, New Series (London, Feb 1924) 258–73.

Fay, Gerard, 'Synge and the Irish; The *Playboy* Riots', *Manchester Guardian* (26 Jan 1957) p. 6.

Fay, William P., 'Le théâtre national irlandais ou les débuts de l'Abbey Theatre', *La revue*, no. 17 (Paris, 1 Sep 1959) 98–100.

Figgis, Darrell, 'J. M. Synge', *Bookman*, XL (London, Apr 1911) 30–3. Reprinted in *Studies and Appreciations* (London: J. M. Dent; New York: Dutton, 1912) pp. 23–33.

'The Art of J. M. Synge', *Fortnightly Review*, XC, New Series (London, Dec 1911) 1056–68. Also in *Forum*, XLVII (N.Y., Jan 1912) 55–70. Reprinted in *Studies and Appreciations* (London: J. M. Dent; New York: Dutton, 1912) pp. 34–59.

Fitzgerald, Maurice, 'The Future of the Peasant Play', *Sinn Fein*, IV, no. 163 (Dublin, 15 Mar 1913) 6–7.

Fitz-Simon, Christopher, 'The Theater in Dublin', *Modern Drama*, II, no. 3 (Dec 1959) 289–94.

Fletcher, Rev. D., 'The Plays of Synge', *Transactions of the Rochdale Literary and Scientific Society*, XI (Rochdale, England, 1912–13) 99–104.

Flood, Jeanne, 'The Pre-Aran Writings of J. M. Synge', *Eire-Ireland; A Journal of Irish Studies*, V, no. 3 (St Paul, Minn., Autumn 1970) 63–80.

'Florence, Jean' [Prof. Blum], 'Le théâtre irlandais (J. M. Synge, Lady Gregory)', *Phalange* (Paris, 20 Jan 1911) 52–61.

'Forthcoming Works', *Irish Book Lover*, IV, no. 7 (London and Dublin, Feb 1913) 128. See also IV, no. 11 (Jun 1913) 198.

'Forty Years of Irish Drama', *The Times Literary Supplement* (London, 13 Apr 1940) pp. 182, 186.

Fox, R. M., 'Realism in Irish Drama', *Irish Statesman*, X (Dublin, 23 Jun 1928) 310–12.

'Wild Riders of Irish Drama', *Theatre Arts*, XXVIII, no. 5 (N.Y., May 1944) 301–4.

'Irish Drama Knocks at the Door', *Life and Letters*, LXI, no. 140 (London, Apr 1949) 16–21.

'Same Program, Fifty Years Later', *American Mercury*, LXXXI (Jul 1955) 43–4.

Fraser, Russell A., 'Ireland Made Him', *Nation*, CXC (N.Y., 20 Feb 1960) 171–3.

Fréchet, René, 'Le thème de la parole dans le théâtre de J. M. Synge', *Études anglaises*, XXI, no. 3 (Paris, Jun–Sep 1968) 243–56.

Freyer, Grattan, 'The Little World of J. M. Synge', *Politics and Letters*, IV (London, Summer 1948) 5–12.

'Funeral of Mr. J. M. Synge', *Irish Times* (Dublin, 27 Mar 1909) p. 8.

'Further Opinion of the Irish Players', *America*, VI (N.Y., 14 Oct 1911) 11–12.

Galsworthy, John, 'Meditation on Finality', *English Review*, XI (London, Jul 1912) 537–41. Reprinted in *Inn of Tranquillity; Studies and Essays* (London: Heinemann, 1912; New York: Scribner's, 1914; St. Clair Shores, Mich.: Scholarly Press, 1970) [on *The Playboy of the Western World*].

'The New Spirit in the Drama', *The Hibbert Journal*, XI, no. 3 (London, Apr 1913) 508–20.

Ganz, Arthur, 'J. M. Synge and the Drama of Art', *Modern Drama*, X, no. 1 (May 1967) 57–68.

Gaskell, Ronald, 'The Realism of J. M. Synge', *Critical Quarterly*, V, no. 3 (Hull, England, Autumn 1963) 242–8.

Gassner, John, *'Deirdre of the Sorrows* by J. M. Synge', *Theatre Arts*, XXXIV, no. 8 (N.Y., Aug 1950) 68–88 [text and commentary].

Gerstenberger, Donna, 'Bonnie and Clyde and Christy Mahon: Playboys All', *Modern Drama*, XIV, no. 2 (Sep 1971) 227–31.

Gibson, Ashley, 'The Irish Players', *T. P.'s Weekly* (London, 10 Jun 1910) 723.

Gill, Michael J., 'Neo-Paganism and the Stage', *New Ireland Review*, XXVII (Dublin, May 1907) 179–87.

'A Glimpse of Synge', *American Playwright*, II (N.Y., Mar 1913) 101.

Glöde, O., 'John M. Synge: *The Aran Islands*', *Englische Studien*, LXI (Leipzig, 1926–7) 301–2.

Gorky, Maxim, 'Observations on the Theatre', *English Review*, XXXVIII (London, Apr 1924) 494–8 [on *The Playboy of the Western World*].

Gosse, Edmund, 'The Playwright of the Western Wild', *Morning Post* (London, 26 Jan 1911) p. 2.

'Gossip', *Irish Book Lover*, III, no. 1 (London and Dublin, Aug 1911) 8.

'Gossip', *Irish Book Lover*, III, no. 8 (London and Dublin, Mar 1912) 133.

Greene, David, 'John Millington Synge: MSS.', *Notes and Queries*, CLXXV, no. 25 (17 Dec 1938) 441.

'An Adequate Text of J. M. Synge', *Modern Language Notes*, LXI (Baltimore, Nov 1946) 466–7.

'*The Shadow of the Glen* and *The Widow of Ephesus*', *PMLA*, LXII (Mar 1947) 233–8.

'The *Playboy* and Irish Nationalism', *The Journal of English and Germanic Philology*, XLVI, no. 2 (Urbana, Ill., Apr 1947) 199–204.

'*The Tinker's Wedding*: A Revaluation', *PMLA*, LXII, no. 3 (Sep 1947) 824–7.

'Synge's Unfinished *Deirdre*', *PMLA*, LXIII, no. 4 (Dec 1948) 1314–21.

'Synge and the Irish', *Colby Library Quarterly*, IV (Waterville, Maine, 1957) 158–66.

'Synge and the Celtic Revival', *Modern Drama*, IV, no. 3 (Dec 1961) 292–9.

'Synge in the West of Ireland', *Mosaic*, V, no. 1 (1971) 1–8.

'J. M. Synge: A Centenary Appraisal', *Eire*, VI, no. 4 (1971) 71–86.

'That Enquiring Man, John Synge', *Nation*, CCXIII (N.Y., 30 Aug 1971) 150–2.

Gregory, Lady, 'The Coming of the Irish Players', *Collier's Magazine*, XLVIII (Springfield, O., 21 Oct 1911) 15, 24.

'A Repertory Theatre', *New York Tribune*, pt V (26 Nov 1911) pp. 6–7.

'The Irish Theatre and the People', *Yale Review*, I, no. 2 (New Haven, Conn., Jan 1912) 188–91.

'Synge', *English Review*, XIII (London, Mar 1913) 556–66. Reprinted in *Our Irish Theatre; A Chapter of Autobiography* (London and New York: G. P. Putnam's, 1913; New York: Capricorn Books, 1965) pp. 119–39.

Gunnell, Doris, 'Le nouveau théâtre irlandais', *La revue*, XCIV (Paris, 1 Jan 1912) 91–106.

Gunning, G. Hamilton, 'The Decline of Abbey Theatre Drama', *Irish Review*, I, no. 12 (Dublin, Feb 1912) 606–9.

H[oughton]., C. H., 'John Synge as I Knew Him', *Irish Statesman*, II, no. 17 (Dublin, 5 Jul 1924) 532–4.

Habart, Michel, 'Le théâtre irlandais', *Théâtre populaire*, no. 9 (Paris, Sep–Oct 1954) 24–43. 43.

Hamel, A. G. van, 'On Anglo-Irish Syntax', *Englische Studien*, XLV (Leipzig, Sep 1912) 272–92.

Hamilton, Clayton, 'The Irish National Theatre', *Bookman*, XXXIV, no. 5 (Jan 1912) 508–16. Reprinted in *Studies in Stagecraft* (New York: Henry Holt; London: Grant Richards, 1914).

'The Players', *Everybody's Magazine*, XXVIII (N.Y., May 1913) 678–80.

Hanighen, Frank C., 'The Irish Players Present –', *Commonweal*, XVII (N.Y., 28 Dec 1932) 237–8.

Hannay, J. O., 'The Stage Irishman: His Origin and Development', *Irish Times* (Dublin, 8 Feb 1912) p. 7 [lecture at the Theatre of the Royal Dublin Society].

Harding, D. W., 'A Note on Nostalgia', *Scrutiny*, I (Cambridge, May 1932) 9–10.

Harrison, Austin, 'Strindberg's Plays', *English Review*, XIII (London, Dec 1912) 80–97 [comparison between Strindberg's *The Crown Bride* and Synge's *Riders to the Sea*].

Hart, William, 'Synge's Ideas on Life and Art: Design and Theory in *The Playboy of the Western World*', *Yeats Studies*, no. 2 (1972) 35–51.

Hawkes, Terence, 'Playboys of the Western World', *Listener*, LXXIV (London, 16 Dec 1965) 991–3 [from a talk in the BBC Third Programme].

Henderson, W. A., 'The Irish Theatre Movement', *Sunday Independent*, XVII, no. 38 (Dublin, 17 Sep 1922) 6.

Henn, T. R., 'John Millington Synge', *Cambridge Review*, L (10 May 1929) 430–2.

'John Millington Synge: A Reconsideration', *Hermathena; A Dublin University Review*, CXII (Autumn 1971) 5–21 [Trinity Monday Discourse delivered on 7 Jun 1971].

Henry, P. L., '*The Playboy of the Western World*', *Philologica Pragensia*, VIII (Prague, 1965) 189–204.

Hoare, John Edward, 'John Synge', *University Magazine*, X (Toronto, Feb 1911) 91–109.

'Ireland's National Drama', *North American Review*, CXCIV (N.Y., Oct 1911) 566–75.

Holloway, Joseph, 'John Millington Synge as Critic of Boucicaultian Irish Drama', *Evening Herald* (Dublin, 10 Jul 1913) p. 2.

Hone, J. M., 'A Memory of *The Playboy*', *Saturday Review*, CXIII (London, 22 Jun 1912) 776–7. Partially reprinted as 'Yeats, Synge and *The Playboy*', *Irish Book Lover*, IV, no. 1 (London and Dublin, Aug 1912) 7–8.

'J. M. Synge', *Everyman*, II, no. 44 (London, 15 Aug 1913) 555.

'How We Spoiled the Irish Actors', *Literary Digest*, XLV, no. 2 (N.Y., 13 Jul 1912) 63.

Howe, P. P., 'The *Playboy* in the Theatre', *Oxford and Cambridge Review*, no. 21 (London, Jul 1912) 37–51.

Hughes, Herbert, 'Synge and Others', *New Age*, VIII, no. 24 (London, 13 Apr 1911) 562–3.

Ide, S., 'February in Koboki Street', *Engeishimpo* (Feb 1914) pp. 170–2.

'Ireland's Greatest Dramatist', *Literary Digest*, XXXVIII, no. 16 (N.Y., 17 Apr 1909) 652 [an obituary article].

'Ireland's Playwright', *Independent*, LXXXIII (N.Y., 27 Sep 1915) 433–4.

'Irish Author and Playwright', *Belfast News-Letter* (25 Mar 1909) p. 8 [obituary].

'Irish Author's Bereavement', *Irish Independent* (Dublin, 31 Oct 1908) p. 6.

'Irish Home Rule in the Drama', *Current Literature*, L (N.Y., Jan 1911) 81–4.

'Irish Literary Movement: The Works of John M. Synge', *Aberdeen Free Press* (6 Feb 1911) p. 3.

'Irish Literary Society', *Irish Book Lover*, II, no. 5 (London and Dublin, Dec 1910) 79–80.

'Irish Literary Society', *Irish Book Lover*, IV, no. 10 (London and Dublin, May 1913) 169–70.

'Irish Opinion on "The Irish Players"', *America*, V (N.Y., 7 Oct 1911) 614—5.

'The Irish Play of Today', *Outlook*, IC (N.Y., 4 Nov 1911) 561—3.

'The Irish Players', *Everybody's Magazine*, XXVI (N.Y., Feb 1912) 231—40.

'The Irish Players in New York', *Outlook*, IC (N.Y., 2 Dec 1911) 801.

'Irish Plays and Players', *Outlook*, IIC (N.Y., 29 Jul 1911) 704.

'Irish Playwright Dead', *Sunday Independent* (Dublin, 28 Mar 1909) p. 8.

'Irish Playwright Dead. Mr. J. M. Synge Passes Away. Loss to Irish Drama', *Dublin Evening Mail* (24 Mar 1909) p. 3.

J., P. [John Palmer], 'The Extra-Occidental Theatre', *Saturday Review*, CXI (London, 25 Feb 1911) 236—7 [Synge and John Masefield compared].

'J. M. Synge', *Evening Sun* (N.Y., 2 Apr 1909) p. 8.

'J. M. Synge, Dramatist', *Glasgow Herald* (16 Feb 1911) p. 12.

'J. M. Synge: His Work and Genius', *Irish Times* (23 Jan 1911) p. 7.

Jacobs, Willis D., 'A Silent Sinner', *American Mercury*, LXXXI (N.Y., Aug 1955) 159—60.

Jochum, K. P. S., 'Maud Gonne on Synge', *Eire*, VI, no. 4 (1971) 65—70.

'John M. Synge', *An Claidheamh Soluis*, XII, no. 8 (Dublin, 30 Apr 1910) 5.

'John M. Synge', *Westminster Gazette* (London, 4 Feb 1911) p. 4.

'John Synge's Art', *Nation*, V, no. 16 (London, 17 Jul 1909) 563–4.

'John Synge's Future Fame', *Irish Book Lover*, I, no. 3 (London and Dublin, Oct 1909) 33–4.

Johnson, Wallace H., 'The Pagan Setting of Synge's *Playboy*', *Renascence*, XIX (1967) 119–21, 150.

Kain, Richard M., 'A Scrapbook of the *"Playboy* Riots" ', *Emory University Quarterly*, XXII, no. 1 (Spring 1966) 5–17.

Kaul, R. K., 'Synge as a Dramatist: An Evaluation', *An English Miscellany*, III (Delhi: St. Stephen's College, 1965) 37–51.

K[avanagh], P[atrick], 'Paris in Aran', *Kavanagh's Weekly*, I, no. 9 (Dublin, 7 Jun 1952) 7.

Kelly, P. J., 'The Early Days of the Irish National Theatre. With Personal Recollections of Synge, Yeats, Moore, Lady Gregory, and Others', *New York Times*, section 4 (1 Jun 1919) p. 2.

Kelly, Seamus, 'Where Motley Is Worn', *Spectator*, CXCVI (London, 20 Apr 1956) 538–40.

Kenny, M., 'The "Irish" Players and Playwrights', *America*, V (N.Y., 30 Sep 1911) 581–2.

'The Irish Pagans', *America*, VI (N.Y., 21 Oct 1911) 31–2.

'The Plays of the "Irish" Players', *America*, VI (N.Y., 4 Nov 1911) 78–9.

Keohler, Thomas, 'The Irish National Theatre', *Dana*, I, no. 10 Dublin, Feb 1905) 317–20; no. 11 (Mar 1905) 351–2.

Kerby, Paul, 'The Source of a Plot', *The Times Literary Supplement* (London, 7 Jul 1921) p.437 [letter to the Editor on *The Shadow of the Glen*].

Kikuchi, K., 'An Approach to Synge's Dramas', *Teikoku Bungaku*, XXIII, no. 5 (1917) 32–48.

Kilroy, James F., 'The Playboy as Poet', *PMLA*, LXXXIII, no. 2 (May 1968) 439–42.

Kilroy, Thomas, 'Synge the Dramatist', *Mosaic*, V, no. 1 (1971) 9–16.

Krause, David, ' "The Rageous Ossean": Patron-Hero of Synge and O'Casey', *Modern Drama*, IV, no. 3 (Dec 1961) 268–91.

'Synge und das irische Melodram', *Theater heute*, V, no. 3 (Hanover, Mar 1964) 62–3.

Krieger, Hans, 'J. M. Synge', *Die neueren Sprachen*, XXIV (Marburg, 1916) 602–5.

Krüger, Werner Adolf, 'John M. Synge', *Die Neue Literatur*, XXXVI, no. 4 (Leipzig, Apr 1935) 229–30.

L., R., 'A Gifted Irishman. Personal Tribute to the Late J. M. Synge', *Daily News* (London, 26 Mar 1909) p.4.

Laan, Thomas F. van, 'Form as Agent in Synge's *Riders to the Sea*', *Drama Survey*, III, no. 3 (Minneapolis, Minn., Feb 1964) 352–66.

Lamm, Martin, 'Um John M. Synge', *Birtingur*, XI, pts 3–4 (Reykjavik, 1965) 56–8.

'The Late Mr. J. M. Synge', *Irish Times* (Dublin, 26 Mar 1909) p.8.

'The Late Mr. J. M. Synge', *Dublin Evening Mail* (26 Mar 1909) p.2.

Lawrence, W. J., 'The Abbey Theatre; Its History and Mystery', *Weekly Freeman*, XCVI (Dublin, 7 Dec 1912) 11–12.

Lengeler, Rainer, 'Phantasie und Komik in Synges *The Playboy of the Western World*', *Germanisch-romanische Monatsschrift*, Neue Folge, XIX (Heidelberg, 1969) 291–304.

Lerner, Laurence, 'Homage to Synge', *Encounter*, XXXVIII, no. 1 (London, Jan 1972) 62–7.

Letts, W. M., 'Synge's Grave', *Westminster Gazette* (London, 20 Dec 1912) p. 2 [poem]. Reprinted in *Bibelot* (Portland, Maine, Jul 1913) 244.

Letts, Winifred, 'The Fays at the Abbey Theatre', *Fortnightly*, no. 978, New Series (London, Jun 1948) 420–3.

'Young Days at the Abbey Theatre', *Irish Writing*, no. 16 (Cork, Sep 1951) 43–6.

Levitt, Paul M., 'The Structural Craftsmanship of J. M. Synge's *Riders to the Sea*', *Eire-Ireland; A Journal of Irish Studies*, IV, no. 1 (Minneapolis, Minn., Spring 1969) 53–61.

Leyburn, Ellen Douglas, 'The Theme of Loneliness in the Plays of Synge', *Modern Drama*, I, no. 2 (Sep 1958) 84–90.

Lintot, Bernard, 'At Number 1, Grub Street', *T. P.'s Weekly*, XVIII (London, 22 Sep 1911) 361.

'Literary and Scientific Society: The Drama of J. M. Synge', *Cork Free Press* (11 Nov 1910) p. 7 [report of D. Corkery's lecture].

Lokhorst, Emmy van, 'Toneelkroniek: Teleurstelling en voldoening', *de Grids*, CXIX, no. 5 (Amsterdam, 1956) 350–4 [disappointment and fulfilment as seen in Synge, Fry, and Philip King].

Love, Harry Melville, 'John Millington Synge', *Colonnade*, VII, no. 7 (The Andiron Club, N.Y., Apr 1914) 225–9.

Lowther, George, 'J. M. Synge and the Irish Revival', *Oxford and Cambridge Review*, no. 25 (London, Nov 1912) 43–59.

Lydon, J. F., 'John Millington Synge: The Man and His Background', *Mosaic*, V, no. 1 (1971) 17–25.

Lynch, Arthur, 'Synge', *Irish Statesman*, XI, no. 7 (Dublin, 20 Oct 1928) 131 [letter to the Editor].

Lynd, Robert, 'Syngolatry', *Daily News and Leader* (London, 14 Jun 1912) p. 8.

McBrien, Peter, 'Dramatic Ideals of Today', *Studies; An Irish Quarterly Review*, XI, no. 42 (Dublin, Jun 1922) 235–42.

M[acDonagh], T[homas], 'J. M. Synge: Irish Dramatist, Writer, Poet', *T. P.'s Weekly*, XIII (London, 9 Apr 1909) 469 [obituary].

Macdonald, H., 'The Playboy in France', *Sinn Fein*, III, no. 106 (Dublin, 10 Feb 1912) 3.

McHugh, Roger, 'Yeats, Synge and the Abbey Theatre', *Studies; An Irish Quarterly Review*, XLI, nos. 163–4 (Dublin, Sep–Dec 1952) 333–40.

'Literary Treatment of the Deirdre Legend', *Threshold*, I, no. 1 (Belfast, Feb 1957) 36–49.

MacKenna, Stephen, 'Synge', *Irish Statesman*, XI, no. 9 (Dublin, 3 Nov 1928) 169–70 [letter to the Editor].

MacLean, Hugh N., 'The Hero as Playboy', *University of Kansas City Review*, XXI, no. 1 (Fall 1954) 9–19.

McMahon, Sean, 'Clay and Worms', *Eire-Ireland; A Journal of Irish Studies*, V, no. 4 (St Paul, Minn., Winter 1970) 116–34.

Maguire, Mary C., 'John Synge', *Irish Review* (Dublin, Mar 1911) 39–43.

Maleh, G., 'Al-Haraka al-Masrahiya al-Irlandiya', *Al-Ma'arifa*, XXXIV (Dec 1964) 376–84 [in Arabic].

Malone, Andrew E., 'The Decline of the Irish Drama', *Nineteenth Century and After*, XCVII, no. 578 (London, Apr 1925) 578–88.

'The Coming of Age of the Irish Drama', *Dublin Review*, CLXXXI, no. 362 (Jul 1927) 101–14. Partially reprinted in *Catholic World*, CXXVI (N.Y., Oct 1927) 109–10.

'The Abbey Theatre Season', *Dublin Magazine*, II, no. 4 (Oct–Dec 1927) 30–8.

Masefield, John, 'John M. Synge', *Contemporary Review*, XCIX (London, Apr 1911) 470–8.

Matsuda, Hiroshi, 'A Note on J. M. Synge's *Poems*', *Hokkaido Eigo-Eibungaku*, XV (Jun 1970) 1–11.

Mencken, Henry L., 'Synge and Others', *Smart Set* (N.Y., London and Paris, Oct 1912) 147–52.

Mennlock, Walter, 'Dramatic Values', *Irish Review*, I, no. 7 (Dublin, Sep 1911) 325–9.

Mercer, Caroline G., 'Stephen Dedalus's Vision and Synge's Peasant Girls', *Notes and Queries*, VII (Dec 1960) 473–4.

Mercier, Vivian, 'Irish Comedy: The Probable and the Wonderful', *University Review*, I, no. 8 (Dublin, Spring 1956) 45–53.

Meyerfeld, Max, 'Letters of John Millington Synge', *The Yale Review*, XIII, no. 4 (Jul 1924) 690–709.

Michie, Donald M., 'Synge and His Critics', *Modern Drama*, XV, no.4 (March 1973) 427–32.

Mikhail, E. H., 'French Influences on Synge', *Revue de littérature comparée*, XLII, no.3 (Paris, Jul–Sep 1968) 429–31.

'Deliberate Workmanship in Synge's *Playboy*', *Colby Library Quarterly*, IX, no.6 (Waterville, Maine, Jun 1971) 322–4.

'Synge's *The Playboy* and Ibsen's *Peer Gynt*: A Parallel', *Colby Library Quarterly*, IX, no.6 (Waterville, Maine, Jun 1971) 324–30.

Miller, Liam, 'The (First) Cuala Edition of *Poems and Translations*', *Long Room*, no.3 (Dublin, Spring 1971) pp.32–7.

Millet, Philippe, 'Un théâtre irlandais', *Le temps* (Paris, 23 Jan 1912) pp.4–5.

Montgomery, K. L., 'Some Writers of the Celtic Renaissance', *Fortnightly Review*, XC, New Series (London, Sep 1911) 545–61.

Moore, George, 'George Moore on the Irish Theatre', *Boston Evening Transcript* (23 Sep 1911) p.8 [letter to the Editor].

'Yeats, Lady Gregory, and Synge', *English Review*, XVI (London, Jan 1914) 167–80; XVI (Feb 1914) 350–64. Reprinted as a chapter in *Hail and Farewell* (London: William Heinemann; N.Y.: Appleton, 1914).

Morris, Lloyd R., 'Four Irish Poets', *Columbia University Quarterly*, XVIII (N.Y., Sep 1916) 332–44.

Moses, Montrose J., 'W. B. Yeats and the Irish Players', *Metropolitan Magazine*, XXXV, no.3 (N.Y., Jan 1912) 23–5, 61–2.

'Dramatists without a Country', *Book-News Monthly* (Philadelphia, Feb 1912) 408–9.

'Mr. J. M. Synge', *The Times* (London, 25 Mar 1909) p. 13 [obituary].

'Mr. J. M. Synge', *Manchester Guardian* (25 Mar 1909) p. 7. [obituary].

'Mr. Roosevelt as a Critic', *Literary Digest*, XLIV, no. 8 (N.Y., 24 Feb 1912) 375–6.

Murphy, Daniel J., 'The Reception of Synge's *Playboy* in Ireland and America: 1907–1912', *Bulletin of the New York Public Library*, LXIV, no. 10 (Oct 1960) 515–33.

Mušek, Karel, 'Irské Literární Divadlo', *Divadelní List Máje*, Ročník III, Číslo 2 (Prague, 2 Nov 1906) 17–19.

'The Aran Islands', *Lumír*, Ročník XXXV, Číslo 8 (Prague, 1910) 383–4.

Nagarkar, Kiran, 'Synge', *Quest*, LVI (Bombay, 1968) 46–8.

'A New Thing in the Theater: Some Impressions of the Much-Discussed "Irish Players"', *Harper's Weekly*, IV (N.Y., 9 Dec 1911) 19.

Nordman, C. A., 'J. M. Synge, Dramatikern', *Finsk Tidskrift för Vitterhet, Vetenskap, Konst Och Politik*, LXXIX (Helsinki, Jul–Dec 1915) 26–70.

'Obituary: Mr. J. M. Synge', *Irish Times* (Dublin, 25 Mar 1909) p. 8.

Observer, 'The Playboy', *Freeman's Journal* (Dublin, 23 Jan 1912) p. 8.

O'Casey, Sean, 'John Millington Synge', *Britansky Soyuznik* (Moscow, Jun 1946). Reprinted in *Blasts and Benedictions*, ed. Ronald Ayling (London: Macmillan; New York: St Martin's Press, 1967) pp. 35–41.

O'Connor, Anthony Cyril, 'Synge and National Drama', *Unitas*, XXVII, no. 2 (Manila, Apr–Jun 1954) 318–25; XXVII, no. 3 (Apr–Jun 1954) 430–44.

O'Connor, Frank, 'All the Olympians', *Saturday Review*, XLIX, no. 50 (N.Y., 10 Dec 1966) 30–2, 99. Reprinted in *The Backward Look; A Survey of Irish Literature* (London: Macmillan, 1967) pp. 183–93; and in *A Short History of Irish Literature; A Backward Look* (New York: Capricorn Books, 1967) pp. 183–93 [same book].

O'Cuisín, Seumas, 'J. M. Synge: His Art and Message', *Sinn Fein*, IV, no. 166 (Dublin, 17 Jul 1909) 1 [substance of a lecture].

O'D., D., 'The Irish National Theatre Company', *United Irishman* (Dublin, 9 Apr 1904) p. 6. See reply by James Connolly (7 May 1904) p. 6; counter-reply by D. O'D. (21 May 1904) p. 3; and counter-counter reply by James Connolly (4 Jun 1904) p. 6.

O'Donnell, Donat, 'The Abbey: Phoenix Infrequent', *Commonweal*, LVII (N.Y., 30 Jan 1953) 423–4.

O'Donoghue, D. J., 'John M. Synge; A Personal Appreciation', *Irish Independent* (Dublin, 26 Mar 1909) p. 4 [obituary].

'The Synge Boom; Foreign Influences', *Irish Independent* (Dublin, 21 Aug 1911) p. 4. See correspondence by J. K. O'Byrne (23 Aug 1911) p. 6; by 'Irishman' (24 Aug 1911) p. 6; by J. K. O'Byrne (26 Aug 1911) p. 6; by Tomas (28 Aug 1911) p. 6; and by J. K. O'Byrne (29 Aug 1911) p. 6.

'John M. Synge', *Irish Book Lover*, III, no. 2 (London and Dublin, Sep 1911) 31.

'Stage Irishman and His Real Creator', *Irish Independent* (Dublin, 12 Feb 1912) p. 4.

O'Faolain, Sean, 'Yeats on Synge', *Irish Statesman*, XI, no. 4

(Dublin, 29 Sep 1928) 71–2. See correspondence by Arthur Lynch, XI, no. 7 (20 Oct 1928) 131; and by Stephen MacKenna, XI, no. 9 (3 Nov 1928) 169–70.

'The Abbey Festival', *New Statesman and Nation*, XVI (London, 20 Aug 1938) 281–2.

O'Hegarty, P. S., 'Synge and Irish Literature', *Dublin Magazine*, VII, no. 1 (Jan–Mar 1932) 51–6.

O h-Eigeartaigh, P. S., 'Dramatic Impressions: I: – Synge', *Irish Nation* (Dublin, 16 Jul 1910) p. 1.

'On the People's Service', *Irish Nation and the Peasant*, I, no. 14 (Dublin, 3 Apr 1909) 5.

O'Neill, George, 'Recent Irish Drama and Its Critics', *New Ireland Review*, XXV (Dublin, Mar 1906) 29–36.

'Some Aspects of Our Anglo-Irish Poets: The Irish Literary Theatre; Foreign Inspiration of Alleged Irish Plays', *Irish Catholic*, XXIV, no. 51 (Dublin, 23 Dec 1911) 5.

'Abbey Theatre Libels', *American Catholic Quarterly*, XXXVII, no. 146 (Philadelphia, Apr 1912) 322–32. Reprinted in *Irish Catholic*, XXV, no. 33 (Dublin, 31 Aug 1912) 6; and XXV, no. 34 (7 Sep 1912) 6.

O'Neill, Michael J., 'Holloway on Synge's Last Days', *Modern Drama*, VI, no. 2 (Sep 1963) 126–30. Reprinted as 'Last Days of J. M. Synge', in *Irish Digest*, LXXX (Dublin, 4 Jun 1964) 76–9.

Orel, Harold, 'Synge's Last Play: "And a Story Will be Told For Ever"', *Modern Drama*, IV, no. 3 (Dec 1961) 306–13.

O'Riordan, Conal, 'Synge in Dutch', *Irish Review*, II, no. 22 (Dublin, Dec 1912) 557–8 [on *The Well of the Saints*].

O'Riordan, John, 'Playwright of the Western World', *Library Review*, XXIII, no. 4 (Glasgow, Winter 1971) 140–5.

O'Ryan, Agnes, 'The Drama of the Abbey Theatre', *Irish Educational Review*, VI, no. 3 (Dublin, Dec 1912) 154–63.

Ó Saothraí, Séamus, 'Synge agus an Ghaeilge', *Díolann Iriseóra* (Dublin, 1970) 83–4.

Ottaway, D. Hugh, '*Riders to the Sea*', *Musical Times*, XCIII, no. 1314 (London, Aug 1952) 358–60 [on the opera by Vaughan Williams].

'Our Scrap Book', *Irish Book Lover*, II, no. 10 (London and Dublin, May 1911) 155; II, no. 12 (Jul 1911) 197; IV, no. 7 (Feb 1913) 127.

P., A., 'John Millington Synge', *Evening Standard and St. James's Gazette* (London, 24 Jan 1911) p. 5.

Paul-Dubois, L., 'Le théâtre irlandais: Synge', *Revue des deux mondes*, XXVII (Paris, 1 May 1935) 637–44.

Pearce, Howard D., 'Synge's *Playboy* as Mock-Christ', *Modern Drama*, VIII, no. 3 (Dec 1965) 303–10.

Peattie, Elia W., 'Synge as Playwright, Poet, and Master of English', *Chicago Daily Tribune* (21 Jan 1911) p. 11.

Phelps, William Lyon, 'The Advance of English Poetry in the Twentieth Century', *Bookman*, XLVI (N.Y., Mar 1918) 58–72.

Pittock, Malcolm, '*Riders to the Sea*', *English Studies*, XLIX (Amsterdam, Oct 1968) 445–9.

Pittwood, Ernest H., 'John Millington Synge', *Holborn Review*, IV, New Series (London, Jul 1913) 489–501.

'*The Playboy*', *Evening Telegraph* (Dublin, 20 Jan 1912) p. 5.

'The *Playboy of the Western World*', *Dramatist*, III (Jan 1912) 224—5.

Podhoretz, Norman, 'Synge's *Playboy*: Morality and the Hero', *Essays in Criticism*, III, no. 3 (Jul 1953) 337—44.

Pope, T. Michael, 'Poetry and the Peasant', *New Witness* (London, 20 Feb 1913) p. 504.

Portyanskaya, N. A., 'Dzh. Sing i B. Shou [J. Synge and B. Shaw], *U.Z.: Irkutskii pedagogicheskii institut*, XXVI (1967) 198—216.

'Post Bag', *Irish Book Lover*, III, no. 1 (London and Dublin, Aug 1911) 14.

Price, Alan, 'A Consideration of Synge's *The Shadow of the Glen*', *Dublin Magazine*, XXVI, New Series, no. 4 (Oct—Dec 1951) 15—24. Partially reprinted in *Synge and Anglo-Irish Drama* (London: Methuen, 1961).

'Synge's Prose Writings: A First View of the Whole', *Modern Drama*, XI, no. 3 (Dec 1968) 221—6.

Pritchett, V. S., 'Books in General', *New Statesman and Nation*, XXI, no. 530 (London, 19 Apr 1941) 413.

Quinn, John, 'Lady Gregory and the Abbey Theatre', *Outlook*, IC (N.Y., 16 Dec 1911) 916—19.

Quinn, Owen, 'No Garland for John Synge', *Envoy; A Review of Literature and Art*, III, no. 11 (Dublin, Oct 1950) 45—51.

R., 'Synge a Yeats', *Jeviste*, II, no. 43 (Prague, 27 Oct 1921) 638—40.

Rabuse, Georg, 'J. M. Synges Verhältnis zur französischen Literatur und besonders zu Maeterlinck', *Herrig's Archiv*, CLXXIV (Brunswick, Germany, 1938) 36—53.

Rahilly, Sean O'Mahony, 'Synge and the Early Days of the Abbey', *Irish Press* (Dublin, 21 Apr 1949) p.4 [interview with Maire O'Neill].

Rajan, Balchandra, 'Yeats, Synge and the Tragic Understanding', *Yeats Studies*, no.2 (1972) 66–79.

'Readers and Writers', *New Age* (London, 7 Aug 1913) 425 [on translating *The Well of the Saints* into German].

Reid, Alec, 'Comedy in Synge and Beckett', *Yeats Studies*, no.2 (1972) 80–90.

Renwick, W. L., 'The Source of a Plot', *The Times Literary Supplement* (London, 22 Jul 1921) p.469 [letter to the Editor on *The Shadow of the Glen*].

Reynolds, Lorna, 'The Rhythms of Synge's Dramatic Prose', *Yeats Studies*, no.2 (1972) 52–65.

Rhodes, Raymond Crompton, 'The Irish National Theatre', *T.P.'s Weekly*, XXI, no.545 (London, 18 Apr 1913) 504 [letter to the Editor].

'*Riders to the Sea*', *Golden Book*, XIII (N.Y., Jun 1931) 80–4 [text and commentary].

Rivoallan, A., 'Dublin au théâtre', *Mercure de France* (Paris, 15 Apr 1937) 299–307.

Roberts, George, 'A National Dramatist', *Shanachie*, II, no.3 (Dublin, Mar 1907) 57–60.

Robinson, Lennox, 'The Birth of a Nation's Theater', *Emerson Quarterly*, XIII, no.2 (Boston, Jan 1933) 3–4, 16–18, 20.

Robinson, Norman L., 'J. M. Synge', *Central Literary Magazine*, XXVIII, no.2 (Birmingham, England, Apr 1927) 53–63.

Rollins, Ronald G., 'Huckleberry Finn and Christy Mahon:

The Playboy of the Western World', *Mark Twain Journal*, XIII, no. 2 (1966) 16–19.

'O'Casey and Synge; The Irish Hero as Playboy and Gunman', *Arizona Quarterly*, XXII, no. 3 (Autumn 1966) 216–22.

Roy, James A., 'J. M. Synge and the Irish Literary Movement', *Anglia*, XXXVII (1913) 129–45.

Ruyssen, Henri, 'Le théâtre irlandais', *Revue germanique*, V (Paris, Jan 1909) 123–5; VII (Jan 1911) 69–70.

'Le théâtre anglais (1911–1912)', *Revue germanique*, VIII (Paris, May–Jun 1912) 290.

R[yan], F[red], 'The Abbey Theatre: *The Playboy of the Western World* and the Abbey Peasant; A Curious Development', *Evening Telegraph* (Dublin, 13 May 1911) p. 5. See reply by Padraic Colum, 'The Irish Peasant in Abbey Theatre Plays', (20 May 1911) p. 5; and counter-reply by Fred Ryan, 'The Irish Peasant and the Abbey Dramatists', (3 Jun 1911) p. 4.

Ryan, Frederick, 'The Cult of the *Playboy*', *Eye-Witness*, II, no. 7 (London, 1 Feb 1912) 206–7.

S., T. P., 'The Stage Irishman at the Abbey', *Peasant and Irish Ireland*, I, no. 48 (Dublin, 4 Feb 1908) 5.

Saddlemyer, Ann (ed.), 'Synge to MacKenna: The Mature Years', *Massachussets Review*, V (Amherst, Winter 1964) 279–95.

'Rabelais *versus* A Kempis: The Art of J. M. Synge', *Komos; A Quarterly of Drama and Arts of the Theatre*, I, no. 3 (Clayton, Victoria, Australia, Oct 1967) 85–96 [condensed from a paper given at the Yeats International Summer School in Sligo, 15 August 1966].

'J. M. Synge – Poet and Playwright', *Ireland of the Welcomes*, XIX, no. 6 (Dublin, Mar–Apr 1971) 6–12.

'Infinite Riches in a Little Room: The Manuscripts of John Millington Synge', *Long Room*, I, no. 3 (Dublin, Spring 1971) 23–31.

'Synge and Some Companions, with a Note Concerning a Walk through Connemara with Jack Yeats', *Yeats Studies*, No. 2 (1972) 18–34.

Salmon, Eric, 'J. M. Synge's *Playboy*: A Necessary Reassessment', *Modern Drama*, XIII, no. 2 (Sep 1970) 111–28.

Salviris, Jacob, 'J. M. Synge', *University Magazine*, XV (Montreal, Oct 1915) 400–7.

Sanderlin, R. Reed, 'Synge's *Playboy* and the Ironic Hero', *Southern Quarterly*, VI (Hattiesburg, Missouri, Apr 1968) 289–301.

'The *Saturday* on Synge', *Irish Book Lover*, II, no. 8 (London and Dublin, Mar 1911) 125–6.

Schoepperle, Gertrude, 'John Synge and His Old French Farce', *North American Review*, CCXIV (N.Y., Oct 1921) 503–13.

Scott-James, R. A., 'J. M. Synge; The Dramatist of Ireland', *Daily News* (London, 1 Feb 1911) p. 3. Reprinted in *Personality in Literature* (London: Martin Secker, 1913) pp. 222–5.

'Scrap Book', *Irish Book Lover*, III, no. 2 (London and Dublin, Sep 1911) 31–2.

Scudder, Vida D., 'The Irish Literary Drama', *Poet Lore*, XVI (Philadelphia, 1905) 40–53.

Sear, H. G., 'Synge and Music', *Sackbut*, III, no. 4 (London, Nov 1922) 119–23.

Selver, P., 'Readers and Writers', *New Age*, XII, no. 15 (London, 7 Aug 1913) 425.

Setterquist, Jan, 'Ibsen and Synge', *Studia Neophilologica*, XXIV, nos. 1–2 (Upsala, 1951–2) 69–154.

Shaw, Bernard, 'A Note on Irish Nationalism', *New Statesman*, Irish Supplement, I, no. 14 (London, 12 Jul 1913) 1–2.

Sherman, Stuart P., 'John Synge', *Nation*, XCV, no. 2478 (N.Y., 26 Dec 1912) 608–11. Also in *Evening Post* (N.Y., 11 Jan 1913) p.6.

Sidnell, M. J., 'Synge's Playboy and the Champion of Ulster', *Dalhousie Review*, XLV, no. 1 (Spring 1965) 51–9.

Siebels, Eva, 'Die Frau in dem Drama des John Synge – ein Spiegel der irischen Seele', *Die Frau*, XLVIII (Berlin, Mar 1941) 178–82.

Skeffington, F. Sheehy, 'The Irish National Theatre', *T.P.'s Weekly*, XXI, no. 547 (London, 2 May 1913) 566 [letter to the Editor].

Skelton, Robin, 'The Poetry of J. M. Synge', *Poetry Ireland*, no. 1 (Dublin, Autumn 1962) pp. 32–44.

'The Death of Synge', *Massachussets Review*, V (Amherst, Winter 1964) 278 [poem].

'Twentieth-Century Irish Literature and the Private Press Tradition: Dun Emer, Cuala, and Dolmen Presses, 1902–1963', *Massachussets Review*, V (Amherst, Winter 1964) 368–77.

'J. M. Synge and *The Shadow of the Glen*', *English*, XVIII, no. 102 (Autumn 1969) 91–97.

Smith, Harry W., 'Synge's "Playboy" and the Proximity of Violence', *Quarterly Journal of Speech*, LV (Chicago, 1969) 381–7.

Smith, Paul, 'Dublin's Lusty Theater', *Holiday*, XXXIII (Philadelphia, Apr 1963) 119–20, 123, 156–9, 161.

Spacks, Patricia Meyer, 'The Making of the *Playboy*', *Modern Drama*, IV, no. 3 (Dec 1961) 314–23.

Starkie, Walter, '*The Playboy* Riots', *Irish Times* (Dublin, 7 Oct 1963) p. 8. Reprinted in *Scholars and Gypsies* (London: John Murray, 1963).

'Memories of John Synge and Jack Yeats', *Yeats Studies*, no. 2 (1972) 91–9.

Stephens, Edward M., 'Synge's Last Play', *Contemporary Review*, CLXXXVI, no. 1068 (London, Dec 1954) 288–93.

Stephens, James, 'I Remember J. M. Synge', *Radio Times* (London, 23 Mar 1928) pp. 590, 611.

Storer, Edward, 'Dramatists of Today: V – J. M. Synge', *British Review*, V (London, Jan–Mar 1914) 73–80. Reprinted in *Living Age*, CCLXXX (Boston, 28 Mar 1914) 777–81.

'The Stormy Debut of the Irish Players', *Current Literature*, LI (N.Y., Dec 1911) 675–6.

'The Story of the Irish Players', *Sunday Record-Herald*, pt 7 (Chicago, 4 Feb 1912) p. 1.

Strong, L. A. G., 'J. M. Synge', *Beacon*, II (London, Jul 1922) 695–701. Reprinted in *Living Age*, CCCXIV (Boston, 9 Sep 1922) 656–60.

'John Millington Synge', *Bookman*, LXXIII (N.Y., Apr 1931) 125–36. Reprinted in *Dublin Magazine*, VII, New Series (Apr–Jun 1932) 12–32.

Sullivan, Mary Rose, 'Synge, Sophocles, and the Un-Making of Myth', *Modern Drama*, XII, no. 3 (Dec 1969) 242–53.

Sultan, Stanley, 'The Gospel According to Synge', *Papers on Language and Literature*, IV, no. 4 (Southern Illinois University, Fall 1968) 428–41.

Suss, Irving, 'The *Playboy* Riots', *Irish Writing*, no. 18 (Cork, Mar 1952) 39–42.

Sutton, Graham, 'John Millington Synge; An Appreciation', *Bookman*, LXIX (London, Mar 1926) 299–301.

Synge, Lanto, 'Uncle John', *Ireland of the Welcomes*, XIX, no. 6 (Dublin, Mar–Apr 1971) 13–17.

'Synge', *Irish Nation* (Dublin, 1 May 1909) p. 2 [obituary article].

'Synge Exhibition in Dublin', *The Times* (London, 17 Apr 1959) p. 7.

'Synge's Dramatic Work', *Cork Examiner* (11 Nov 1910) p. 8.

Taylor, Herbert, 'The Plays of J. M. Synge', *Manchester Quarterly: An Illustrated Journal of Literature and Art*, CXIV (Apr 1910) 160–9.

Tennyson, Charles, 'Irish Plays and Playwrights', *Quarterly Review*, CCXV, no. 428 (London, Jul 1911) 227–34.

'The Rise of the Irish Theatre', *Contemporary Review*, C (London, Aug 1911) 240–7.

Téry, Simone, 'J. M. Synge et son oeuvre', *Revue anglo-américaine*, II, no. 1 (Paris, Oct 1924) 204–16.

Tobin, Michael, 'The Ponderings of a Playgoer', *Iris Hibernia*, IV, no. 3 (Fribourg, Switzerland, 1960) 27–39.

Tonson, Jacob, 'Books and Persons; An Occasional Causerie', *New Age*, IX, no. 16 (London, 17 Aug 1911) 374—5. See replies by An Irish Playgoer, 'The Abbey Theatre', IX, no. 18 (31 Aug 1911) 431; and by Sidheog Ni Annain, 'The Abbey Theatre', IX, no. 19 (7 Sep 1911) 454.

Townshend, George, 'The Irish Drama', *Drama Magazine* (Chicago, Aug 1911) 93—104.

Triesch, Manfred, 'Some Unpublished J. M. Synge Papers', *English Language Notes*, IV, no. 1 (Boulder, Colo., Sep 1966) 49—51.

Trividic, C., 'John Millington Synge devant l'opinion irlandaise', *Etudes anglaises*, VII, no. 2 (Paris, Apr 1954) 185—89.

'The Troublous *Playboy*', *Literary Digest*, XLIII, no. 25 (N.Y., 16 Dec 1911) 1152—3.

Tupper, James W., 'J. M. Synge and His Work', *Dial*, LIV (Chicago, 16 Mar 1913) 233—5.

UaF., R., 'J. M. Synge', *Inis Fáil*, no. 53 (London, Apr 1909) p. 12 [obituary article].

Ua Fuaráin, Eoghan, 'The Anglo-Irish Dramatic Movement', *Irisleabhar Muighe Nuadhad*, I, no. 4 (Maynooth, An Cháisg [Easter] 1910) 6—16.

Untermeyer, Louis, 'J. M. Synge and the Playboy of the Western World', *Poet Lore*, XIX (Boston, Sep 1908) 364—7.

'The Late J. M. Synge', *New York Times Book Review*, Saturday Review of Books Section, (17 Apr 1909) p. 247.

'The Virile Poet', *Nation*, IX, no. 22 (London, 26 Aug 1911) 767—8.

'Vital Drama', *The Times Literary Supplement* (London, 13 Apr 1940) p. 183 [editorial].

Walbrook, H. M., 'Irish Dramatists and Their Countrymen', *Fortnightly Review*, XCIV (London, Nov 1913) 957–61. Reprinted in *Living Age*, CCLXXIX (Boston, 27 Dec 1913) 789–93.

Warner, Alan, 'The Poet as Watcher', *Threshold*, no. 22 (Belfast, Summer 1969) 64–70.

'Astringent Joy: The Sanity of Synge', *Wascana Review*, VI, no. 1 (Regina, Sask., 1971) 5–13.

Watkins, Ann, 'The Irish Players in America: Their Purpose and Their Art', *The Craftsman*, XXI (N.Y., Jan 1912) 352–63.

Wauchope, George Armstron, 'The New Irish Drama', *Bulletin of the University of South Carolina*, no. 168 (Columbia, 1 Oct 1925) 1–11.

Webber, John E., 'The Irish Players', *Canadian Magazine*, XXVIII (Toronto, Mar 1912) 471–81.

Weygandt, Cornelius, 'The Irish Literary Revival', *Sewanee Review*, XII, no. 4 (Oct 1904) 420–31.

'The Art of the Irish Players and a Comment on Their Plays', *Book-News Monthly* (Philadelphia, Feb 1912) 379–81.

White, H. O., 'John Millington Synge', *Irish Writing*, no. 9 (Cork, Oct 1949) 57–61 [a talk broadcast by the B.B.C. on the Northern Ireland Home Service and later rebroadcast on the Third Programme].

Williams, Clive, 'Pestalozzi and John Synge', *Hermathena; A Dublin University Review*, CVI (Spring 1968) 23–39.

Woods, Anthony S., 'Synge Staged at Home by the Fireside', *Catholic World*, CXLI (N.Y., Apr 1935) 46–52.

'The Work of J. M. Synge', *Spectator* (London, 1 Apr 1911) 482–3.

'The Works of J. M. Synge', *Birmingham Daily Post* (1 Feb 1911) p. 4.

'The Writings of J. M. Synge', *Freeman's Journal* (Dublin, 23 Jan 1912) p. 8.

Yamamoto, Shuji, 'Synge no Mihappyo Gikyoku', *Eigo Seinen*, CXV (Tokyo, 1969) 138–9 [on the unpublished play *When the Moon Has Set*].

Yeats, Jack B., 'The Tinker's Curse', *Irish Homestead* (Dublin, 1 Dec 1906) Special Art Supplement [picture].

'Memories of Synge', *Irish Nation and The Peasant*, I, no. 33 (Dublin, 14 Aug 1909) 7. Reprinted in *Synge and the Ireland of His Time*, by W. B. Yeats (Dublin: Cuala Press, 1911).

'The Playboy', *A Broadside*, II, no. 4 (Churchtown, Dundrum, Sep 1909) 3 [picture].

'Synge and the Irish; Random Reflections on a Much-Discussed Dramatist from the Standpoint of a Fellow-Countryman', *Harper's Weekly*, LV (N.Y., 25 Nov 1911) 17.

Yeats, W. B., 'The Irish National Theatre and Three Sorts of Ignorance', *United Irishman*, X (Dublin, 24 Oct 1903) 2.

'John M. Synge and the Ireland of His Time', *Forum*, XLVI (N.Y., Aug 1911) 179–200. Reprinted in *Synge and the Ireland of His Time* (Dublin: Cuala Press, 1911).

'The Theater of Beauty', *Harper's Weekly*, LV (N.Y., 11 Nov 1911) 11.

'On Those Who Dislike the Playboy', *Irish Review*, I, no. 10 (Dublin, Dec 1911) 476 [poem].

'The Irish Drama', *Twentieth Century Magazine*, V (Boston, 1911) 12–15.

'A People's Theatre; A Letter to Lady Gregory', *Irish Statesman* (Dublin, 29 Nov 1919) 547–9; and (6 Dec 1919) 572–3. Also in *Dial*, LXVIII, no. 4 (Chicago, Apr 1920) 458–68. Reprinted in *Explorations* (London: Macmillan, 1962) pp. 244–59; and in *The Theory of the Modern Stage; An Introduction to Modern Theatre and Drama*, ed. Eric Bentley (Harmondsworth: Penguin Books, 1968) pp. 327–38.

'A Memory of Synge', *Irish Statesman* (5 Jul 1924) 530–2.

'A Defence of the Abbey Theatre', *Dublin Magazine*, I, no. 2 (Apr–Jun 1926) 8–12.

'The Death of Synge and Other Pages from an Old Diary', *London Mercury*, XVII (Apr 1928) 637–51; and in *Dial*, LXXXIV (Chicago, Apr 1928) 271–88. Reprinted in book form as *Death of Synge* (Dublin: Cuala Press, 1928). Reprinted in *Dramatis Personae* (London: Macmillan, 1936); in *Autobiography of William Butler Yeats* (London: Macmillan, 1938); and in *Autobiographies* (London: Macmillan, 1955).

'Yeats, Synge and *The Playboy*', *Irish Book Lover*, IV, no. 1 (London and Dublin, Aug 1912) 7–8.

'Young Irish Playwright. Death of Mr. John M. Synge', *Irish Independent* (Dublin, 25 Mar 1909) p. 4.

Z[abel], M. D., 'Synge and the Irish', *Poetry; A Magazine of Verse*, XLII, no. 2 (Chicago, May 1933) 101–6.

(c) REVIEWS OF PLAY PRODUCTIONS
[arranged in chronological order]

The Shadow of the Glen:

'Irish National Theatre', *Irish Times* (Dublin, 9 Oct 1903) p. 8 [at the Molesworth Hall].

'Two New Plays. Irish National Theatre', *Irish Daily Independent and Nation* (Dublin, 9 Oct 1903) p. 6.

'Irish National Theatre Society', *Daily Express* (Dublin, 9 Oct 1903) p. 5.

'Irish National Theatre Society', *Freeman's Journal* (Dublin, 9 Oct 1903) pp. 5–6.

'National Theatre Society', *Dublin Evening Mail* (9 Oct 1903) p. 2.

'Irish National Theatre Society: Production of Two New Plays', *Evening Telegraph* (Dublin, 9 Oct 1903) p. 3.

'The Irish National Theatre', *Irish News and Belfast Morning News* (9 Oct 1903) p. 5.

Yeats, J. B., 'Ireland Out of the Dock', *United Irishman* (Dublin, 10 Oct 1903) p. 2.

Chanel, 'Plays with Meanings', *Leader* (Dublin, 17 Oct 1903) pp. 124–5.

[Review of *In the Shadow of the Glen*], *United Irishman* (Dublin, 17 Oct 1903) p. 1.

K., T. M., 'The Irish National Theatre Society', *New Ireland* (London, 17 Oct 1903) p. 5.

Yeats, W. B., 'The Irish National Theatre and Three Sorts of Ignorance', *United Irishman* (Dublin, 24 Oct 1903) p. 2.

Yeats, J. B., 'The Irish National Theatre Society', *United Irishman* (Dublin, 31 Oct 1903) p. 7.

Grein, J. T., 'The Irish Theatre at the Royalty', *Sunday Times* (London, 27 Mar 1904) p. 8.

'Four Irish Plays; National Sentiment at the Royalty Theatre', *Daily Mail* (London, 28 Mar 1904) p. 2.

A., L. F., 'Irish Plays; The Irish National Theatre at the Royalty', *Daily Chronicle* (London, 28 Mar 1904) p. 9.

'Royalty Theatr   *Standard* (London, 28 Mar 1904) p. 3.

S., E. F., 'The Irish National Theatre Society', *Westminster Gazette* (London, 28 Mar 1904) p. 4.

'Irish National Theatre Society; Performance at the Royalty', *Morning Post* (London, 28 Mar 1904) p. 8.

Nevinson, Henry W., 'The Irish Plays', *Spectator*, X (London, 2 Apr 1904) 12–13.

'The Irish Theatre', *Athenaeum* (London, 2 Apr 1904) 444.

L., R. W., 'The Passing Show', *Today* (London, 6 Apr 1904) 264.

Beerbohm, Max, 'Some Irish Plays and Players', *Saturday Review*, XCVII (London, 9 Apr 1904) 455–7.

'National Drama. The Abbey Theatre', *Irish Daily Independent and Nation* (Dublin, 28 Dec 1904) p. 6.

'The Abbey Theatre: Last Night's Performances', *Irish Daily Independent and Nation* (Dublin, 29 Dec 1904) p. 6.

'The Irish National Theatre', *Manchester Guardian* (2 Jan 1905) p. 3.

'*In the Shadow of the Glen*', *United Irishman*, XIII, no. 306 (Dublin, 7 Jan 1905) 5.

'All Ireland', *United Irishman*, XIII, no. 309 (Dublin, 28 Jan 1905) 1 [correspondence]; no. 310 (4 Feb 1905) 1 [correspondence].

Synge, J. M., 'A Letter on the Subject of *In the Shadow of the Glen*', *United Irishman*, XIII (Dublin, 11 Feb 1905) 1.

Moore, George, 'The Irish Literary Theatre', *Irish Times* (Dublin, 13 Feb 1905) p. 6.

'Plays in the Abbey Theatre', *Independent* (Dublin, 21 Jan 1907) p. 6.

'The Abbey Theatre', *Freeman's Journal* (Dublin, 21 Jan 1907) p. 4.

'The Abbey Theatre', *Daily Express* (Dublin, 21 Jan 1907) p. 6.

'The Abbey Theatre', *Evening Telegraph* (Dublin, 21 Jan 1907) p. 2.

'Three Hours' Fun. Triple Bill at the Abbey. Mr. Synge in Another Aspect', *Irish Independent* (Dublin, 18 Oct 1907) p. 4.

Cox, J. H., 'Three Hours' Fun. Triple Bill at the Abbey. Mr. Synge in Another Aspect', *Evening Herald* (Dublin, 18 Oct 1907) p. 5.

'The Abbey Theatre: A Triple Bill', *Evening Telegraph* (Dublin, 18 Oct 1907) p. 2.

'The Abbey Theatre', *Daily Express* (Dublin, 19 Oct 1907) p. 6.

'The Abbey Theatre', *Freeman's Journal* (Dublin, 9 Mar 1908) p. 5.

The Shadow of the Glen

'The Abbey Theatre', *Daily Express* (Dublin, 9 Mar 1908) p. 6.

'The Abbey Theatre: Four Plays in New Casts', *Evening Telegraph* (Dublin, 9 Mar 1908) p. 2.

'Amusements: The Abbey Company at the Theatre Royal', *Irish News and Belfast Morning News* (1 Dec 1908) p. 3.

'Theatre Royal: Visit of the Abbey Players. A Triple Bill', *Northern Whig* (Belfast, 1 Dec 1908) p. 2.

'Theatre Royal: The Irish Players', *Ulster Echo* (Belfast, 1 Dec 1908) p. 3.

'Manchester Amusements: Gaiety Theatre', *Manchester Courier* (16 Feb 1909) p. 8.

'Irish Plays: Notes on Nationalism at the Gaiety Theatre', *Manchester Chronicle* (16 Feb 1909) p. 2.

M., A. N., 'Gaiety Theatre', *Manchester Guardian* (16 Feb 1909) p. 7.

Cox, J. H., 'Quadruple Bill. Abbey Theatre Plays', *Irish Independent* (Dublin, 9 Mar 1909) p. 4.

'Irish Plays', *Morning Leader* (London, 8 Jun 1909) p. 3.

'Court Theatre', *Morning Post* (London, 10 Jun 1909) p. 7.

'Irish Plays. Intellectual Drama at the Court Theatre', *Standard* (London, 10 Jun 1909) p. 7.

W., J., 'Royal Court Theatre', *Westminster Gazette* (London, 10 Jun 1909) p. 3.

C., P., 'More Irish Plays in London', *Manchester Guardian*, London ed. (11 Jun 1909) p. 14.

'Irish National Co.', *Daily News* (London, 11 Jun 1909) p. 10.

Beerbohm, Max, 'Irish Players', *Saturday Review*, CVII (London, 12 Jun 1909) 748.

Harrison, Austin, 'A People's Drama. The Irish Plays at the Court Theatre', *Observer* (London, 13 Jun 1909) p.6.

Clifton, Arthur, 'Court Theatre: The Irish National Theatre Society', *Court Journal and Fashionable Gazette* (London, 16 Jun 1909) 872–3.

'Irish Play Season', *Stage* (London, 17 Jun 1909) 18.

Archer, William, 'The First-Fruit of the Endowment', *Nation*, V, no.12 (London, 19 Jun 1909) 419–21.

'The Irish National Theatre at the Court', *Illustrated London News*, CXXXIV (19 Jun 1909) 908.

'Irish Drama. Court (Irish National Theatre)', *Athenaeum* (London, 19 Jun 1909) 740.

'The Irish Players', *Irish News and Belfast Morning News* (5 Aug 1909) p.8.

'Grand Opera House: The Abbey Players', *Northern Whig* (Belfast, 5 Aug 1909) p.11.

'Irish Players in Leeds', *Yorkshire Observer* (Bradford, 18 Apr 1910) p.9.

'The Abbey Theatre', *Evening Telegraph* (Dublin, 7 Oct 1910) p.2.

Mantle, Burns, 'News of the Theaters: An Irish Fantasy', *Chicago Daily Tribune* (1 Nov 1910) p.8 [at the Grand Opera].

Bennett, James O'Donnell, 'Mrs. Fiske Presents Two Plays', *Chicago Record-Herald* (1 Nov 1910) p.8.

'Gaiety Theatre: *In the Shadow of the Glen*', *Manchester Courier* (24 Feb 1911) p. 12.

Grein, J. T., 'Court: The Irish Players', *Sunday Times* (London, 18 Jun 1911) p. 6.

'The Court Theatre', *Academy* (London, 24 Jun 1911) 785–6.

'Irish Players' Triumph', *Evening Express* (Liverpool, 11 Jul 1911) p. 7.

'Irish Players Happy Choice for Plymouth Theatre's Dedication', *Boston Journal* (24 Sep 1911) p. 3.

'Simple and Real', *Boston Sunday Globe* (24 Sep 1911) p. 9.

Hale, Philip, 'Boston's New Theatre Opens', *Sunday Herald* (Boston, 24 Sep 1911) p. 4.

Williams, S. C., 'The Abbey Players at the Plymouth', *Boston Daily Advertiser* (25 Sep 1911) p. 5.

'Irish Players Delight Boston', *Christian Science Monitor* (25 Sep 1911) p. 4.

'The Irish Players', *Boston Evening Transcript* (25 Sep 1911) p. 12.

Williams, S. C., 'Irish Players Open Plymouth Theatre', *Boston Evening Record* (25 Sep 1911) p. 6.

Biggers, Earl Derr, 'The New Plays', *Boston Traveler* (25 Sep 1911) p. 4.

Kenny, M., 'The Plays of the "Irish" Players', *America*, VI, no. 4 (N.Y., 4 Nov 1911) 78–9.

'Delightfully Artistic Are Irish Players', *New Haven Evening Register*, Last ed. (7 Nov 1911) p. 13.

'New School of Acting', *Irish Independent* (Dublin, 17 Nov 1911) p.3 [at the Abbey Theatre].

'Abbey Theatre', *Freeman's Journal* (Dublin, 17 Nov 1911) p.9.

'Abbey Theatre: Dramatic School Pupils Performance', *Daily Express* (Dublin, 17 Nov 1911) p.6.

'Abbey Theatre: Pupils' Performance; Address by Mr. W. B. Yeats', *Evening Telegraph* (Dublin, 17 Nov 1911) p.5.

Crawford, Mary Caroline, 'The Irish Players', *Theatre Magazine*, XIV (N.Y., Nov 1911) 157–8.

'The Irish Players', *Evening Post* (N.Y., 16 Dec 1911).

'Irish Players Again: Seen in One Act Play by Synge', *Brooklyn Daily Eagle* (16 Dec 1911) p.9.

'Gallery, In Ugly Mood, Jeers New Synge Play', *World* (N.Y., 16 Dec 1911) p.5.

W., A., 'The Drama', *New York Tribune* (16 Dec 1911) p.7.

Sherwin, Louis, 'The Shadow of the Glen', *New York Globe and Commercial Advertiser* (16 Dec 1911) p.6.

Mailly, William, 'The Shadow of the Glen', *New York Call* (18 Dec 1911) p.3.

'The Shadow of the Glen', *New York Dramatic Mirror*, LXVI (20 Dec 1911) 6–7.

Hall, O. L., 'Irish Co. in Three Plays', *Chicago Daily Journal* (22 Feb 1912) p.8.

Leslie, Amy, 'Four Fine Irish Plays', *Chicago Daily News* (22 Feb 1912) p.14.

Hatton, Frederic, 'Triple Bill Enhances Irish Players' Week', *Chicago Evening Post* (22 Feb 1912) p.5.

'The Irish Players', *Pall Mall Gazette* (London, 21 Jun 1912) p.5 [at the Court].

'The Irish Players at the Court', *Illustrated London News*, CXL (22 Jun 1912) 958.

'The Court: Irish Plays', *Stage* (London, 27 Jun 1912) 17.

'The Irish Drama', *Athenaeum*, no.4418 (London, 29 Jun 1912) 741.

Point, Jack, 'Two New Plays Produced Last Night at the Abbey', *Evening Herald* (Dublin, 25 April 1913) p.4.

'The Abbey Theatre', *Evening Telegraph* (Dublin, 25 Apr 1913) p.4.

F., J., 'Frank Beauty in Synge Play', *New York World-Telegram* (4 Nov 1932) [at the Martin Beck Theatre].

Atkinson, Brooks, 'The Play. In Which the Dubliners Mount Two One-Act Plays and One of Two Acts', *New York Times* (4 Nov 1932) p.25.

'*The Shadow of the Glen*: Synge on Television', *The Times* (London, 12 Aug 1954) p.9.

Wiggin, Maurice, 'Television: Tall Tales', *Sunday Times* (London, 15 Aug 1954) p.9.

Hope-Wallace, Philip, 'Drama', *Listener*, LII (London, 19 Aug 1954) 296–7.

Atkinson, Brooks, 'The Theatre: Three Plays by Synge', *New York Times* (7 Mar 1957) p.24 [by the Irish Players at Theater East].

Kerr, Walter, 'Three Plays by John Synge Given at the Theater East', *New York Herald Tribune* (7 Mar 1957) p.16.

Atkinson, Brooks, 'Three Plays by Synge', *New York Times* (17 Mar 1957) Section 2, p.1.

'Off-Broadway Shows: Three Plays by Synge', *Variety* (N.Y., 20 Mar 1957) 72.

'Three Plays', *Catholic World*, CLXXXV (N.Y., May 1957) 148.

'Irish Plays in Edinburgh', *The Times* (London, 29 Aug 1957) p.3.

'Mr. Behan Back in Ribald Mood', *The Times* (London, 30 Jul 1963) p.13 [by the New Pike Company at the Theatre Royal, Stratford E.].

Kenyon, Michael, 'Festival of Irish Comedy at the Theatre Royal, Stratford E.', *Guardian* (London, 30 Jul 1963) p.7.

Darlington, W. A., 'Irish Plays Fail to Inspire', *Daily Telegraph and Morning Post* (London, 30 Jul 1963) p.12.

Shulman, Milton, 'A Drop of Irish, but the Flavour Is Weak', *Evening Standard* (London, 30 Jul 1963) p.4.

Barker, Felix, 'A Drop of Irish', *Evening News and Star* (London, 30 Jul 1963) p.3.

D., P., 'Behan Broadside; Festival of Irish Comedy (Theatre Royal, Stratford, E.)', *Daily Worker* (London, 31 Jul 1963) p.2.

Marriott, R. B., 'At Stratford East: Irish Comedy with Synge and Behan', *Stage and Television Today* (London, 1 Aug 1963) 7.

Hobson, Harold, 'Theatre', *Sunday Times* (London, 4 Aug 1963) p.25.

Tynan, Kenneth, 'Dubliners in the East End', *Observer* (London, 4 Aug 1963) p. 17.

Gellert, Roger, 'O'Booze', *New Statesman*, LXVI (London, 9 Aug 1963) 178–9.

Trewin, J. C., 'Period Pieces', *Illustrated London News*, CCXLIII (10 Aug 1963) 216.

Riders to the Sea:

'Irish National Theatre Society', *Irish Times* (Dublin, 26 Feb 1904) p. 5 [at the Molesworth Hall].

'Irish National Theatre', *Irish Daily Independent and Nation* (Dublin, 26 Feb 1904) p. 5.

'Irish National Theatre Society. A New Play Produced', *Freeman's Journal* (Dublin, 26 Feb 1904) p. 6.

'Irish National Theatre Society', *Evening Telegraph* (Dublin, 26 Feb 1904) p. 3.

C., E. T., 'Mr. Synge's New Play', *Irish Times* (Dublin, 27 Feb 1904) p. 6 [letter to the Editor].

Chanel, 'The National Theatre', *Leader* (Dublin, 5 Mar 1904) pp. 27–8.

Grein, J. T., 'The Irish Theatre at the Royalty', *Sunday Times* (London, 27 Mar 1904) p. 8.

A., L. F., 'Irish Plays; The Irish National Theatre at the Royalty', *Daily Chronicle* (London, 28 Mar 1904) p. 9.

'Four Irish Plays; National Sentiment at the Royalty Theatre', *Daily Mail* (London, 28 Mar 1904) p. 2.

'Royalty Theatre', *Standard* (London, 28 Mar 1904) p. 3.

S., E. F., 'The Irish National Theatre Society', *Westminster Gazette* (London, 28 Mar 1904) p.4.

'Irish National Theatre Society; Performance at the Royalty', *Morning Post* (London, 28 Mar 1904) p.8.

Nevinson, Henry W., 'The Irish Plays', *Speaker*, X (London, 2 Apr 1904) 12–13.

'The Irish Theatre', *Athenaeum* (London, 2 Apr 1904) 444.

L., R. W., 'The Passing Show', *Today* (London, 6 Apr 1904) 264.

Beerbohm, Max, 'Some Irish Plays and Players', *Saturday Review*, XCVII (London, 9 Apr 1904) 455–7.

'Irish National Theatre', *Gael* (N.Y., Apr 1904) 139.

'National Theatre Society', *Daily Express* (Dublin, 22 Jan 1906) p.7.

'New Irish Comedy', *Evening Telegraph* (Dublin, 22 Jan 1906) p.6 [*Eloquent Dempsy* preceded by *Riders to the Sea*].

'The Abbey Theatre', *Irish Independent* (Dublin, 23 Jan 1906) p.6.

'The New Theatre', *Oxford Times* (8 Jun 1907) p.12.

A., W., 'The Irish Actors', *Tribune* (London, 12 Jun 1907) p.7.

'Irish Plays in London', *Stage* (London, 13 Jun 1907) p.9.

'Abbey Theatre', *Irish Times* (Dublin, 4 Aug 1908) p.6.

'Before the Footlights. Irish Tragedy and Comedy', *Irish Independent* (Dublin, 4 Aug 1908) p.6.

'The Abbey Theatre: *Riders to the Sea*', *Freeman's Journal* (Dublin, 4 Aug 1908) p. 5.

'Abbey Theatre', *Daily Express* (Dublin, 4 Aug 1908) p. 6.

'The Abbey', *Evening Herald* (Dublin, 4 Aug 1908) p. 4.

'The Abbey Theatre: *Riders to the Sea*', *Evening Telegraph* (Dublin, 4 Aug 1908) p. 2.

'Theatre Royal: The Irish Players', *Belfast News-Letter* (4 Dec 1908) p. 9.

'Theatre Royal: The Abbey Theatre Company in Four Plays', *Irish News and Belfast Morning News* (4 Dec 1908) p. 5.

'Theatre Royal: Visit of the Abbey Company', *Northern Whig* (Belfast, 4 Dec 1908) p. 9.

'Theatre Royal: Abbey Theatre Company', *Ulster Echo* (Belfast, 4 Dec 1908) p. 3.

M., C. E., 'Gaiety Theatre', *Manchester Guardian*, London ed. (18 Feb 1909) p. 4.

'Irish Plays', *Morning Leader* (London, 8 Jun 1909) p. 3 [at the Court Theatre].

'Court Theatre', *Morning Post* (London, 10 Jun 1909) p. 7.

'Irish Plays. Intellectual Drama at the Court Theatre', *Standard* (London, 10 Jun 1909) p. 7.

W., J., 'Royal Court Theatre', *Westminster Gazette* (London, 10 Jun 1909) p. 3.

C., P., 'More Irish Plays in London', *Manchester Guardian*, London ed. (11 Jun 1909) p. 14.

'Irish National Theatre Co.', *Daily News* (London, 11 Jun
  1909) p. 10.

Beerbohm, Max, 'Irish Players', *Saturday Review*, CVII
  (London, 12 Jun 1909) 748.

D., T. B., 'Irish Plays at the Court', *Outlook*, XXIII (London,
  12 Jun 1909) 810.

Harrison, Austin, 'A People's Drama. The Irish Plays at the
  Court Theatre', *Observer* (London, 13 Jun 1909) p. 6.

'The Irish Theatre; Dublin at the Court', *Referee* (London,
  13 Jun 1909) p. 2.

Clifton, Arthur, 'Court Theatre: The Irish National Theatre',
  Court Journal (London, 16 Jun 1909) pp. 872–3.

'Irish Play Season', *Stage* (London, 17 Jun 1909) p. 18.

'The Irish National Theatre at the Court', *Illustrated London
  News*, CXXXIV (19 Jun 1909) 908.

Archer, William, 'The First-Fruits of the Endowment', *Nation*,
  V, no. 12 (London, 19 Jun 1909) 419–21.

'Irish Drama. Court (Irish National Theatre)', *Athenaeum*
  (London, 19 Jun 1909) 740.

'Amusement: Grand Opera House', *Belfast News-Letter* (5 Apr
  1910) p. 8.

'Amusements: The Abbey Theatre Company at the Opera
  House', *Irish News and Belfast Morning News* (5 Apr 1910)
  p. 8.

'Grand Opera House: The Abbey Players', *Northern Whig*
  (Belfast, 5 Apr 1910) p. 11.

'Irish Players in New Bill', *Christian Science Monitor* (3 Oct 1911) p. 5.

P., H. T., 'More Irish Plays', *Boston Evening Transcript* (3 Oct 1911) p. 14.

'*Riders to the Sea* at Plymouth Theatre', *Boston Daily Advertiser* (3 Oct 1911) p. 5.

'Plymouth Theatre', *Boston Post* (3 Oct 1911) p. 9.

C., J. V., 'New Bill by Irish Players', *Boston Evening Record* (3 Oct 1911) p. 6.

Hale, Philip, 'Two Successes at Plymouth: Irish Players Delight Audience with the Grim Tragedy "Riders to the Sea"', *Boston Herald* (3 Oct 1911) p. 5.

'Irish Players in New Bill', *Boston Journal* (3 Oct 1911) p. 9.

Biggers, Earl Derr, 'The New Plays', *Boston Traveler* (4 Oct 1911) p. 4.

Kenny, M., 'The Plays of the "Irish" Players', *America*, VI, no. 4 (N.Y., 4 Nov 1911) 78–9.

'Notes of the Stage', *New York Press* (4 Dec 1911) p. 10.

'Irish Players Again: Synge's Tragedy *Riders to the Sea* Proves Most Effective of Company's Repertoire', *Brooklyn Daily Eagle* (5 Dec 1911) p. 6.

'Maxine Elliott's – Irish Players: *Riders to the Sea*', *New York Dramatic Mirror*, LXVI (13 Dec 1911) 7.

Eaton, Walter Prichard, 'Viewing Irish Players in the Light of Reason', *Sunday Record-Herald* (Chicago, 17 Dec 1911) pt. VII, p. 3.

Leslie, Amy, 'Varied Bill at Grand: Tragic Hour With Synge', *Chicago Daily News* (13 Feb 1912) p. 14.

Hall, O. L., 'Irish Co. in Three Plays', *Chicago Daily Journal* (14 Feb 1912) p. 7.

Hammond, Percy, 'Music and the Theatres', *Chicago Daily Tribune* (15 Feb 1912) p. 9.

Bennett, James O'Donnell, 'Drama and Music: Ireland's Smiles and Tears', *Chicago Record-Herald* (15 Feb 1912) p. 6.

'*Riders to the Sea* by J. M. Synge', *Green Book Album*, VII (Chicago, Feb 1912) 292–3.

'Abbey Theatre', *Irish Times* (Dublin, 8 Mar 1912) p. 10.

'The Abbey Theatre', *Irish Independent* (Dublin, 8 Mar 1912) p. 6.

'Abbey Theatre', *Daily Express* (Dublin, 8 Mar 1912) p. 7.

'The Abbey Theatre: Four Plays', *Evening Herald* (Dublin, 8 Mar 1912) p. 2.

'Plays at the Abbey', *Evening Telegraph* (Dublin, 8 Mar 1912) p. 4.

'The Abbey Theatre', *Dublin Evening Mail* (9 Mar 1912) p. 3.

'The Irish Players', *Pall Mall Gazette* (London, 28 Jun 1912) p. 5 [at the Court].

'Irish Tragedy and Comedy', *Athenaeum* (London, 6 Jul 1912) 24.

'The Irish Players', *New York Evening Post* (1 Mar 1913) p. 7.

'The Abbey Theatre', *Irish Times* (Dublin, 14 Mar 1913) p. 5.

'Abbey Theatre', *Freeman's Journal* (Dublin, 14 Mar 1913) p. 7.

'A New Play at the Abbey Theatre', *Evening Telegraph* (Dublin, 14 Mar 1913) p. 6 [*The Cuckoo's Nest* preceded by *Riders to the Sea*].

'Dramatic Gossip', *Athenaeum* (London, 4 Jul 1914) 28.

Firkins, O. W., 'Drama: Rostand and Synge', *Weekly Review*, III (N.Y., 18 Aug 1920) 155–6 [by the Celtic Players at the Bramhall Playhouse].

'*L'appel de la mer*. A Synge Libretto', *The Times* (London, 22 Apr 1924) p. 10 [opera by Henri Rabaud in Paris].

Buchanan, Paul S., 'The First University Theatre Tournament', *Drama*, XV (Chicago, Feb 1925) 106 [by West Virginia University].

'Court Theatre', *The Times* (London, 28 May 1927) p. 10.

'Court Theatre: *Riders to the Sea* by J. M. Synge', *Daily Telegraph* (London, 28 May 1927) p. 12.

P., J. B., 'Mr. O'Casey's New Play', *Daily Chronicle* (London, 28 May 1927) p. 4 [*The Shadow of a Gunman* followed by *Riders to the Sea*].

B., E. A., 'Sean O'Casey Early Play', *Daily News* (London, 28 May 1927) p. 5 [*The Shadow of a Gunman* preceded by *Riders to the Sea*].

'The Irish Players', *Morning Post* (London, 28 May 1927) p. 10.

Birrell, Francis, 'Court Theatre: *Riders to the Sea*', *Nation*, XLI, no. 9 (London, 4 Jun 1927) 304.

Watts, Richard, Jr., '*Riders to the Sea*. Irish Players Offer Synge Drama on Double Bill', *New York Herald Tribune* (5 Nov 1932) p. 16 [at the Martin Beck Theater].

Carroll, Sydney W., 'An Irish Gem', *Sunday Times* (London, 15 Dec 1935) p.6 [a Flanagan Hurst production financed by Miss Gracie Fields].

Greene, Graham, 'The Cinema: *Riders to the Sea*. Privately Shown', *Spectator* (London, 20 Dec 1935) p.1028.

H., J. K., 'Irish Repertorians Offer Three Plays', *New York Times* (15 Feb 1937) p.13 [at the Ninety-Second Street Y.M.H.A.].

'The Arts Theatre, Cambridge', *The Times* (London, 23 Feb 1938) p.12.

'Three Operas at the Arts Theatre, Cambridge', *New Statesman and Nation*, XV, no.366 (London, 26 Feb 1938) 328.

Toye, Francis, 'The Charm of Music', *Illustrated London News*, CXCII (12 Mar 1938) 428.

Atkinson, Brooks, 'American Negro Theatre Acts J. M. Synge's *Riders to the Sea*', *New York Times* (4 Feb 1949) p.30 [at the Harlem Children's Centre].

Atkinson, Brooks, 'The Theatre: Three Plays by Synge', *New York Times* (7 Mar 1957) p.24 [by the Irish Players at Theater East].

Kerr, Walter, 'Three Plays by John Synge Given at the Theater East', *New York Herald Tribune* (7 Mar 1957) p.16.

Atkinson, Brooks, 'Three Plays by Synge', *New York Times* (17 Mar 1957) section 2, p.1.

'Off-Broadway Shows: Three Plays by Synge', *Variety* (N.Y., 20 Mar 1957) 72.

'Three Plays', *Catholic World*, CLXXXV (N.Y., May 1957) 148.

'A Superb Glimpse of Tragic Style', *The Times* (London, 29 Sep 1960) p. 16 [on B.B.C. Television].

Lewis, Peter, 'Teleview', *Daily Mail* (London, 29 Sep 1960) p. 16.

Cookman, Anthony, 'O'Neill and Synge', *Listener*, LXIV (London, 6 Oct 1960) 596—7.

The Well of the Saints:

'Irish National T' atre: *The Well of the Saints* by Mr. J. M. Synge', *Irish Times* (Dublin, 6 Feb 1905) p. 7.

'The Abbey Theatre: *The Well of the Saints*', *Irish Independent* (Dublin, 6 Feb 1905) p. 7.

'Irish National Theatre. Mr. Synge's New Play', *Freeman's Journal* (Dublin, 6 Feb 1905) p. 5.

M'C., F., 'Irish National Theatre: *The Well of the Saints*', *Evening Herald* (Dublin, 6 Feb 1907) p. 3.

'Irish National Theatre Society: *The Well of the Saints*', *Daily Express* (Dublin, 6 Feb 1905) p. 6.

M., R., 'At the Abbey Theatre: Production of *The Well of the Saints*', *Dublin Evening Mail* (6 Feb 1905) p. 2.

'The National Theatre: Mr. Synge's New Play', *Evening Telegraph* (Dublin, 6 Feb 1905) p. 5.

'All Ireland', *United Irishman*, XIII (Dublin, 11 Feb 1905) 1 [editorial].

Keohler, Thomas, 'The Irish National Theatre', *Dana*, I, no. 11 (Dublin, Mar 1905) 351—2 [at the Abbey].

Lebeau, Henry, 'Les spectacles du mois — Mars 1905 — etranger:

Irlande, Dublin: *The Well of the Saints'*, *Revue d'art dramatique et musical* (Paris, 15 Apr 1905) 56–60.

'A Lover of the West' [Henry Lebeau]. *'The Well of the Saints'*, *Dana*, I, no. 12 (Dublin, Apr 1905) 365–8 [in French].

'St. George's Hall: Performances of the National Theatre Society', *Athenaeum* (London, 2 Dec 1905) 771–2.

'Abbey Theatre', *Irish Times* (Dublin, 15 May 1908) p. 6.

'Plays at the Abbey Theatre', *Irish Independent* (Dublin, 15 May 1908) p. 6.

'The Abbey Theatre: *The Well of the Saints'*, *Freeman's Journal* (Dublin, 15 May 1908) p. 10.

'The Abbey Theatre', *Daily Express* (Dublin, 15 May 1908) p. 6.

'The Abbey Theatre', *Evening Telegraph* (Dublin, 30 Oct 1908) p. 2.

'The Abbey Theatre', *Freeman's Journal* (Dublin, 30 Oct 1908) p. 10.

'Abbey Theatre', *Daily Express* (Dublin, 30 Oct 1908) p. 4.

'Mr. J. M. Synge', *Dublin Evening Mail* (30 Oct 1908) p. 3.

'More Irish Plays', *Manchester Chronicle* (17 Feb 1909) p. 3.

'Gaiety Theatre: Grave and Gay', *Manchester Courier* (17 Feb 1909) p. 9.

'The Irish Players: A Remarkable Production at the Gaiety Theatre', *Manchester Evening News* (17 Feb 1909) p. 7.

A., J. E., 'Gaiety Theatre: The Irish Plays', *Manchester Guardian*, London ed. (17 Feb 1909) p. 7.

'Abbey Theatre', *Irish Times* (Dublin, 14 May 1909) p. 6.

'The Abbey Theatre', *Freeman's Journal* (Dublin, 14 May 1909) p. 10.

'Irish Plays', *Morning Leader* (London, 8 Jun 1909) p. 3.

W., J., 'Royal Court Theatre', *Westminster Gazette* (London, 9 Jun 1909) p. 3.

'The Abbey Theatre Company in London', *Pall Mall Gazette* (London, 9 Jun 1909) p. 5.

'Irish Triple Bill', *Daily News* (London, 10 Jun 1909) p. 5.

'Irish Play Season', *Stage* (London, 10 Jun 1909) 17.

'The Irish Plays', *The Times* (London, 12 Jun 1909) p. 8.

Harrison, Austin, 'A People's Drama. The Irish Plays at the Court Theatre', *Observer* (London, 13 Jun 1909) p. 6.

'Court: The Irish Plays', *Sunday Times* (London, 13 Jun 1909) p. 4.

'The Irish Theatre; Dublin at the Court', *Referee* (London, 13 Jun 1909) 2.

'The Irish Theatre (Court)', *New Age*, V, no. 8 (London, 17 Jun 1909) 162.

'The Irish National Theatre at the Court', *Illustrated London News*, CXXXIV (19 Jun 1909) 908.

Archer, William, 'The First-Fruit of the Endowment', *Nation*, V, no. 12 (London, 19 Jun 1909) 419–21.

'Irish Drama. Court (Irish National Theatre)', *Athenaeum* (London, 19 Jun 1909) 740.

'Grand Opera House: The Visit of the Abbey Theatre Company', *Belfast News-Letter* (6 Apr 1910) p. 9.

'Grand Opera House: "The Well of the Saints" ', *Northern Whig* (Belfast, 6 Apr 1910) p. 11.

'The Irish Players', *Boston Evening Transcript* (23 Sep 1911) p. 9.

'Plymouth Theatre', *Boston Daily Advertiser* (26 Sep 1911) p. 5.

'Irish Players at Plymouth', *Boston Herald* (26 Sep 1911) p. 5.

'New Plays at the Plymouth', *Boston Post* (27 Sep 1911) p. 6.

' "Well of Saints" Superb Comedy', *Boston Journal* (27 Sep 1911) p. 7.

Williams, S. C., 'Abbey Players in New Bill', *Boston Evening Record* (27 Sep 1911) p. 6.

Williams, S. C., 'The Abbey Players Score Again', *Boston Daily Advertiser* (27 Sep 1911) p. 5.

P., H. T., 'Two More Irish Plays', *Boston Evening Transcript* (27 Sep 1911) p. 19.

'The Theatrical World: Irish Players Change Bill', *Christian Science Monitor* (27 Sep 1911) p. 12.

Biggers, Earl Derr, 'The New Plays', *Boston Traveler* (28 Sep 1911) p. 4.

Kenny, M., 'The Plays of the "Irish" Players', *America*, VI, no. 4 (N.Y., 4 Nov 1911) 78–79.

McConaughy, J. W., 'The New Play', *New York Evening Journal* (24 Nov 1911) p. 27.

'Irish Players As Wild Westerners', *New York Times* (24 Nov 1911) p. 13.

'On Both Sides of the Footlights', *Evening Telegram* (N.Y., 24 Nov 1911) p. 10.

'Irish Players Consist Largely of Humbug', *Brooklyn Daily Eagle* (24 Nov 1911) p. 6.

'Irish Players in Plays by Bernard Shaw and J. M. Synge', *New York Tribune* (24 Nov 1911) p. 7.

'Irish Players Interesting', *New York Commercial* (24 Nov 1911) p. 2.

'Music and Drama: The Irish Players', *Evening Post* (N.Y., 24 Nov 1911) p. 9.

Mailly, William, 'Drama', *New York Call* (25 Nov 1911) p. 4.

'Acting of the Irish Players', *New York Times* (26 Nov 1911) p. 3.

DeFoe, Louis V., '*The Well of the Saints*', *New York World* (26 Nov 1911).

'*The Well of the Saints*', *New York Dramatic Mirror*, LXVI (29 Nov 1911) 9.

'Drama', *Nation*, XCIII (N.Y., 30 Nov 1911) 528–9.

Stevens, Ashton, ' "Well of Saints" Is Grim, Gray Comedy', *Chicago Examiner* (28 Feb 1912) p. 7.

Hall, O. L., 'News and Gossip of the Theatres', *Chicago Daily Journal* (28 Feb 1912) p. 7.

Hatton, Frederic, 'Irish Players Reveal Poetical Synge Play', *Chicago Evening Post* (28 Feb 1912) p. 5.

Hammond, Percy, 'The Well of the Saints by the Irish Players', *Chicago Daily Tribune* (29 Feb 1912) p. 7.

Leslie, Amy, 'Three New Irish Bits', *Chicago Daily News* (29 Feb 1912) p. 5.

Delamarter, Eric, 'With the Irish Players', *Inter Ocean* (Chicago, 29 Feb 1912) p. 6.

'The Irish Players at the Court Theatre', *The Times* (London, 18 Jun 1912) p. 10.

'Irish Plays at the Court', *Standard* (London, 18 Jun 1912) p. 5.

'The Irish Players', *Pall Mall Gazette* (London, 18 Jun 1912) p. 5.

'The Irish Players', *Morning Post* (London, 18 Jun 1912) p. 10.

'The Court: Irish Plays', *Stage* (London, 20 Jun 1912) 17–18.

'The Irish Players at the Court', *Illustrated London News*, CXL (22 Jun 1912) 958.

'Four Irish Plays', *Athenaeum* (London, 22 Jun 1912) p. 715.

'At the Play: Court', *Observer* (London, 23 Jun 1912) p. 7.

M., K., 'Plays and Players: The Irish Players in Two Revivals', *Boston Evening Transcript* (10 Apr 1913) p. 13.

Atkinson, Brooks, 'The Play: The Well of the Saints', *New York Times* (22 Jan 1932) p. 15 [by the Irish Theatre at the Barbizon Plaza Hotel].

'Blind Principals Add to Pathos of Tenderly Beautiful Irish Play', *New York World-Telegram* (22 Jan 1932).

DeCasseres, Benjamin, 'Broadway to Date: The Well of the

Saints', *Arts and Decoration*, XXXVI (N.Y., Mar 1932) 42, 63.

N., L., 'Again the Abbey', *New York Times* (22 Nov 1934) p. 26 [at the Golden Theatre].

Rathbun, Stephen, 'A Double Bill: *The Well of the Saints*', *New York Sun* (22 Nov 1934) p. 22.

Ross, George, 'Dubliners in 2 Plays with Moral', *New York World-Telegram* (22 Nov 1934) p. 30.

'The Arts', *Stage* (London, 11 Mar 1943) 4.

'Arts Theatre: *The Well of the Saints* by J. M. Synge', *The Times* (London, 18 Mar 1943) p. 6.

Agate, James, 'Ibsen, Synge and Shaw. *The Well of the Saints*: Arts', *Sunday Times* (London, 21 Mar 1943) p. 2.

Redfern, James, '*The Well of the Saints* at the Arts Theatre Club', *Spectator* (London, 26 Mar 1943) 291.

'Plays at the Arts Theatre', *New Statesman and Nation*, XXV, no. 632 (London, 3 Apr 1943) 224–5.

H., E. M., '*The Well of the Saints*', *Theatre World*, XXXVIII (London, Apr 1943) 6.

'New Lindsey Theatre: *The Well of the Saints* by J. M. Synge', *The Times* (London, 28 Apr 1954) p. 6.

L., L., 'Irish Realism and Fancy', *Daily Telegraph* (London, 28 Apr 1954) p. 8.

Frank, Elizabeth, 'Two Pieces of Irish Enchantment. *The Well of the Saints*: New Lindsey', *News Chronicle* (London, 28 Apr 1954) p. 3.

'The New Lindsey: *The Well of the Saints*', *Stage* (London, 29 Apr 1954) 10.

Atkinson, Brooks, '*The Well of the Saints*', *New York Times* (11 Apr 1959) p. 15 [by the Gate Theatre off-Broadway].

Malcolm, Donald, 'The Theatre: *The Well of the Saints*', *New Yorker*, XXXV (18 Apr 1959) 82–3.

'Early Stages', *Catholic World*, CLXXXIX (N.Y., Jun 1959) 243.

Hope-Wallace, Philip, 'Old Vic: Abbey Theatre', *Guardian* (London, 4 Aug 1970) p. 6.

Callan, Paul, 'At the Old Vic', *Evening Standard* (London, 4 Aug 1970) p. 13.

Frame, Colin, 'Verbal Gems and a Load of Codswallop: *The Well of the Saints*', *Evening News* (London, 4 Aug 1970) p. 3.

Billington, Michael, 'Simplicity of Synge. Old Vic: *The Well of the Saints*', *The Times* (London, 5 Aug 1970) p. 7.

S., L. G., 'Abbey at Old Vic', *Stage* (London, 6 Aug 1970) 15.

Hobson, Harold, 'Theatre: The Abbey Theatre in *The Well of the Saints* (Old Vic)', *Sunday Times* (London, 9 Aug 1970) p. 21.

Breyden, Ronald, 'Theatre', *Observer* (London, 9 Aug 1970) p. 20.

Cushman, Robert, 'Theatre: *The Well of the Saints* (Old Vic)', *Spectator* (London, 15 Aug 1970) 163–4.

Trewin, J. C., 'Theatre', *Illustrated London News*, CCLVII (15 Aug 1970) 31.

The Playboy of the Western World:

'The Abbey Theatre: Mr. Synge's New Play', *Evening Telegraph* (Dublin, 25 Jan 1907) p.3.

'Platform and Stage', *Irish Times* (Dublin, 26 Jan 1907) p.9.

'The Abbey Theatre: Mr. Synge's New Play', *Freeman's Journal* (Dublin, 26 Jan 1907) p.10.

'Abbey Theatre', *Irish Times* (Dublin, 28 Jan 1907) p.7.

Jacques, 'A Queer Hero in Mr. Synge's New Play', *Irish Independent* (Dublin, 28 Jan 1907) p.4.

'The Abbey Theatre: *The Playboy of the Western World*', *Freeman's Journal* (Dublin, 28 Jan 1907) p.10.

'The Abbey Theatre: Mr. Synge's New Play', *Daily Express* (Dublin, 28 Jan 1907) p.6.

D., H. S., 'A Dramatic Freak. First Night at the Abbey Theatre', *Dublin Evening Mail* (28 Jan 1907) p.2.

'The Abbey Theatre: *The Playboy of the Western World*; A Revolting Caricature', *Evening Telegraph* (Dublin, 28 Jan 1907) p.2.

A Western Girl, 'To the Editor of the *Evening Telegraph*', *Evening Telegraph* (Dublin, 28 Jan 1907) p.2.

'Dublin', *Northern Whig* (Belfast, 28 Jan 1907) p.8.

'An Impression of *The Playboy*', *Irish Times* (Dublin, 29 Jan 1907) p.8 [letter to the Editor].

' "The Playboy of the West" ', *Irish Times* (Dublin, 29 Jan 1907) p.5.

'The Abbey Theatre: Uproarious Scenes. Protests against

Mr. Synge's Play', *Freeman's Journal* (Dublin, 29 Jan 1907) p. 7.

'Disturbance at the Abbey Theatre', *Morning Mail* (Dublin, 29 Jan 1907) p. 3.

F., A., ' "I Don't Care a Rap". Mr. Synge's Defence. His Play an Extravaganza', *Dublin Evening Mail* (29 Jan 1907) p. 2 [interview].

'*The Playboy* at the Abbey. "Kill the Author". Indignant Audience. Disorderly Scenes', *Evening Herald* (Dublin, 29 Jan 1907) p. 2.

'Abbey Theatre *Playboy*; Uproarious Scenes Last Night. Mr. Synge's Play Hooted and the Performance Stopped', *Evening Telegraph* (Dublin, 29 Jan 1907) p. 2 [plus correspondence].

'A Queer Country: An Irish Play Hissed Down', *Cork Constitution* (29 Jan 1907) p. 5.

'The Abbey Theatre Disturbance', *Dublin Evening Mail* (29 Jan 1907) p. 2 [editorial].

'The Abbey Theatre in Dublin: Mr. J. M. Synge's New Comedy Hissed', *Pall Mall Gazette* (London, 29 Jan 1907) p. 10.

H., P., 'Dramatic Criticism', *Dublin Evening Mail* (29 Jan 1907) p. 5 [letter to the Editor].

'Scene at a Dublin Theatre', *Cork Examiner* (29 Jan 1907) p. 5.

'Disturbances at the Abbey Theatre', *Daily Express* (Dublin, 29 Jan 1907) p. 6.

'Abbey Theatre Scene; Interview with Mr. W. B. Yeats', *Evening Telegraph* (Dublin, 29 Jan 1907) p. 4.

'Uproar in a Dublin Theatre', *Belfast News-Letter* (29 Jan 1907) p.7.

'Police In', *Irish Independent* (Dublin, 29 Jan 1907) p.5.

'An Alleged Irish Comedy', *Irish News and Belfast Morning News* (29 Jan 1907) p.5.

'Dublin Theatre Scenes', *Globe* (London, 30 Jan 1907) p.3.

'The National Theatre Company', *Irish Times* (Dublin, 30 Jan 1907) p.6 [editorial].

'The "Playboy" at the Abbey', *Evening Herald* (Dublin, 30 Jan 1907) p.5

'The Abbey Theatre', *Morning Mail* (Dublin, 30 Jan 1907) p.4.

Pat, 'That Dreadful Play', *Irish Times* (Dublin, 30 Jan 1907) p.6.

'Abbey Theatre Scenes. More Uproar Last Night', *Freeman's Journal* (Dublin, 30 Jan 1907) pp.7–8.

'The Abbey Theatre: Further Disorderly Scenes: Mr. Yeats and the Critics', *Daily Express* (Dublin, 30 Jan 1907) p.5.

'Last Night's Row at the Abbey. Disturbers Charged in the Police Court', *Dublin Evening Mail* (30 Jan 1907) p.2.

'This Evening's London Papers: *The Playboy of the Western World*', *Dublin Evening Mail* (30 Jan 1907) p.3.

'Abbey Scenes Sequel. Prosecution in Police Court. Mr. Yeats Describes the Disturbance', *Evening Herald* (Dublin, 30 Jan 1907) pp.1–2.

'An Unpopular Play: Uproar at the Irish Theatre', *Birmingham Daily Mail* (30 Jan 1907) p.5.

'Disturbance in an Irish Theatre', *Birmingham Daily Post* (30 Jan 1907) p. 7.

'Abbey Theatre Scenes. More Uproar Last Night. Mr. Synge's Play Produced under Police Protection', *Evening Telegraph* (Dublin, 30 Jan 1907) p. 2 [plus correspondence].

'Irish Theatre: More Disturbances', *Cork Constitution* (30 Jan 1907) p. 5.

'Abbey Theatre: More Scenes', *Cork Examiner* (30 Jan 1907) p. 6.

'The Previous Scenes', *Irish Independent* (Dublin, 30 Jan 1907) p. 5.

' "Playboy of the West" ', *Irish Times* (Dublin, 30 Jan 1907) p. 8.

'Another Scene at the Abbey Theatre', *Northern Whig* (Belfast, 30 Jan 1907) p. 9.

'Police-Protected Drama; *Playboy* Prosecutions. Charges in Police Court', *Evening Telegraph* (Dublin, 30 Jan 1907) p. 3.

'Mr. Synge's Disgusting Travesty', *Irish News and Belfast Morning News* (30 Jan 1907) p. 8.

'*The Playboy of the Western World*: More Disturbances at the Abbey Theatre', *Irish Times* (Dublin, 31 Jan 1907) p. 5.

Synge, J. M., '*The Playboy*', *Irish Times* (Dublin, 31 Jan 1907) p. 5 [letter to the Editor].

'The Abbey Theatre Disorders: Why Society Boycotts the Institution', *Pall Mall Gazette* (London, 31 Jan 1907) p. 7.

Duncan, Ellen, '*The Playboy*', *Irish Times* (Dublin, 31 Jan 1907) p. 5 [letter to the Editor].

'Scenes at the Abbey Theatre: Renewal of Disturbances', *Daily Express* (Dublin, 31 Jan 1907) p. 5.

'The Abbey Theatre: More Uproar. Great Display of Police', *Freeman's Journal* (Dublin, 31 Jan 1907) pp. 7–8.

'The "Playboy" Scenes', *Irish Independent* (Dublin, 31 Jan 1907) p. 5 [plus correspondence].

'Abbey Theatre Scenes. Another Police Prosecution', *Evening Herald* (Dublin, 31 Jan 1907) p. 2.

'Dublin's Unpopular Play', *Belfast News-Letter* (31 Jan 1907) p. 11.

' "Pegeen Mike" – A Parricide', *Irish News and Belfast Morning News* (31 Jan 1907) p. 4 [editorial].

'Scenes in a Dublin Theatre', *Northern Whig* (Belfast, 31 Jan 1907) p. 11.

'Irish National Theatre: Extraordinary Scenes in Dublin', *Aberdeen Free Press* (31 Jan 1907) p. 6.

'Statement by Mr. W. B. Yeats', *Aberdeen Free Press* (31 Jan 1907) p. 6.

'La Linge', ' "The Playboy" at the Abbey', *Dublin Evening Mail* (31 Jan 1907) p. 2 [letter to the Editor].

M., A. M., 'Art in Trouble. Two Plays and a Row', *Evening Herald* (Dublin, 31 Jan 1907) p. 4.

'*The Playboy*', *Evening Herald* (Dublin, 31 Jan 1907) p. 5 [includes cartoons].

'The Law and the Drama. Last Night's Row at the Abbey', *Dublin Evening Mail* (31 Jan 1907) pp. 3–4.

'Scenes at the Abbey Theatre', *Morning Mail* (Dublin, 31 Jan 1907) p.3.

'Under Police Protection. Another Night in the Abbey', *Evening Telegraph* (Dublin, 31 Jan 1907) p.2 [plus correspondence].

'Police and *The Playboy*; Another Prosecution', *Evening Telegraph* (Dublin, 31 Jan 1907) p.3 [plus correspondence].

'Dublin', *Stage* (London, 31 Jan 1907) 2.

'Notes and Comments', *Cork Examiner* (31 Jan 1907) p.5.

'*The Playboy of the Western World*: Comparative Quiet at the Abbey Theatre', *Irish Times* (Dublin, 1 Feb 1907) p.6.

Colum, Padraic, '*The Playboy*', *Irish Times* (Dublin, 1 Feb 1907) p.6 [letter to the Editor].

'The Abbey Theatre: A Rather Quiet Night. Two Arrests', *Freeman's Journal* (Dublin, 1 Feb 1907) p.5.

'*The Playboy* Has a Quieter Time at the Abbey. But Two Arrests Were Made. Author and Mr. Yeats Interviewed', *Evening Herald* (Dublin, 1 Feb 1907) p.5.

'Mr. Wall Invited to the Abbey. Last Night's Row', *Dublin Evening Mail* (1 Feb 1907) p.2.

'The Scenes at the Abbey Theatre', *Morning Mail* (Dublin, 1 Feb 1907) p.4.

Colum, Padraic, 'Letter to the Editor', *Dublin Evening Mail* (1 Feb 1907) p.2.

'A Comedy in Court', *Irish Independent* (Dublin, 1 Feb 1907) p.5.

Power, Ambrose, 'Letter to the Editor', *Dublin Evening Mail* (1 Feb 1907) p. 2.

'Crito', 'Letter to the Editor', *Dublin Evening Mail* (1 Feb 1907) p. 2.

'Abbey Theatre Play: Interview with Mr. W. B. Yeats', *Dublin Evening Mail* (1 Feb 1907) p. 5.

'Abbey Street "Parricide"; A Fairly Quiet Hearing Under Police Protection', *Evening Telegraph* (Dublin, 1 Feb 1907) pp. 2–3 [plus correspondence].

'Abbey Theatre Play: A Fair Hearing Accorded; Interview with Mr. W. B. Yeats', *Daily Express* (Dublin, 1 Feb 1907) p. 5.

'The Abbey Theatre: Continued Disturbances', *Cork Constitution* (1 Feb 1907) p. 3.

'Abbey Theatre: Another Prosecution', *Cork Examiner* (1 Feb 1907) p. 6.

'Irish National Theatre: More Disorderly Scenes', *Aberdeen Free Press* (1 Feb 1907) p. 6.

'Abbey Theatre', *Irish Times* (Dublin, 2 Feb 1907) p. 5.

'Uproarious Scenes in a Theatre', *Glasgow Observer* (2 Feb 1907) p. 6.

'The Abbey Theatre: One Arrest', *Freeman's Journal* (Dublin, 2 Feb 1907) p. 2.

'Tumult in a Theatre', *Irish Weekly Independent* (Dublin, 2 Feb 1907) pp. 1, 5.

Avis, 'The Playboys in the Abbey', *Leader* (Dublin, 2 Feb 1907) pp. 387–8.

Griffith, Arthur, 'The Language of the Play', *Freeman's Journal* (Dublin, 2 Feb 1907) p. 2 [letter to the Editor].

B., M. P., 'Rafferty at the New Play', *Saturday Herald* (Dublin, 2 Feb 1907) p. 3.

Gwynn, Stephen, 'Mr. Boyle and Mr. Synge', *Freeman's Journal* (Dublin, 2 Feb 1907) p. 2 [letter to the Editor].

'*The Playboy* at the Abbey', *Saturday Herald* (Dublin, 2 Feb 1907) pp. 1–2.

'Matinee at the Abbey Theatre. *The Playboy*'s Reception', *Evening Herald* (Dublin, 2 Feb 1907) p. 2.

'More Peaceful Now', *Irish Independent* (Dublin, 2 Feb 1907) p. 5.

'Abbey Theatre Disturbances. Another Prosecution. Amusing Evidence', *Dublin Evening Mail* (2 Feb 1907) p. 3.

'The Play-boy of the Western World', *Irish Truth* (Dublin, 2 Feb 1907) pp. 6795–6.

'The New Play at the Abbey Theatre', *Dublin Evening Mail* (2 Feb 1907) p. 4.

'The Abbey Theatre Disturbance: Mr. Wall and the Rights of Playgoers', *Daily Express* (Dublin, 2 Feb 1907) p. 7.

'The Abbey Theatre', *Sinn Féin* (Dublin, 2 Feb 1907) p. 2.

'Under Police Protection; Another Night in the Abbey', *Evening Telegraph* (Dublin, 2 Feb 1907) p. 3 [plus correspondence].

'The Author Interviewed', *Weekly Freeman* (Dublin, 2 Feb 1907) p. 6.

'Another *Playboy* Matinee', *Evening Telegraph* (Dublin, 2 Feb 1907) p. 5.

'Monday Night at the Abbey Theatre', *Leader* (Dublin, 2 Feb 1907) pp. 384–5.

'*The Playboy of the Western World*', *Evening Telegraph* (Dublin, 2 Feb 1907) p. 6 [correspondence].

Quine, Sean, 'Talk Upon Topics', *Irish Weekly and Ulster Examiner* (Belfast, 2 Feb 1907) p. 1.

'To the Point', *I* 'ı *Weekly and Ulster Examiner* (Belfast, 2 Feb 1907) p. 4.

'An Alleged Irish Comedy: Scenes in the Abbey Theatre', *Irish Weekly aı*.' *Ulster Examiner* (Belfast, 2 Feb 1907) p. 5.

'Abbey Theatre: Further Prosecutions', *Cork Examiner* (2 Feb 1907) p. 5.

'A Queer Comedy: An Irish Play Hissed Down', *Cork Weekly News* (2 Feb 1907) p. 3.

'The Abbey Theatre: Audience Overawed by Police. Interview with Mr. Yeats', *Freeman's Journal* (Dublin, 4 Feb 1907) p. 4 [plus correspondence].

'Exit *The Playboy*', *Irish Independent* (Dublin, 4 Feb 1907) p. 5.

O'Donoghue, D. J., 'Letter to the Editor', *Freeman's Journal* (Dublin, 4 Feb 1907) p. 4.

'The Abbey Theatre', *Daily Express* (Dublin, 4 Feb 1907) p. 7.

Boyle, William, 'Letter to the Editor', *Freeman's Journal* (Dublin, 4 Feb 1907) p. 4.

'Abbey Theatre: Another Prosecution', *Cork Constitution* (4 Feb 1907) pp. 5–6.

'Passing of "The Parricide" ', *Evening Telegraph* (Dublin, 4 Feb 1907) p. 2 [plus correspondence].

'Abbey Theatre: More Prosecutions', *Cork Examiner* (4 Feb 1907) p. 8.

'The National Drama', *Evening Telegraph* (Dublin, 4 Feb 1907) p. 4.

'Dublin', *Northern Whig* (Belfast, 4 Feb 1907) p. 7.

J., P., 'Ireland on the Stage', *Irish News and Belfast Morning News* (4 Feb 1907) p. 4 [editorial].

'The Freedom of the Play. Discussion at the Abbey Theatre', *Irish Times* (Dublin, 5 Feb 1907) p. 8.

'The Abbey Theatre Disturbances: Mr. Yeats on Mr. Synge's Play: Lively Debate', *Daily Express* (Dublin, 5 Feb 1907) p. 8.

'Parricide and Public. Discussion at the Abbey Theatre', *Freeman's Journal* (Dublin, 5 Feb 1907) pp. 7–8.

'Freedom of the Drama', *Irish Independent* (Dublin, 5 Feb 1907) p. 4 [editorial].

'A Lover of Liberty', 'The Freedom of the Theatre', *Freeman's Journal* (Dublin, 5 Feb 1907) p. 7 [letter to the Editor].

'The Abbey Theatre Disturbances', *Morning Mail* (Dublin, 5 Feb 1907) p. 3.

'*The Playboy* at the Abbey. Merits and Demerits Debated', *Evening Herald* (Dublin, 5 Feb 1907) p. 5 [includes cartoons].

'Playboy', *Irish Independent* (Dublin, 5 Feb 1907) pp. 5–6.

'The Parricide and the People; Discussion in the Abbey. Mr. Yeats's Defence', *Evening Telegraph* (Dublin, 5 Feb 1907) p. 2 [plus correspondence].

'Abbey Theatre: More Scenes', *Cork Examiner* (5 Feb 1907) p. 6.

'Mr. Synge's Secret', *Dublin Evening Mail* (5 Feb 1907) p. 2.

Yeats, W. B., 'Mr. Boyle's Plays', *Evening Telegraph* (Dublin, 6 Feb 1907) p. 3 [letter to the Editor].

Dillon, Edward, 'A Contradiction', *Evening Telegraph* (Dublin, 6 Feb 1907) p. 3 [letter to the Editor].

'Resolutions of Protest', *Evening Telegraph* (Dublin, 6 Feb 1907) p. 3.

'Anti-"Playboy" Protests from Indignant Connachtmen', *Irish Independent* (Dublin, 6 Feb 1907) p. 5 [plus correspondence] pp. 4, 7.

Dillon, Edward, 'The Disturbance at the Abbey Theatre', *Irish Times* (Dublin, 7 Feb 1907) p. 6 [letter to the Editor].

'The Man That Killed His Father', *Evening Telegraph* (Dublin, 8 Feb 1907) p. 2.

' "Playboy of the Western World" ', *Irish Weekly Independent* (Dublin, 9 Feb 1907) p. 6.

'The Freedom of the Theatre', *Sinn Féin* (Dublin, 9 Feb 1907) pp. 2–3.

'The "Playboy" Disturbances', *Irish Weekly and Ulster Examiner* (Belfast, 9 Feb 1907) p. 12.

'The Abbey Theatre Debate', *Irish Truth* (Dublin, 9 Feb 1907) pp. 6811–12.

'Yeats's Fishy Yarn: Curious Genesis of the "Playboy" ', *Irish Weekly and Ulster Examiner* (Belfast, 9 Feb 1907) p. 12.

'Abbey Theatre: Another Prosecution', *Cork Weekly News* (9 Feb 1907) p. 5.

'Mr. Synge's "Playboy" ', *Irish People* (Dublin, 9 Feb 1907) p. 6.

O'Dempsey, Michael, 'Letter to the Editor', *Irish Times* (Dublin, 11 Feb 1907) p. 8.

Horniman, E. E. F., 'Abbey Theatre Affairs', *Evening Telegraph* (Dublin, 12 Feb 1907) p. 2 [letter to the Editor].

'Lionising a Murderer', *Connaught Champion* (Galway, 16 Feb 1907) p. 2.

'The Western Peasant', *Freeman's Journal* (Dublin, 26 Feb 1907) p. 6 [editorial].

'Vindicated', *Connaught Champion* (Galway, 2 Mar 1907) p. 4 [editorial].

Brooks, Sydney, 'The Irish Peasant as a Dramatic Issue', *Harper's Weekly*, LI (N.Y., 9 Mar 1907) 344.

Boyle, William, 'Irish Drama', *Glasgow Observer* (6 Apr 1907) p. 5.

'An Irish Comedy in Dublin Last January', *Chicago Evening Post* (20 Apr 1907) p. 6.

'The New Theatre', *Oxford Times* (8 Jun 1907) p. 12.

'The Drama', *Nation* (London, 8 Jun 1907) 560–1.

'Irish Plays in London', *Daily Mail* (London, 11 Jun 1907) p. 7 [at Great Queen Street Theatre].

B[aughan], E. A., 'Irish Plays', *Daily News* (London, 11 Jun 1907) p. 6.

'An Irish Comedy', *Daily Graphic* (London, 11 Jun 1907) p. 7.

'Great Queen Street Theatre', *Morning Post* (London, 11 Jun 1907) p. 11.

'The Irish National Theatre in London; A Mayo Problem Play', *Pall Mall Gazette* (London, 11 Jun 1907) p. 4.

'Great Queen-Street Theatre', *Globe* (London, 11 Jun 1907) p. 5.

W., J., 'Great Queen Street', *Westminster Gazette* (London, 11 Jun 1907) p. 2.

'Mr. Synge's Slander on the Irish Peasantry: "The Parricide" Greeted with Saxon Cheers', *Evening Telegraph* (Dublin, 11 Jun 1907) p. 2.

'London Correspondence', *Freeman's Journal* (Dublin, 11 Jun 1907) p. 7.

'A Much Criticised Irish Play', *Standard* (London, 11 Jun 1907) p. 9.

'*The Playboy* in London', *Irish Independent* (Dublin, 11 Jun 1907) p. 6.

'Great Queen Street Theatre: *The Playboy of the Western World*', *Morning Post* (London, 11 Jun 1907) p. 11.

'The Irish National Theatre', *Pall Mall Gazette* (London, 11 Jun 1907) p. 4.

'London Correspondence: An Irish Play', *Sussex Daily News* (Brighton, 11 Jun 1907) p. 8.

'London Letter: An Irish Comedy', *Bristol Daily Mercury* (11 Jun 1907) p. 4.

'Irish Plays in London', *Northern Whig* (Belfast, 11 Jun 1907) p. 11.

A., W., 'The Irish Actors', *Tribune* (London, 11 Jun 1907) p. 7.

'Theatrical Novelties in London', *Birmingham Daily Post* (12 Jun 1907) p. 5.

' "The Playboy" in London: A Sheaf of Press Criticism', *Dublin Evening Mail* (12 Jun 1907) p. 2.

'London Correspondence', *Irish Times* (Dublin, 12 Jun 1907) pp. 6–7.

'Irish Plays in London', *Stage* (London, 13 Jun 1907) 9.

'London Correspondence', *Freeman's Journal* (Dublin, 15 Jun 1907) p. 7.

Shore, W. T., 'The Playboy of the Western World', *Academy* (London, 15 Jun 1907) p. 586.

Grein, J. T., 'Great Queen Street: *The Playboy of the Western World*', *Sunday Times* (London, 16 Jun 1907) p. 4.

'Amusements', *News of the World* (London, 16 Jun 1907) p. 12.

'The Irish Season at the Great Queen Street Theatre', *Observer* (London, 16 Jun 1907) p. 4.

Grein, J. T., 'Great Queen Street: *The Playboy of the Western World*', *Sunday Times* (London, 16 Jun 1907) p. 4.

'The Irish National Theatre', *Reynolds's Newspaper* (London, 16 Jun 1907) p. 4.

Palamede, 'Irish Plays', *Referee* (London, 16 Jun 1907) p. 3.

S., E. F., 'The Stage from the Stalls', *Sketch* (London, 19 Jun 1907) p. 300.

Guest, L. Haden, 'The Irish Theatre', *New Age* (London, 20 Jun 1907) pp. 124—5.

S., M. T., '*The Playboy of the Western World*: An Irish Literary Play', *Catholic Weekly* (London, 21 Jun 1907) p. 3.

P., 'Among the Mummers', *John Bull* (London, 22 Jun 1907) pp. 602—3.

'Vedette', 'Round the Theatres', *Illustrated Sporting and Dramatic News* (London, 22 Jun 1907) p. 694.

Jingle, 'Irish Plays at the Court Theatre', *Bystander* (London, 22 Jun 1907) pp. 598—600.

Momus, 'Irish Plays in London', *Gentlewoman* (London, 22 Jun 1907) p. 862.

O h-Eigeartaigh, P. S., 'Playboy Week in London', *Peasant and Irish Ireland* (Dublin, 22 Jun 1907) p. 5.

'Theatrical Notes', *Pall Mall Gazette* (London, 24 Jun 1907) p. 1.

Wylie, Bertie, '*The Playboy of the Western World*', *Pall Mall Gazette* (London, 27 Jun 1907) p. 2 [letter to the Editor].

'Two Irish Plays', *Athenaeum* (London, 5 Oct 1907) 415—6.

Bennett, James O'Donnell, '*The Playboy of the Western World* for the First Time in America', *Record-Herald* (Chicago, 11 Apr 1909) pt 5, p. 4.

Bennett, James O'Donnell, 'News of the Stage', *Record-Herald* (Chicago, 14 Apr 1909) p.8.

B[ennett], J[ames] O'D[onnell], 'Music and the Drama: A Note about "The Playboy"', *Record-Herald* (Chicago, 17 Apr 1909) p.8.

Lawrence, W. J., '*The Playboy of the Western World*. Proposed Revival at the Abbey Theatre', *Evening Telegraph* (Dublin, 19 May 1909) p.3.

'*The Playboy of the Western World*', *Evening Telegraph* (Dublin, 20 May 1909) p.3.

'J. M. Synge and "The Playboy"', *Evening Telegraph* (Dublin, 26 May 1909) p.5.

'Abbey Theatre', *Irish Times* (Dublin, 28 May 1909) p.6.

Jacques, 'The *Playboy* Again', *Irish Independent* (Dublin, 28 May 1909) p.6.

'The Abbey Theatre', *Freeman's Journal* (Dublin, 28 May 1909) p.8.

'The Abbey Theatre: Revival of *The Playboy*', *Daily Express* (Dublin, 28 May 1909) p.6.

Point, Jack, '*The Playboy* Again at the Abbey', *Evening Herald* (Dublin, 28 May 1909) p.4.

'The Abbey Theatre', *Evening Telegraph* (Dublin, 28 May 1909) p.5.

'Mr. Synge's Art and Message', *Evening Telegraph* (Dublin, 29 May 1909) p.7.

'Court Theatre', *Daily Telegraph* (London, 8 Jun 1909) p.4.

'Irish Plays at the Court', *Daily Mail* (London, 8 Jun 1909) p.8.

'Irish Plays at the Court', *Daily Express* (London, 8 Jun 1909)
   p. 5.

'Irish Plays in London', *Daily News* (London, 8 Jun 1909) p. 3.

'Irish Plays', *Morning Leader* (London, 8 Jun 1909) p. 3.

'Court Theatre', *Morning Post* (London, 8 Jun 1909) p. 10.

'The Abbey Theatre Company in London: *The Playboy of the
   Western World*', *Pall Mall Gazette* (London, 8 Jun 1909)
   p. 5.

W., J., 'Irish Plays at the Court Theatre', *Westminster Gazette*
   (London, 8 Jun 1909) p. 2.

C., P., 'The Irish Company in London', *Manchester Guardian*,
   London ed. (8 Jun 1909) p. 7.

'Court Theatre: The Irish Plays', *Globe* (London, 8 Jun 1909)
   p. 5.

'Irish Plays', *Evening Standard and St. James's Gazette*
   (London, 8 Jun 1909) p. 6.

' "The Playboy of the West": Production in London', *Evening
   Telegraph* (Dublin, 9 Jun 1909) p. 3.

'Irish Plays. Intellectual Drama at the Court Theatre', *Standard*
   (London, 10 Jun 1909) p. 7.

'Irish Play Season', *Stage* (London, 10 Jun 1909) p. 17.

'Dublin's National Theatre Company in London', *Daily
   Chronicle* (London, 12 Jun 1909) p. 7.

'Irish Theatre Society at the Court', *Illustrated London News*,
   CXXXIV (12 Jun 1909) 870.

D., T. B., 'Irish Plays at the Court', *Outlook*, XXIII (London, 12 Jun 1909) 810.

'Irish Drama. Court (Irish National Theatre Society): *The Playboy of the Western World* by J. M. Synge', *Athenaeum* (London, 12 Jun 1909) p. 712.

Harrison, Austin, 'A People's Drama. The Irish Plays at the Court Theatre', *Observer* (London, 13 Jun 1909) p. 6.

'The Irish Theatre; Dublin at the Court', *Referee* (London, 13 Jun 1909) p. 2.

'New Theatre: The Irish Players', *Oxford Review* (15 Jun 1909) p. 3.

Clifton, Arthur, 'Court Theatre: The Irish National Theatre Society', *Court Journal* (London, 16 Jun 1909) 872–3.

'The Irish Theatre (Court)', *New Age*, V, no. 8 (London, 17 Jun 1909) 162.

'The Abbey Theatre Company at the Court', *Pall Mall Gazette* (London, 18 Jun 1909) p. 5.

Archer, William, 'The First-Fruits of the Endowments', *Nation*, V, no. 12 (London, 19 Jun 1909) 419–21.

'The Irish Players at the New Theatre', *Oxford Times* (19 Jun 1909) p. 10.

'Abbey Theatre Co.: *The Playboy* and Other Pieces at the Grand Opera House', *Irish News and Belfast Morning News* (4 Aug 1909) p. 5.

'Grand Opera House: "The Playboy of the Western World" ', *Northern Whig* (Belfast, 4 Aug 1909) p. 12.

'Grand Opera House: *The Playboy of the Western World*', *Belfast News-Letter* (4 Aug 1909) p. 10.

'Grand Opera House: The Abbey Company', *Ulster Echo*
(4 Aug 1909) p. 3.

'The Abbey Players in Belfast: *The Playboy*', *Irish Nation and The Peasant*, I, no. 33 (Dublin, 14 Aug 1909) 7.

Mac. C., S., 'Localising Synge's "Playboy" ', *Irish Nation*
(Dublin, 21 Aug 1909) p. 7.

'Irish Plays: *The Playboy of the Western World* at the Gaiety',
Daily Dispatch (Manchester, 23 Nov 1909) p. 4.

'At the Theatre: The Irish Players at the Gaiety', *Manchester Chronicle* (23 Nov 1909) p. 3.

'Manchester Amusements: Gaiety Theatre', *Manchester Courier*
(23 Nov 1909) p. 10.

'Amusements: Irish Plays at the Gaiety', *Manchester Evening News* (23 Nov 1909) p. 6.

M., A. N., 'Gaiety Theatre: *The Playboy of the Western World*',
Manchester Guardian, London ed. (23 Nov 1909) p. 9.

H., '*The Playboy of the Western World*', *Manchester Catholic Herald* (27 Nov 1909) p. 1.

'The Irish Players: Some Notes about the Company Who Visit Leeds This Week', *Yorkshire Evening Post* (Leeds, 13 Apr 1910) p. 4.

'Irish Players in Leeds', *Yorkshire Observer* (Bradford, 15 Apr 1910) p. 7.

A., J. E., 'Gaiety Theatre', *Manchester Guardian*, London ed.
(19 Apr 1910) p. 11.

'Public Amusements', *Weekly Times* (London, 5 Jun 1910)
p. 4.

Dukes, Ashley, 'The Irish Plays', *New Age*, VII, no. 7 (London, 16 June 1910) 160–81.

MacCarthy, Desmond, 'The Irish National Theatre', *Saturday Review* (London, 18 Jun 1910) pp. 782–3.

'Opera House: Abbey Theatre Company in "Deirdre" and "The Playboy of the Western World" ', *Cork Constitution* (30 Aug 1910) p. 6.

'Opera House', *Cork Free Press* (30 Aug 1910) p. 8.

'Opera House: Abbey Theatre Plays', *Cork Examiner* (30 Aug 1910) p. 7.

'Opera House', *Cork Examiner* (1 Sep 1910) p. 7.

O'Connor, Eily, '*The Playboy of the Western World*', *Cork Constitution* (2 Sep 1910) p. 8 [letter to the Editor].

'The *Playboy* Again', *Leader* (Dublin, 3 Sep 1910) p. 53.

Ray, R. J., '*The Playboy of the Western World*', *Cork Constitution* (4 Sep 1910) p. 10 [letter to the Editor].

O'Connor, Eily, '*The Playboy of the Western World*', *Cork Constitution* (6 Sep 1910) p. 8 [letter to the Editor].

J., M., '*The Playboy of the Western World*', *Cork Constitution* (6 Sep 1910) p. 8 [letter to the Editor].

Ray, R. J., '*The Playboy*', *Cork Constitution* (7 Sep 1910) p. 8 [letter to the Editor].

R., T. B., '*The Playboy*', *Cork Constitution* (8 Sep 1910) p. 6. [letter to the Editor].

J., M., '*The Playboy*', *Cork Constitution* (9 Sep 1910) p. 6. [letter to the Editor].

L., W. A., 'The Playboy', *Irish Nation* (Dublin, 17 Sep 1910) p. 2.

Hamilton, Clayton, 'Significant Plays of Recent London Season: *The Playboy of the Western World*', *Bookman*, XXXII (N.Y., Oct 1910) 145–6.

Cahill, Patrick K., '*The Playboy of the Western World*', *Evening Telegraph* (Dublin, 3 May 1911) p. 6 [letter to the Editor].

'Abbey Theatre Players at Shakespeare Festival: 'Playboy of the West' Creates Unfavourable Impression', *Evening Telegraph* (Dublin, 4 May 1911) p. 2.

'*The Playboy of the Western World*', *Evening Telegraph* (Dublin, 5 May 1911) p. 2 [correspondence].

'Notes: The Rowdiness of Drama', *Evening Standard and St. James's Gazette* (London, 6 May 1911) p. 3.

'Notes of the Week', *Saturday Review*, CXI (London, 6 May 1911) 540.

' "The Playboy" at Stratford-on-Avon', *Evening Telegraph* (Dublin, 8 May 1911) p. 6.

Morrison, G. E., 'The Irish Players at Stratford', *Saturday Review*, CXI (London, 20 May 1911) 616 [letter to the Editor].

'The *Playboy* in England', *Leader* (Dublin, 3 Jun 1911) p. 365.

'Royal Court Theatre', *The Times* (London, 6 Jun 1911) p. 10.

'Irish Players: Court Theatre', *Daily Telegraph* (London, 6 Jun 1911) p. 11.

'The Irish Players', *Daily Mail* (London, 6 Jun 1911) p. 6.

'Ireland in London: Irish National Company at the Court Theatre', *Daily Chronicle* (London, 6 Jun 1911) p.5.

L., R., 'Irish Plays', *Daily News* (London, 6 Jun 1911) p.5.

'Court Theatre', *Standard* (London, 6 Jun 1911) p.9.

W., J., 'The Irish Theatre', *Westminster Gazette* (London, 6 Jun 1911) p.5.

'The Irish Players', *Pall Mall Gazette* (London, 6 Jun 1911) p.7.

'Court Theatre', *Morning Post* (London, 6 Jun 1911) p.8.

'The Irish Players', *Evening Standard and St. James's Gazette* (London, 6 Jun 1911) p.22.

'The Court: The Abbey Street Players', *Stage* (London, 8 Jun 1911) p.18.

J., P. [John Palmer], 'The Irish Players', *Saturday Review*, CXI (London, 10 Jun 1911) 705–7.

'The Court Theatre', *Academy* (London, 10 Jun 1911) 723–4.

'Court: The Irish Players', *Observer* (London, 11 Jun 1911) p.9.

'Dramatic Gossip', *Referee* (London, 11 Jun 1911) p.2.

'The Irish Players', *T.P.'s Weekly*, XVII (London, 16 Jun 1911) 744.

Inkster, Leonard, 'The Irish Players', *Saturday Review*, CXI (London, 17 Jun 1911) 746 [letter to the Editor].

M., H. W., 'Half-Truth and Truth', *Nation*, IX, no.12 (London, 17 Jun 1911) 430–1.

J., P. [John Palmer], 'The Acting of the Irish Players', *Saturday Review*, CXI (London, 24 Jun 1911) 770–1.

McNulty, Edward, 'The Irish Players', *Saturday Review*, CXI (London, 24 Jun 1911) 777 [letter to the Editor].

Fay, F. J., 'The Irish Players', *Saturday Review*, CXII (London, 1 Jul 1911) 17 [letter to the Editor].

Inkster, Leonard, 'The Irish Players', *Saturday Review*, CXII (London, 1 Jul 1911) 17 [letter to the Editor].

Ervine, St. John G., '*The Playboy of the Western World*', *Saturday Review*, CXII (London, 8 Jul 1911) 48–9 [letter to the Editor].

McNulty, Edward, 'Synge – The Ragman', *Saturday Review*, CXII (London, 8 Jul 1911) 49 [letter to the Editor].

'Drama', *Nation*, XCIII (N.Y., 12 Oct 1911) 346–7.

'Plymouth Theatre', *Boston Evening Record* (14 Oct 1911) p. 6.

'Attractions at the Theatre: "The Playboy of the Western World" at the Plymouth', *Boston Sunday Globe* (15 Oct 1911) p. 58.

'Irish Protest "Playboy" ', *Boston Evening Record* (16 Oct 1911) p. 5.

'Singe's [*sic*] Playboy Pleases', *Boston Evening Record* (17 Oct 1911) p. 5.

P., H. T., 'The Embattled "Playboy" ', *Boston Evening Transcript* (17 Oct 1911) p. 12.

Biggers, Earl Derr, 'The New Plays', *Boston Traveler* (17 Oct 1911) p. 6.

'Approves the Irish Play', *Boston Evening Transcript* (17 Oct 1911) p.3.

'Doesn't Need Expurgation. Boston Opinion of *The Playboy*', *Boston Globe* (17 Oct 1911) p.9.

Hale, Philip, 'Double Bill at the Plymouth: Scattered Hissing at "Playboy of the Western World" Resented by the Audience', *Boston Herald* (17 Oct 1911) p.12.

'*The Playboy of the Western World*', *Christian Science Monitor* (17 Oct 1911) p.4.

Crosby, E. H., 'New Plays Last Evening', *Boston Post* (17 Oct 1911) p.9.

'Irish Actors Give "Playboy" ', *Boston Journal* (17 Oct 1911) p.4.

'Irish Play Wins Censor', *Boston American* (17 Oct 1911) p.1.

Young, Nicholas, 'Finished Acting by Irish Players: "The Playboy of the Western World" at Plymouth Big Hit Despite Interruptions', *Boston American* (17 Oct 1911) p.14.

'The Irish Players: The Victory for "The Playboy" ', *Boston Evening Transcript* (18 Oct 1911) p.23.

'Ask "Playboy's" Withdrawal', *Boston Herald* (18 Oct 1911) p.2.

'Condemn Play by the Irish Players', *Boston Post* (18 Oct 1911) p.7.

'No Booing at Irish Players', *Boston Post* (18 Oct 1911) p.7.

'Drama: "National" Plays', *Nation*, XCIII (N.Y., 19 Oct 1911) 376–7.

The Playboy of the Western World

'Protests the Irish Players: Central Council Terms the "Playboy" Infamous', *Boston Post* (24 Oct 1911) p. 5.

'Condemns the Playboy', *Gaelic American* (N.Y., 28 Oct 1911) p. 2.

'A Representative Irish Visitor', *America*, VI, no. 3 (N.Y., 28 Oct 1911) 64.

'News of the Theatre: Providence and "The Playboy" ', *Boston Evening Transcript* (31 Oct 1911) p. 13.

'Boston Irishme Protest', *Gaelic American* (N.Y., 4 Nov 1911) p. 10.

'*The Playboy* in England', *Academy and Literature*, LXXXI (London, Nov 1911) 671–2 [by the Dramatic Company of Letchworth].

'New Plays That Open Next Week', *Globe and Commercial Advertiser* (N.Y., 25 Nov 1911) p. 5.

Conway, James P., '*The Playboy of the Western World*', *New York Sun* (25 Nov 1911) p. 8 [letter to the Editor].

'Acting of the Irish Players', *New York Times* (26 Nov 1911) p. 3.

'The Irish Players and Their Audiences', *New York Sun* (26 Nov 1911).

'Seumas MacManus Raps the *Playboy*', *New York Press* (27 Nov 1911).

'Col. Roosevelt To See Play', *Globe and Commercial Advertiser* (N.Y., 28 Nov 1911) p. 1.

'Riot in Theatre over an Irish Play', *New York Times* (28 Nov 1911) pp. 1, 3.

'But the Play Was Produced', *Evening Sun* (N.Y., 28 Nov 1911) p. 6 [editorial].

'Big Police Guard for Irish Play', *Evening Sun* (N.Y., 28 Nov 1911) pp. 1, 7.

' "The Playboy" in New York', *Boston Evening Transcript* (28 Nov 1911) p. 22.

'Irish Lawyers Ask Mayor to Stop Play Which Caused Riot', *Evening Telegram* (N.Y., 28 Nov 1911) p. 1.

W., A., 'Synge's *Playboy of the Western World* at Maxine Elliott's Theatre', *New York Tribune* (28 Nov 1911) p. 7.

'*Playboy* Mobbed', *New York Sun* (28 Nov 1911) pp. 1–2.

Sherwin, Louis, 'Dramatic Reviewers at Odds Over Synge's Work, *The Playboy of the Western World*', *Globe and Commercial Advertiser* (N.Y., 28 Nov 1911) p. 7.

'How Bad Is "The Play Boy of the Western World" ', *Evening Mail* (N.Y., 28 Nov 1911) p. 8.

'*The Playboy of the Western World*', *New York Gaelic-American* (28 Nov 1911).

' "Playboy" To Go on in Spite of Rioters', *Brooklyn Daily Eagle* (28 Nov 1911) p. 3.

'Stop Irish Play, Is Plea to Mayor', *Evening Mail* (N.Y., 28 Nov 1911) pp. 1–3.

'*The Playboy of the Western World*', *New York Evening Post* (28 Nov 1911) p. 9.

' "Playboy" Causes Riot: Irish Players in Drama That Caused Wild Riot in Theater Last Evening', *Brooklyn Daily Eagle* (28 Nov 1911) p. 6.

'Audience in Riot Hurls Potatoes at Irish Players', *New York Press* (28 Nov 1911) pp. 1–2.

'The *Playboy* Riots. Wild Scenes Described. Mayor Asked to Stop the Play', *Irish Independent* (Dublin, 29 Nov 1911) p. 6.

'The *Playboy* Row', *New York Times* (29 Nov 1911) p. 10 [editorial].

'*The Playboy* As a Play, Not As a Riot', *Evening Sun* (29 Nov 1911) p. 8.

'Mayor Decides Irish Play Is Quite Harmless', *Evening Telegram* (N.Y., 29 Nov 1911) p. 2.

Benjamin, M. W., 'The Irish Play', *New York Evening Post* (29 Nov 1911) [letter to the Editor].

'A Rousing Playboy Riot. Unparalleled Disorder at the Maxine Elliott Theatre', *New York Dramatic Mirror*, LXVI (29 Nov 1911) 7, 11.

'Throw Out 7 At "Playboy" ', *Sun* (N.Y., 29 Nov 1911) pp. 1–2.

'Pursuing "The Playboy" ', *Boston Evening Transcript* (29 Nov 1911) p. 22.

Mailly, William, 'Drama', *New York Call* (29 Nov 1911) p. 4.

Bunbury, C., '*The Playboy of the Western World*', *New York Times* (30 Nov 1911) [letter to the Editor].

'The Consputation of Synge', *Sun* (N.Y., 30 Nov 1911) p. 6 [correspondence].

'Drama', *Nation*, XCIII (N.Y., 30 Nov 1911) 528–9.

'The "Playboy" Uproar: Mayor Will Take No Action', *Irish Independent* (Dublin, 30 Nov 1911) p.6.

'The Irish Players in New York', *Outlook*, XCIX (N.Y., 2 Dec 1911) 801.

'Synge and *The Playboy*', *New York Evening Post* (2 Dec 1911).

'New York's Protest Against A Vile Play', *Gaelic American*, VIII (N.Y., 2 Dec 1911) 1, 8.

F., L. C., 'The Irish Players', *Daily People* (N.Y., 3 Dec 1911) p.2.

W., A., 'The Playgoer', *New York Tribune* (3 Dec 1911), pt 5, p.6.

'Maxine Elliott's – Irish Players: *The Playboy of the Western World*', *New York Dramatic Mirror*, LXVI (6 Dec 1911) 6.

DeFoe, Louis V., '*The Playboy*, Despite Its Foes, Gives Synge a Place in Ireland's Hall of Fame', *World* (N.Y., 8 Dec 1911) p.5.

'*The Playboy of the Western World*', *New York Gaelic-American* (9 Dec 1911) p.4.

'A Great Irish Play and Some Irishmen', *Outlook*, XCIX (N.Y., 9 Dec 1911) 843–4.

'*The Playboy of the Western World*', *Sun* (N.Y., 10 Dec 1911) p.2.

W., H. M., 'Theatrical Notes: The Irish Players in New York', *Pall Mall Gazette* (London, 11 Dec 1911) p.4.

Metcalfe, J. S., 'Drama', *Life*, LVIII, no.1520 (N.Y., 14 Dec 1911) 1090.

'The Troublous *Playboy*', *Literary Digest*, XLIII, no. 25 (N.Y., 16 Dec 1911) 1152–3.

'The Irish Players', *Outlook*, XCIX (N.Y., 16 Dec 1911) 915–19.

Eaton, Walter Prichard, 'Viewing Irish Players in the Light of Readon', *Sunday Record-Herald* (Chicago, 11 Dec 1911) pt 7, p. 3.

'*The Playboy of the Western World*', *New York Journal* (18 Dec 1911).

Parsons, Chauncey L., 'Lady Gregory: Guiding Genius of the Irish Players', *New York Dramatic Mirror* (27 Dec 1911) p. 5.

'Ireland', *America*, VI, no. 12 (N.Y., 30 Dec 1911) 267.

'The Stormy Debut of the Irish Players', *Current Literature*, LI (N.Y., Dec 1911) 675–6.

'Irish Play Halted by More Disorder. Eggs and Pie Hurled at Performers in *The Playboy* at Adelphi Last Night', *Evening Bulletin*, LXV, no. 239 (Philadelphia, 17 Jan 1912) p. 1.

'*The Playboy*: Irish Company Arrested in America', *Pall Mall Gazette* (London, 18 Jan 1912) p. 1.

'*The Playboy*: Another American Surprise; Players Arrested', *Evening Telegraph* (Dublin, 19 Jan 1912) p. 3.

'Notes of the Day: The Irish Players', *Pall Mall Gazette* (London, 19 Jan 1912) p. 7.

Ryan, Frederick, 'An Irish View. Why the Playboy Has Excited Hostility', *Daily News* (London, 19 Jan 1912) p. 1.

'Abbey Players Co. Arrested. Synge's *Playboy* the Cause', *Irish Independent* (Dublin, 19 Jan 1912) p. 5.

'*The Playboy*', *Evening Telegraph* (Dublin, 20 Jan 1912) p. 5.

'*Playboy* Fiasco. Extraordinary Proceedings in Court. Company Released', *Daily News* (London, 20 Jan 1912) p. 5.

'Irish Play Is Again Halted by "Riots"; Police Arrest 14', *North American* (Philadelphia, 20 Jan 1912) pp. 1, 6, 8.

'Irish Players in Fight for Freedom', *Public Ledger* (Philadelphia, 20 Jan 1912) p. 1.

'Lady Gregory Denies Harm in "The Playboy" ', *Chicago Examiner* (27 Jan 1912) p. 4.

'Irish Players Will Produce "Playboy" Despite Protest', *Chicago Sunday Examiner* (28 Jan 1912) pt 1, p. 9.

'*The Playboy of the Western World* and the Trouble It Made', *Sun* (N.Y., 28 Jan 1912) p. 7.

'Irish Delay Play Protest', *Chicago Daily Journal* (28 Jan 1912) p. 5.

'Mayor Will Prohibit Play: Lady Gregory Defends It', *Chicago Daily Journal* (30 Jan 1912) p. 3.

' "Playboy" May Not Play Here', *Chicago Daily Socialist* (30 Jan 1912) p. 1.

'*The Playboy of the Western World* and Why It Stirs the Irish Wrath', *Chicago Daily Journal* (31 Jan 1912) p. 3.

'Threaten Injunction to Foil Ban on Play', *Chicago Daily Journal* (31 Jan 1912) p. 3.

'*The Playboy of the Western World*', *New York Dramatic Mirror*, LXVII (31 Jan 1912) 20.

'Mayor Studies "Playboy" To Determine Its Morality', *Chicago Examiner* (31 Jan 1912) p. 3.

'Truce on Irish Play Until Mayor Reads It', *Chicago Record-Herald* (31 Jan 1912) p. 13.

'The Mayor and the "Play Boy" ', *Chicago Record-Herald* (31 Jan 1912) p. 14 [editorial].

'*The Playboy of the Western World*', *Theatre Magazine*, XV (N.Y., Jan 1912) ii, vii.

'*The Playboy of the Western World*', *American Playwright*, I (N.Y., Jan 1912) 24–5.

White, M., Jr., 'The Worth-While Irish Players', *Munsey's Magazine*, XLVI (N.Y., Jan 1912) 588–9.

'Irish Play Ban Void, City Lawyer Holds', *Chicago Record-Herald* (1 Feb 1912) p. 1.

'Nullifies Order to Stop "Playboy" ', *Chicago Daily Tribune* (1 Feb 1912) p. 19.

'Rules on *Playboy* Row', *Chicago Daily Journal* (1 Feb 1912) p. 3.

'*The Playboy*: Collapse of Case Against the Irish Actors', *Daily News* (London, 2 Feb 1912) p. 2.

Hackett, Francis, 'Says "Playboy" Foes Have Had Their Day', *Chicago Evening Post* (3 Feb 1912) p. 3.

'Mrs. Cudahy Disavows "Playboy" ', *Chicago Sunday Examiner* (4 Feb 1912) pt 1, pp. 1, 9.

' "Playboy" Is Merely Stupid', *Chicago Sunday Examiner* (4 Feb 1912) pt 1, p. 9.

'Mrs. John Cudahy Praised for Snubbing "The Playboy" ', *Chicago Examiner* (5 Feb 1912) p. 10.

'Says "Playboy" Libels Women: [Seamas] MacManus Assails the Drama', *Chicago Examiner* (6 Feb 1912) p. 4.

Hammond, Percy, 'First Performance in Chicago of *The Playboy of the Western World*; No Riots', *Chicago Daily Tribune* (7 Feb 1912) p. 13.

Hatton, Frederic, 'Bouquets, Not Bricks, Greet "The Playboy" ', *Chicago Evening Post* (7 Feb 1912) p. 5.

'Peace at Irish Play', *Chicago Record-Herald* (7 Feb 1912) p. 1.

Leslie, Amy, 'Synge with His Types; *Playboy*, a Bitter, Ugly Thrust of Humor', *Daily News* (Chicago, 7 Feb 1912) p. 14.

Hall, O. L., 'Act *Playboy* without Fight', *Chicago Daily Journal* (7 Feb 1912) p. 5.

' "Playboy of the Western World" Draws Throngs of Chicago Society Folk', *Chicago Examiner* (7 Feb 1912) p. 7.

' "Playboy" Again Given Without Disturbance', *Chicago Examiner* (8 Feb 1912) p. 7.

Bennett, James O'Donnell, 'The Theatre: "The Playboy of the Western World" ', *Chicago Record-Herald* (8 Feb 1912) p. 8.

Ruhl, Arthur A., 'A New Kind of Magic', *Collier's*, XLVIII (N.Y., 10 Feb 1912) 33–4.

'The Irish Players', *Everybody's Magazine*, XXVI (N.Y., Feb 1912) 231–40.

'*The Playboy of the Western World* by J. M. Synge', *Green Book Album*, VII (Chicago, Feb 1912) 288–9.

DeFoe, Louis V., 'Mindwinter in the Theatres', *Red Book Magazine*, XVIII (Chicago, Feb 1912) 753–62.

'The Matter with the *Playboy*', *Papyrus* (N.Y., Feb 1912) 18–21.

Ryan, J. E., 'A Playboy Post Mortem', *Chicago Citizen* (2 Mar 1912) p.3 [letter to the Editor].

'Editorial Notes', *Forum*, XLVI (N.Y., Mar 1912) 380–1.

'Loyalists Welcome the Playboys', *Gaelic American* (N.Y., 13 Apr 1912) p.4.

P., C., 'The Irish Players in Philadelphia', *New Drama*, no.1 (Boston, Apr 1912) 15–16.

'Irish Plays at the Court Theatre', *The Times* (London, 4 Jun 1912) p.7.

'Court Theatre: Irish Players', *Daily Telegraph* (London, 4 Jun 1912) p.9.

'Dublin Players in London: *The Playboy* at the Court Theatre', *Daily News* (London, 4 Jun 1912) p.2.

'*The Playboy*', *Daily Mail* (London, 4 Jun 1912) p.4.

L., S. R., 'Irish Players at the Court Theatre; A Worthy London Welcome to *The Playboy*', *Daily Chronicle* (London, 4 Jun 1912) p.7.

'*The Playboy* in London', *Daily Express* (London, 4 Jun 1912) p.5.

'Irish Players; Opening Performance at the Court Theatre', *Standard* (London, 4 Jun 1912) p.4.

S., E. F., 'The Irish National Theatre at the Court', *Westminster Gazette* (London, 4 Jun 1912) p.3.

W., H. M., 'The Irish Players: Last Night's Welcome at the Court Theatre', *Pall Mall Gazette* (London, 4 Jun 1912) p.5.

'The Irish Players', *Morning Post* (London, 4 Jun 1912) p.7.

'The Irish Plays and Players', *Evening News* (London, 4 Jun
1912) p. 4.

'The Court: Irish Plays', *Stage* (London, 6 Jun 1912) 18.

'The Irish Players', *Athenaeum* (London, 8 Jun 1912) 663–4.

Grein, J. T., 'The Irish Players', *Sunday Times* (London, 9 Jun
1912) p. 6.

'Court: The Irish Players', *Observer* (London, 9 Jun 1912) p. 7.

'The Irish Players at the Court', *Illustrated London News*, CXL
(22 Jun 1912) 958.

Palmer, John, 'The Success of the Irish Players', *Saturday
Review* (London, 13 Jul 1912) 42–3.

'Abbey Theatre', *Irish Times* (Dublin, 29 Aug 1912) p. 7.

'The Abbey Theatre: Mixed Reception of *The Playboy*',
Freeman's Journal (Dublin, 29 Aug 1912) p. 4.

'The Abbey Theatre', *Daily Express* (Dublin, 29 Aug 1912)
p. 6.

'The Abbey Theatre: Mixed Reception of *The Playboy*',
Evening Telegraph (Dublin, 29 Aug 1912) p. 4.

Hatton, Frederic, '*Playboy* Brings Many to Fine Arts Theater',
Chicago Evening Post (2 Jan 1913) p. 11.

'Playboy Critics Won Over', *Montreal Daily Herald* (28 Jan
1913) p. 5 [at His Majesty's].

Enfield, Edward, 'Failed to Realize That Play Is Comedy',
Montreal Daily Herald (28 Jan 1913) p. 4 [letter to the
Editor].

'Objects to Repertoire of the Irish Players', *Montreal Daily Herald* (28 Jan 1913) p.4 [letter to the Editor].

Holloway, Joseph, *'The Playboy* in Canada; A Fuss over Its Production. Views of the Critics', *Evening Herald* (Dublin, 12 Feb 1913) p.4.

'Irish Players at the Court', *Daily Graphic* (London, 2 Jun 1914) p.6.

'Court Theatre: The Irish Players', *Daily Telegraph* (London, 2 Jun 1914) p.11.

L., S. R., 'Irish Players; Abbey Theatre Company at the Court', *Daily Chronicle* (London, 2 Jun 1914) p.5.

'Irish Players at the Court', *Daily News and Leader* (London, 2 Jun 1914) p.2.

'Court Theatre', *Standard* (London, 2 Jun 1914) p.9.

'The Irish Theatre', *Pall Mall Gazette* (London, 2 Jun 1914) p.7.

'Court Theatre: The Irish Players' Season', *Morning Post* (London, 2 Jun 1914) p.9.

'The Playboy', *Evening Standard and St. James's Gazette* (London, 2 Jun 1914) p.13.

'The Court: The Irish Players', *Stage* (London, 4 Jun 1914) p.22.

'Dramatic Gossip', *Athenaeum* (London, 6 Jun 1914) p.804.

Grein, J.T., 'Royal Court: The Irish Players', *Sunday Times* (London, 7 Jun 1914) p.6.

'At the Play: Court', *Observer* (London, 7 Jun 1914) p.11.

'The Irish Players at the Court', *Illustrated London News*, CXLIV (13 Jun 1914) 1032.

Clark, B. H., '*The Playboy of the Western World* in Paris', *Colonnade*, XI (Jan 1916) 23—6.

'Act Synge's Comedy. Repertory Theatre Gives *Playboy of the Western World* at Bramhall', *New York Times* (17 Apr 1921) p. 23.

'Play That Caused Riots Revived by Irish in Peace', *World* (N.Y., 17 Apr 1921) p. 2.

Broun, Heywood, 'Even Without a Riot *Playboy* Proves Exciting', *New York Tribune* (18 Apr 1921) p. 6.

Towse, J. Ranken, '*The Playboy* Again', *New York Evening Post* (18 Apr 1921) p. 9.

'Synge's Irish Play at the Bramhall Well Received', *New York Clipper*, LXIX (20 Apr 1921) 23.

Firkins, O. W., 'Drama: Synge's *Playboy*', *Weekly Review*, IV (N.Y., 12 May 1921) 496—7.

Young, Stark, 'After the Play', *New Republic*, XXVII (N.Y., 22 Jun 1921) 117.

'*The Playboy* Revived; Mr. Synge's Best Comedy at the Court Theatre', *Daily Chronicle* (London, 26 Jul 1921) p. 7.

'Irish Players Return; Revival Last Night of *The Playboy of the Western World*', *Daily Mirror* (London, 26 Jul 1921) p. 3.

M., S. P. B., '*The Playboy* Returns', *Daily Express* (London, 26 Jul 1921) p. 4.

'*Playboy* Revival', *Daily Mail* (London, 26 Jul 1921) p. 8.

B., E. A., 'The Irish Players; Brilliant Performance at the Court Theatre', *Daily News* (London, 26 Jul 1921) p. 5.

R.-S., N. G., 'Irish Players: Their Season at the Court Theatre', *Westminster Gazette* (London, 26 Jul 1921) p. 6.

L., S. R., '*The Playboy*; Synge's Masterpiece at the Court', *Pall Mall Gazette* (London, 26 Jul 1921) p. 9.

'The Irish Players; Strong Fare at the Court', *Morning Post* (London, 26 Jul 1921) p. 8.

'The *Playboy* Again; Irish Players' Great Success at the Court', *Evening Standard* (London, 26 Jul 1921) p. 12.

'*The Playboy of the Western World*, Revival at the Court', *The Times* (London, 27 Jul 1921) p. 8.

'The Court: *The Playboy of the Western World*', *Stage* (London, 28 Jul 1921) 14.

'The Irish Players in *The Playboy of the Western World* at the Court Theatre', *Spectator* (London, 30 Jul 1921) 141.

Carroll, Sydney W., 'Court: *The Playboy of the Western World*', *Sunday Times* (London, 31 Jul 1921) p. 4.

G., H., 'Court: *The Playboy of the Western World* by J. M. Synge', *Observer* (London, 31 Jul 1921) p. 7.

MacGowan, Kenneth, 'Broadway Bows to By-Ways', *Theatre Arts Magazine*, V, no. 3 (N.Y., Jul 1921) 181.

'Bramhall: *The Playboy of the Western World*', *Theatre*, XXXIV (N.Y., Jul 1921) 14.

'*The Playboy of the Western World*', *Saturday Review*, CXXXII (London, 6 Aug 1921) 177–8.

MacCarthy, Desmond, 'The Irish Players', *New Statesman*, XVII (London, 6 Aug 1921) 494.

'*The Playboy of the Western World* at the Court', *Illustrated London News*, CLIX (13 Aug 1921) 230.

Turner, W. J., '*The Playboy of the Western World*. Court', *London Mercury*, IV, no. 23 (Sep 1921) 537–9.

McQ., L. J., 'How Synge Wrote *The Playboy*', *Bookman*, LX, no. 360 (Sep 1921) 267–8.

'Synge Revival at the Royalty: *The Playboy of the Western World*', *The Times* (London, 13 Oct 1925) p. 14.

Griffith, Hubert, '*The Playboy* Again; Royalty Theatre Revival As Good As Ever', *Daily Chronicle* (London, 13 Oct 1925) p. 11.

'Synge's *Playboy*; Poet's Classic Revived at Royalty Theatre by the Irish Players', *Daily Mirror* (London, 13 Oct 1925) p. 22.

B., E. A., 'Brilliant Acting; *The Playboy of the Western World*', *Daily News* (London, 13 Oct 1925) p. 8.

P., A., '*The Playboy*; Brilliant Irish Production at the Royalty', *Daily Sketch* (London, 13 Oct 1925) p. 2.

M., S. P. B., 'Magic of a Great Play; Perfect Acting in *The Playboy of the Western World*', *Daily Graphic* (London, 13 Oct 1925) p. 2.

B., E. W., 'The Royalty Theatre: Popular Revival of *The Playboy*', *Westminster Gazette* (London, 13 Oct 1925) p. 7.

'*The Playboy*; Synge's Comedy Revived by the Original Company', *Morning Post* (London, 13 Oct 1925) p. 14.

G., H., '*The Playboy* Revived Again', *Evening Standard* (London, 13 Oct 1925) p. 3.

'The Royalty: *The Playboy* Returns', *Stage* (London, 15 Oct 1925) 18.

Agate, James, 'Royalty: *The Playboy of the Western World*', *Sunday Times* (London, 18 Oct 1925) p. 6.

G., H., '*The Playboy of the Western World* by J. M. Synge', *Observer* (London, 18 Oct 1925) p. 11.

Shand, John, 'A Company of Good Actors', *New Statesman*, XXVI (London, 24 Oct 1925) 47.

Omicron, 'From Alpha to Omega', *Nation*, XXXVIII, no. 4 (London, 24 Oct 1925) 150.

S., W. N., '*The Playboy* Again', *Theatre World*, II, no. 10 (London, Nov 1925) 61.

Atkinson, Brooks, 'The Play: Playboying the Western World', *New York Times* (3 Jan 1930) p. 20 [by the Irish Players at the Irish Theatre in the Village].

Watts, Richard, Jr., '*The Playboy of the Western World*', *New York Herald Tribune* (3 Jan 1930) p. 14.

Watts, Richard, Jr., 'Burgess Meredith Triumphs in Brilliant Irish Comedy', *New York Herald Tribune* (4 Jan 1930) p. 28.

'Revival', *Time*, XV (13 Jan 1930) 18.

'Criterion Theatre: *The Playboy of the Western World* by J. M. Synge', *The Times* (London, 29 Oct 1930) p. 12.

D[arlington], W. A., 'Famous Irish Play Revived: *The Playboy of the Western World*; Fine Acting at the Criterion', *Daily Telegraph* (London, 29 Oct 1930) p. 6.

'Old Play's Return; *The Playboy of the Western World* in London Again', *Daily Mirror* (London, 29 Oct 1930) p. 3.

C., J., '*The Playboy*; When the Wit of Western World Begins to See Its Humour', *Daily Sketch* (London, 29 Oct 1930) p. 3.

'Synge's *Playboy* Revived', *News Chronicle* (London, 29 Oct 1930) p. 9.

'*The Playboy* Revived', *Morning Post* (London, 29 Oct 1930) p. 12.

'*The Playboy* Revived', *Evening Standard* (London, 29 Oct 1930) p. 17.

'The Criterion: *The Playboy of the Western World*', *Stage* (London, 30 Oct 1930) 14.

H., H., 'Criterion: *The Playboy of the Western World* by J. M. Synge', *Observer* (London, 2 Nov 1930) p. 15.

'*The Playboy of the Western World* at the Criterion', *Illustrated London News*, CLXXVII (8 Nov 1930) 848.

Gore-Browne, Robert, 'Plays Sacred and Profane. *The Playboy of the Western World* by J. M. Synge. Criterion Theatre', *Saturday Review*, CL (London, 8 Nov 1930) 592.

Shipp, Horace, 'Plays with Ideas', *English Review*, LI (London, Dec 1930) 782–5.

Atkinson, Brooks, 'The Play: Synge and Lady Gregory in the Abbey Theatre Bill', *New York Times* (21 Oct 1932) p. 25 [by the Irish Players at the Martin Beck Theatre].

Watts, Richard, Jr., '*The Playboy of the Western World*. Poetical Farce by Synge Given at the Martin Beck', *New York Herald Tribune* (21 Oct 1932) p. 12.

R., G., 'Synge's Irish Play Staged to Perfection', *New York World-Telegram* (21 Oct 1932).

Watts, Richard, Jr., 'Irish Players Offer Synge Drama on Double Bill', *New York Herald Tribune* (5 Nov 1932) p. 16.

Hanighen, Frank C., 'The Irish Players Present — ', *Commonweal*, XVII (N.Y., 28 Dec 1932) 237–8.

Williams, Herschel, 'Mid-Channel. Broadway in Review: *The Playboy of the Western World*', *Theatre Arts Monthly*, XVII, no. 1 (N.Y., Jan 1933) 12–14.

Atkinson, Brooks, 'The Play: Abbey Theatre Troupe Turns to *The Playboy of the Western World*', *New York Times* (22 Nov 1937) p. 14 [at the Ambassador Theatre].

Drake, Herbert, '*The Playboy of the Western World*. J. M. Synge's Play Presented by the Abbey Players', *New York Herald Tribune* (22 Nov 1937) p. 12.

'Abbey Troupe Again Offers *Playboy*', *New York Journal and American* (22 Nov 1937) p. 10.

R., G., '*Playboy* Appears Once More on Broadway', *New York World-Telegram* (22 Nov 1937) p. 20.

Bolton, Whitney, 'Abbey Players Score In Ambassador Comedy', *Morning Telegraph* (N.Y., 23 Nov 1937) p. 3.

'Mercury Theatre: *The Playboy of the Western World* by J. M. Synge', *The Times* (London, 28 Jan 1939) p. 10.

Darlington, W. A., '*The Playboy* at the Mercury; Strong Irish Cast', *Daily Telegraph and Morning Post* (London, 28 Jan 1939) p. 10.

Hale, Lionel, 'Young Actor's Skill in Synge Revival; *The Playboy of the Western World* by J. M. Synge. Mercury Theatre', *News Chronicle* (London, 28 Jan 1939) p. 11.

'*The Playboy* Again', *Evening News* (London, 28 Jan 1939)
    p. 5.

'*The Playboy of the Western World* by J. M. Synge (Mercury)',
    John O'London's Weekly, XL (3 Feb 1939) 703.

'*The Playboy of the Western World* at the Mercury', *New
    Statesman and Nation*, XVII, no. 415 (London, 4 Feb 1939)
    169.

H., H., 'Mercury: *The Playboy of the Western World* by John
    Millington Synge', *Observer* (London, 5 Feb 1939) p. 13.

Cookman, A. V., 'The Theatre: *The Playboy of the Western
    World* by J. M. Synge. Mercury', *London Mercury*, XXXIX,
    no. 233 (Mar 1939) 530–1.

'Mercury Theatre: *The Playboy of the Western World* by J. M.
    Synge', *The Times* (London, 2 Oct 1939) p. 6.

'*The Playboy* at Notting Hill', *Daily Sketch* (London, 2 Oct
    1939) p. 12.

'The Mercury: *The Playboy of the Western World*', *Stage*
    (London, 5 Oct 1939) 8.

Brown, Ivor, 'Duchess: *The Playboy of the Western World* by
    J. M. Synge', *Observer* (London, 29 Oct 1939) p. 11.

'*The Playboy of the Western World* at the Duchess', *New
    Statesman and Nation*, XVIII, no. 454 (London, 4 Nov 1939)
    644.

'*The Playboy of the Western World*', *Life*, XXI (5 Aug 1946)
    82–3 [at Summer Theatre, Dennis, Mass.].

Atkinson, Brooks, '*The Playboy of the Western World*', *New
    York Times* (28 Oct 1946) p. 18 [by Theatre Incorporated
    at the Booth Theatre].

Barnes, Howard, 'The Playboy of the Western World', *New York Herald Tribune* (28 Oct 1946) p. 12.

Watts, Richard, Jr., 'The Playboy of the Western World', *New York Post* (28 Oct 1946).

Hawkins, William, 'Meredith Stars in *Playboy*', *New York World-Telegram* (28 Oct 1946) p. 12.

Garland, Robert, 'The Playboy of the Western World', *New York Journal-American* (28 Oct 1946) p. 8.

Kronenberger, Louis, 'Synge's Fine Folk Satire', *PM* (N.Y., 28 Oct 1946) p. 18.

Morehouse, Ward, 'The Playboy of the Western World', *Sun* (N.Y., 28 Oct 1946) p. 14.

Chapman, John, 'Good Writing, Well-Spoken, Makes New *Playboy* Revival an Event', *Daily News* (N.Y., 28 Oct 1946) p. 35.

Gibbs, Wolcott, 'The Theatre: Gaels and Gagmen', *New Yorker*, XXII (2 Nov 1946) 57.

'The Aldrich Playboy', *Newsweek*, XXVIII (N.Y., 4 Nov 1946) 85.

'The Theater: Old Play in Manhattan', *Time*, XLVIII (4 Nov 1946) 38.

Phelan, Kappo, 'The Playboy of the Western World', *Commonweal*, XLV (N.Y., 8 Nov 1946) 95.

Krutch, Joseph Wood, 'Drama', *Nation*, CLXIII (N.Y., 9 Nov 1946) 536.

Young, Stark, 'Synge and Webb', *New Republic*, CXV (N.Y., 11 Nov 1946) 628.

Colum, Padraic, 'Praise for *Playboy*', *New York Times* (24 Nov 1946) section 2, p. 1 [letter to the Drama Editor].

'*The Playboy of the Western World*', *Catholic World*, CLXIV (N.Y., Dec 1946) 262–3.

'*The Playboy of the Western World*', *Harper's Bazaar*, LXXX (N.Y., Dec 1946) 220.

'*The Playboy of the Western World*', *New York Theatre Critics' Reviews* (1946) p. 287.

Gilder, Rosamond, 'Broadway in Review: *The Playboy of the Western World*', *Theatre Arts*, XXXI, no. 1 (N.Y., Jan 1947) 21–2.

'Mercury Theatre: *The Playboy of the Western World* by J. M. Synge', *The Times* (London, 12 Mar 1948) p. 7.

G., R. P. M., '*The Playboy* Revived', *Daily Telegraph and Morning Post* (London, 12 Mar 1948) p. 5.

F., E., 'The Playboy Again; *The Playboy of the Western World*: Mercury Theatre', *News Chronicle* (London, 12 Mar 1948) p. 3.

'The Mercury: *Playboy of the Western World*', *Stage* (London, 18 Mar 1948) p. 4.

Trewin, J. C., 'At the Theatre', *Observer* (London, 21 Mar 1948) p. 2.

Trewin, J. C., 'Lovers' Meeting', *Illustrated London News*, CCXII (3 Apr 1948) 386.

M., H. G., '*Playboy of the Western World*', *Theatre World*, XLIV (London, Apr 1948) 10.

'*The Playboy of the Western World* at the Mercury Theatre', *Theatre World*, XLIV (London, May 1948) 27–8.

'The Paris Festival: Thirty Plays in Six Weeks', *The Times* (London, 7 Jul 1954) p.12.

Cusack, Cyril, '*The Playboy of the Western World*', *The Times* (London, 20 Jul 1954) p.9 [letter to the Editor].

'Irish Play in East Berlin', *The Times* (London, 21 Aug 1956) p.4 [at the Schiffbauerdamm Theatre].

'The Theatre Workshop: *The Playboy of the Western World* by J. M. Synge', *The Times* (London, 17 Jan 1957) p.3.

Darlington, W. A., '*The Playboy* Lacks Poetry; Uninspired Revival', *Daily Telegraph and Morning Post* (London, 17 Jan 1957) p.8.

Barber, John, 'The Playboy Talks Like Romeo', *Daily Express* (London, 17 Jan 1957) p.5.

Dent, Alan, 'Peter Pan Playboy Is 50 Years Old', *News Chronicle* (London, 17 Jan 1957) p.3.

Hobson, Harold, 'Irish Drama', *Sunday Times* (London, 20 Jan 1957) p.13.

'Impressive Synge Revival', *Stage* (London, 24 Jan 1957) p.9.

Watt, David, 'Irish Brose: *The Playboy of the Western World* by J. M. Synge (Theatre Royal, Stratford, East)', *Spectator* (London, 25 Jan 1957) p.114.

Worsley, T. C., 'Minority Culture', *New Statesman and Nation*, LIII (London, 26 Jan 1957) 97–8.

Trewin, J. C., 'Round the Parish', *Illustrated London News*, CCXXX (26 Jan 1957) 150.

M., H. G., 'Theatre Royal, Stratford E.: *The Playboy of the Western World*', *Theatre World*, LIII, no.385 (London, Feb 1957) 10.

Morgan, Jane, '*Playboy of the Western World*', *Plays and Players*, IV, no. 6 (London, Mar 1957) 17, 20.

Fallon, Gabriel, 'Dublin's Theatre Festival', *Threshold*, I, no. 3 (Belfast, Autumn 1957) 75–81.

Atkinson, Brooks, '*Playboy* Opens. Synge Satire Revived at 7 Arts Center', *New York Times* (9 May 1958) p. 19.

Kerr, Walter, 'Off Broadway: *The Playboy*, Synge Play, Revived at Tara Theater', *New York Herald Tribune* (9 May 1958) p. 12.

Coleman, Robert, '*Playboy* Delightful Comedy', *New York Mirror* (9 May 1958) pp. 30–1.

McHarry, Charles, 'Irish Players Give *Playboy*', *Daily News* (N.Y., 9 May 1958) p. 58.

Bolton, Whitney, 'A Robust Production of *Playboy*', *Morning Telegraph* (N.Y., 10 May 1958) p. 3.

Hayes, Richard, 'The Road to the Isles', *Commonweal*, LXVIII (N.Y., 20 Jun 1958) 303–4.

'*The Playboy of the Western World*', *Catholic World*, CLXXXVII (N.Y., Jul 1958) 312–3.

K., '*The Heart's a Wonder* at Gaiety Theatre', *Irish Times* (Dublin, 5 Aug 1958) p. 4.

'Irish Classic as a Musical', *The Times* (London, 7 Aug 1958) p. 4.

'Synge Set to Music in *The Heart's a Wonder*', *Stage* (London, 7 Aug 1958) 9.

'Irish Comedy Lost in Song: *The Heart's a Wonder*', *The Times* (London, 19 Sep 1958) p. 6 [at the Westminster].

Darlington, W. A., '*Playboy* as a Musical of Charm; Irish Airs Used', *Daily Telegraph and Morning Post* (London, 19 Sep 1958) p. 12.

D., P., 'This Is Rather Irish', *Daily Mirror* (London, 19 Sep 1958) p. 16.

Wilson, Cecil, 'As Oirish a Night as Onny Man Could Wish', *Daily Mail* (London, 19 Sep 1958) p. 11.

'*The Playboy* Is Set to Music', *Daily Worker* (London, 19 Sep 1958) p. 3.

'Synge Musical Opens: London Sees New Version of His Drama *Playboy*', *New York Times* (19 Sep 1958) p. 23.

Dent, Alan, 'Synge a Song of Auld Oireland', *News Chronicle* (London, 19 Sep 1958) p. 3.

Shulman, Milton, 'It's a Rare Old Night for the Oirish', *Evening Standard* (London, 19 Sep 1958) p. 15.

Barker, Felix, 'Not Such a Darlin' Irish Experiment', *Evening News* (London, 19 Sep 1958) p. 4.

Hobson, Harold, 'Theatre', *Sunday Times* (London, 21 Sep 1958) p. 11.

Tynan, Kenneth, 'At the Theatre', *Observer* (London, 21 Sep 1958) p. 17.

'They Have Lost the Only Playboy: *The Heart's a Wonder*', *Stage* (London, 25 Sep 1958) p. 9.

Robinson, Robert, 'The Arts and Entertainment', *New Statesman*, LVI (London, 27 Sep 1958) 408.

Brien, Alan, 'Words without Music: *The Heart's a Wonder* (Westminster)', *Spectator* (London, 3 Oct 1958) pp. 435–6.

Trewin, J. C., 'Words and Music', *Illustrated London News*, CCXXXIII (4 Oct 1958) 578.

M., H. G., 'Westminster: *The Heart's a Wonder*', *Theatre World*, LIV, no. 405 (London, Oct 1958) 11.

'Dramatic Structure Undermined. *The Playboy of the Western World*', *The Times* (London, 27 Nov 1958) p. 6 [by Cliff Owen for Granada].

G., R. P. M., 'Television: Natural Style in *Playboy*; Lifelike Acting', *Daily Telegraph and Morning Post* (London, 27 Nov 1958) p. 12.

Smith, Andrew, 'On TV Last Night', *Daily Herald* (London, 27 Nov 1958) p. 3.

Sear, Richard, 'A Magnificent Playboy', *Daily Mirror* (London, 27 Nov 1958) p. 16.

Black, Peter, 'Teleview', *Daily Mail* (London, 27 Nov 1958) p. 12.

Purser, Philip, 'Yet Another Brave Try Fails', *News Chronicle* (London, 27 Nov 1958) p. 3.

Wiggin, Maurice, 'Television: Hogwash and Poteen', *Sunday Times* (London, 30 Nov 1958) p. 16.

Richardson, Maurice, 'Television and Radio: Inaudible Irish Oedipus', *Observer* (London, 30 Nov 1958) p. 16.

Deadman, Derek, '*The Heart's a Wonder*', *Plays and Players*, VI, no. 2 (London, Nov 1958) 15.

C., M., '*The Playboy of the Western World* (Granada Television)', *Stage* (London, 4 Dec 1958) p. 7.

Holt, Edgar, 'Plays of the Week', *Radio Times*, CXLIII (London, 15 May 1959) 7.

'Reality and Joy: Radio Production of *The Playboy*', *The Times* (London, 19 May 1959) p.3.

Rodger, Ian, 'Drama', *Listener*, LXI (London, 28 May 1959) 959.

'Dublin's Theatre Festival Opened', *Irish Times* (Dublin, 13 Sep 1960) p.7.

N., '*Playboy of the Western World* at the Gaiety', *Irish Times* (Dublin, 13 Sep 1960) p.5.

'Pegeen Mike's Play', *The Times* (London, 16 Sep 1960) p.16.

'New Plays Dominate Dublin Festival', *Stage and Television Today* (London, 22 Sep 1960) p.14.

'Siobhan McKenna Returns in *The Playboy*', *Stage and Television Today* (London, 6 Oct 1960) p.1.

'Strong Acting in *The Playboy*. Synge's Masterpiece in London', *The Times* (London, 13 Oct 1960) p.18 [at the Piccadilly].

Darlington, W. A., 'Reminder of Irish Poetry; Perfect Blend in *Playboy*', *Daily Telegraph and Morning Post* (London, 13 Oct 1960) p.16.

'The Irish Roar Like a Gale', *Daily Herald* (London, 13 Oct 1960) p.3.

Levin, Bernard, 'What Gabble, Bedad! Siobhan McKenna Is Just Superb', *Daily Express* (London, 13 Oct 1960) p.16.

Richards, Dick, 'First Night. Rich!', *Daily Mirror* (London, 13 Oct 1960) p.26.

'Synge's *Playboy* Opens in London', *Daily Worker* (London, 13 Oct 1960) p.3.

Dent, Alan, 'Radiant, Ecstatic Siobhan', *News Chronicle* (London, 13 Oct 1960) p. 5.

Shulman, Milton, 'An Enchanting Experience – Even If the Irish Does Floor You', *Evening Standard* (London, 13 Oct 1960) p. 19.

Barker, Felix, 'At the Theatre', *Evening News* (London, 13 Oct 1960) p. 7.

Hobson, Harold, '*The Playboy of the Western World*. Piccadilly', *Sunday Times* (London, 16 Oct 1960) p. 35.

Tynan, Kenneth, 'Farce with Tears', *Observer* (London, 16 Oct 1960) p. 26.

Johns, Eric, 'The Universal Appeal of *The Playboy*', *Stage and Television Today* (London, 20 Oct 1960) p. 6.

Gascoigne, Bamber, 'Between Two Schools: *The Playboy of the Western World* (Piccadilly)', *Spectator* (London, 21 Oct 1960) p. 601.

Brooks, Jeremy, 'Theatre in Decline?', *New Statesman*, LX (London, 22 Oct 1960) 602.

Trewin, J. C., 'Irish and Russian', *Illustrated London News*, CCXXXVII (29 Oct 1960) 768.

Trilling, Ossin, 'Report from Dublin; Irish Drama Dominates the 1960 Theatre Festival', *Theatre World*, LVI, no. 430 (London, Nov 1960) 33.

S., F., 'Piccadilly: *The Playboy of the Western World*', *Theatre World*, LVI, no. 430 (London, Nov 1960) 16, 49.

Roberts, Peter, '*The Playboy of the Western World*', *Plays and Players*, VIII, no. 3 (London, Dec 1960) 11.

'Irish Actors to Tour Europe', *The Times* (London, 5 Sep 1961) p. 15.

Gill, Brendan, 'The Theatre: Growing Old', *New Yorker*, XLVI (16 Jan 1971) 75 [by the Repertory Theatre of Lincoln Center].

Kalem, T. E., 'Synge's Wake', *Time*, XCVII (18 Jan 1971) 37.

Kroll, Jack, 'The Old Glory', *Newsweek*, LXXVII (18 Jan 1971) 79.

Hewes, Henry, 'Singed Hero', *Saturday Review*, LIV (N.Y., 23 Jan 1971) 75–6.

Clurman, Harold, 'Theatre', *Nation*, CCXII, no. 4 (N.Y., 25 Jan 1971) 124–5.

Kauffmann, Stanley, '*The Playboy of the Western World*', *New Republic*, CLXIV (Washington, 30 Jan 1971) 24, 35.

The Tinker's Wedding:

'The Afternoon Theatre: *The Tinker's Wedding*', *The Times* (London, 12 Nov 1909) p. 13.

'Afternoon Theatre: *The Tinker's Wedding*', *Daily Telegraph* (London, 12 Nov 1909) p. 8.

'The Afternoon Theatre: Mr. Synge's Play', *Daily Chronicle* (London, 12 Nov 1909) p. 5.

Baughan, E. A., 'Holbrooke's Lyric Drama', *Daily News* (London, 12 Nov 1909) p. 5.

'*The Tinker's Wedding*', *Daily Mail* (London, 12 Nov 1909) p. 8.

'Comedy and Opera', *Daily Graphic* (London, 12 Nov 1909) p. 2.

S., E. F., 'The Tinker's Wedding at the Afternoon Theatre',
Westminster Gazette (London, 12 Nov 1909) p. 3.

'Irish Comedy and English Opera', *Pall Mall Gazette* (London,
12 Nov 1909) p. 6.

'His Majesty's: The Afternoon Theatre; *The Tinker's Wedding*',
Morning Post (London, 12 Nov 1909) p. 8.

'The Afternoon Theatre's Second Season: *The Tinker's
Wedding*', *Evening News* (London, 12 Nov 1909) p. 4.

'Afternoon Theatre: *The Tinker's Wedding*', *Observer*
(London, 14 Nov 1909) p. 8.

'The Afternoon Theatre', *Stage* (London, 18 Nov 1909) p. 11.

'*The Tinker's Wedding* at the Afternoon Theatre', *Illustrated
London News*, CXXXV (20 Nov 1909) 720.

'Afternoon Theatre (His Majesty's). *The Tinker's Wedding*',
Athenaeum (London, 20 Nov 1909) pp. 631–2.

M., K., '*The Tinker's Wedding*', *Boston Evening Transcript*
(18 Oct 1911) p. 23.

Kenny, M., 'The Plays of the "Irish" Players', *America*, VI,
no. 4 (N.Y., 4 Nov 1911) 78–9.

Atkinson, Brooks, 'The Theatre: Three Plays by Synge', *New
York Times*, 7 Mar 1957) p. 24 [by the Irish Players at
Theater East].

Kerr, Walter, 'Three Plays by John Synge Given at the Theater
East', *New York Herald Tribune* (7 Mar 1957) p. 16.

Atkinson, Brooks, 'Three Plays by Synge', *New York Times*
(17 Mar 1957) section 2, p. 1.

"Off-Broadway Shows: Three Plays by Synge', *Variety* (N.Y., 20 Mar 1957) p. 72.

Wyatt, Euphemia Van Rensselaer, 'Three Plays', *Catholic World*, CLXXXV (N.Y., May 1957) 148.

'Mr. Behan Back in Ribald Mood', *The Times* (London, 30 Jul 1963) p. 13 [by the New Pike Company at the Theatre Royal, Stratford, E.].

Kenyon, Michael, 'Festival of Irish Comedy at the Theatre Royal, Stratford, E.', *Guardian* (London, 30 Jul 1963) p. 7.

Darlington, W. A., 'Irish Plays Fail to Inspire', *Daily Telegraph and Morning Post* (London, 30 Jul 1963) p. 12.

Shulman, Milton, 'A Drop of Irish, but the Flavour Is Weak', *Evening Standard* (London, 30 Jul 1963) p. 4.

Barker, Felix, 'A Drop of the Irish', *Evening News and Star* (London, 30 Jul 1963) p. 3.

D., P., 'Behan's Broadside; Festival of Irish Comedy (Theatre Royal, Stratford, E.)', *Daily Worker* (London, 31 Jul 1963) p. 2.

Marriott, R. B., 'At Stratford East: Irish Comedy with Synge and Behan', *Stage and Television Today* (London, 1 Aug 1963) p. 7.

Hobson, Harold, 'Theatre', *Sunday Times* (London, 4 Aug 1963) p. 25.

Tynan, Kenneth, 'Dubliners in the East End', *Observer* (London, 4 Aug 1963) p. 17.

Gellert, Roger, 'O'Booze', *New Statesman*, LXVI (London, 9 Aug 1963) 178–9.

Trewin, J. C., 'Period Pieces', *Illustrated London News*, CCXLIII (10 Aug 1963) 216.

'Theatre Festival Without a Policy', *The Times* (London, 9 Oct 1963) p. 16 [at the Pike Theatre in Dublin].

Deirdre of the Sorrows:

'Deirdre of the Sorrows', *Irish Times* (Dublin, 14 Jan 1910) p. 10.

'A Saddening Play: *Deirdre of the Sorrows*', *Irish Independent* (Dublin, 14 Jan 1910) p. 7.

'The Abbey Theatre: Production of Mr. J. M. Synge's Post-humous Work', *Freeman's Journal* (Dublin, 14 Jan 1910) p. 5.

'The Abbey Theatre: Production of Mr. Synge's Last Play', *Daily Express* (Dublin, 14 Jan 1910) p. 5.

'Deirdre', *Sinn Féin* (Dublin, 14 Jan 1910) pp. 1, 3.

'The Abbey Theatre: Production of Mr. J. M. Synge's Post-humous Work', *Evening Telegraph* (Dublin, 14 Jan 1910) p. 2.

'Synge's *Deirdre* at the Abbey', *Irish Nation* (Dublin, 15 Jan 1910) p. 5.

D., H. S., '*Deirdre of the Sorrows*. Mr. Synge's Last Play', *Dublin Evening Mail* (15 Jan 1910) p. 5.

'Provincial Production', *Stage* (London, 20 Jan 1910) p. 23.

Firin, 'Synge's *Deirdre* at the Abbey', *Irish Nation* (Dublin, 22 Jan 1910) p. 1.

'Dramatic Gossip', *Athenaeum* (London, 22 Jan 1910) p. 108.

'Deirdre', *Sinn Féin* (Dublin, 22 Jan 1910) p. 1.

'Gaiety Theatre: *Deirdre of the Sorrows*', *Manchester Courier* (21 Apr 1910) p. 12.

'Irish Players at the Gaiety Theatre', *Manchester Evening News* (21 Apr 1910) p. 6.

'*Deirdre of the Sorrows*: First Manchester Performance of J. M. Synge's Last Play', *Daily Dispatch* (Manchester, 21 Apr 1910) p. 3.

M., C. E., 'Gaiety Theatre', *Manchester Guardian*, London ed. (21 Apr 1910) p. 6.

'Abbey Theatre', *Irish Times* (Dublin, 29 Apr 1910) p. 5.

'The Abbey Theatre: Mr. Synge's *Deirdre*', *Freeman's Journal* (Dublin, 29 Apr 1910) p. 9.

'The Abbey Theatre: Revival of *Deirdre*', *Daily Express* (Dublin, 29 Apr 1910) p. 6.

'The Abbey Theatre: Mr. Synge's *Deirdre*', *Evening Telegraph* (Dublin, 29 Apr 1910) p. 2.

'Royal Court Theatre', *The Times* (London, 31 May 1910) p. 12.

'*Deirdre of the Sorrows*', *Morning Leader* (London, 31 May 1910) p. 1.

'Irish Players; Delightful Performance of Miss Maire O'Neill', *Daily Mail* (London, 31 May 1910) p. 8.

C., G., 'Court Theatre', *Star* (London, 31 May 1910) p. 2.

'Irish Drama in London; Mr. Synge's *Deirdre* Produced at the Court', *Daily News* (London, 31 May 1910) p. 6.

'Court Theatre', *Daily Telegraph* (London, 31 May 1910) p. 12.

'Irish Players; The Late J. M. Synge's Last Play at the Court', *Daily Chronicle* (London, 31 May 1910) p. 1.

'Irish National Theatre', *Standard* (London, 31 May 1910) p. 8.

'Court Theatre: *Deirdre of the Sorrows*', *Globe* (London, 31 May 1910) p. 10.

S., E. F., 'The Irish National Theatre Society', *Westminster Gazette* (London, 31 May 1910) p. 4.

'Court Theatre: Irish National Theatre Society', *Morning Post* (London, 31 May 1910) p. 10.

'The Irish Players: The Class of Drama in Which the Green Isle Excels', *Evening News* (London, 1 Jun 1910) p. 2.

'The Irish Players at the Court', *Pall Mall Gazette* (London, 1 Jun 1910) p. 5.

'The Court: *Deirdre of the Sorrows*', *Stage* (London, 2 Jun 1910) p. 16.

'*Deirdre of the Sorrows* at the Court', *Illustrated London News*, CXXXVI (4 Jun 1910) 854.

Stair, Owen, 'The Theatre: Irish Plays at the Court Theatre', *Outlook* (London, 4 Jun 1910) p. 819.

Dunsany, Lord, '*Deirdre of the Sorrows*', *Saturday Review*, CIX (London, 4 Jun 1910) 719–20.

'Irish National Theatre: *Deirdre of the Sorrows*', *Era* (London, 4 Jun 1910) p. 13.

Archer, William, 'The Art of the Artless', *Nation*, VII, no. 10 (London, 4 Jun 1910) 346–7.

'Things Theatrical', *Sporting Times* (London, 4 Jun 1910) p. 4.

'Irish Drama', *Athenaeum* (London, 4 Jun 1910) p. 684.

'Irish Plays', *Lloyd's Weekly News* (London, 5 Jun 1910) p. 9.

Grein, J. T., 'Court: Irish National Players. *Deirdre of the Sorrows*', *Sunday Times* (London, 5 Jun 1910) p. 6.

'Court: The Irish Players', *People* (London, 5 Jun 1910) p. 4.

'Court: Irish Plays and Players', *Observer* (London, 5 Jun 1910) p. 8.

Mordred, 'The Irish National Theatre', *Referee* (London, 5 Jun 1910) p. 2.

'Amusement Notes', *Financial News* (London, 6 Jun 1910) p. 8.

Clifton, Arthur, 'Court Theatre', *Court Journal* (London, 8 Jun 1910) p. 749.

H., P. P., 'At the Theatre', *Justice* (London, 11 Jun 1910) p. 8.

H., P. P., 'Irish Plays', *Literary Post* (London, 15 Jun 1910) pp. 202–3.

Dukes, Ashley, 'The Irish Plays', *New Age*, VII, no. 7 (London, 16 Jun 1910) 160–1.

'Our Captious Critic: *Deirdre of the Sorrows* at the Court Theatre', *Illustrated Sporting and Dramatic News* (London, 18 Jun 1910) p. 662.

'Opera House: Abbey Theatre Company in "Deirdre" and "The Playboy of the Western World"', *Cork Constitution* (30 Aug 1910) p. 6.

'Opera House', *Cork Weekly News* (3 Sep 1910) p. 6.

'A Synge Tragedy, Indeed', *New York Times* (26 Sep 1920) section 6, p. 1 [by the Celtic Players at the Bramhall Playhouse].

'New Synge Play Badly Put on by Celtic Players', *New York Clipper*, LXVIII (29 Sep 1920) 19.

Firkins, O. W., 'Drama: Synge at the Bramhall Playhouse', *Weekly Review*, III (N.Y., 6 Oct 1920) 297–8.

Atkinson, Brooks, 'Synge Premiere: *Deirdre of the Sorrows*', *New York Times* (15 Dec 1949) p. 51 [by the Abbe Practical Workshop at New York's Roerich Museum].

Garland, Robert, '*Deirdre of the Sorrows*', *New York Journal-American* (15 Dec 1949) p. 24.

Watts, Richard, Jr., '*Deirdre of the Sorrows*', *New York Post* (15 Dec 1949).

Gassner, John, 'The Theatre Arts', *Forum*, CXIII (Philadelphia, Jan 1950) 27.

'Cambridge Amateur Dramatic Club: *Deirdre of the Sorrows*', *The Times* (London, 17 Oct 1956) p. 3.

Gelb, Arthur, 'Theatre: *Deirdre of the Sorrows*. Synge's Irish Classic Is Acted at Gate', *New York Times* (15 Oct 1959) p. 46.

Malcolm, Donald, 'Off Broadway: Near Myth', *New Yorker*, XXXV (24 Oct 1959) 91–2 [at the Gate].

'*Deirdre of the Sorrows*', *America*, CII (N.Y., 14 Nov 1959) 217.

(d) UNPUBLISHED MATERIAL

Abbey Theatre, Dublin, 'Programmes, 1902–1913', National Library of Ireland, Dublin.

Abood, Edward F., 'The Reception of the Abbey Theater in America, 1911–14', Ph.D. dissertation, University of Chicago, 1963.

Allt, G. D. P., 'The Anglo-Irish Literary Movement in Relation to Its Antecedents', Ph.D. dissertation, Cambridge University, 1952.

Auberg, Arild, 'The Quest for Literary Synthesis in the Works of John Millington Synge', Ph.D. dissertation, University of Oslo, 1972.

Aufhauser, Annemarie, 'Sind Die Dramen Von John Millington Synge Durch Franzqesische Vorbilder Beeinflusst', Ph.D. dissertation, Muenchen University, 1935.

Bernardbehan, Brother Merrill, 'Anglo-Irish Literature', M.A. thesis, University of Montreal, 1939.

Berrow, J. H., 'A Study of the Background Treatment and Presentation of Irish Character in British Plays from the Late 19th Century to the Present Day', M.A. thesis, University of Wales, Swansea, 1966.

Butler, Henry J., 'The Abbey Theatre and the Principal Writers Connected Therewith' (Aug 1925), MS 2263: National Library of Ireland, Dublin.

Byars, John Arthur, 'The Heroic Type in the Irish Legendary Dramas of W. B. Yeats, Lady Gregory, and J. M. Synge: 1903–1910', Ph.D. dissertation, University of North Carolina, 1963.

Carden, Mary, 'The Few and the Many', Ph.D. dissertation, University College Dublin, 1967.

Carmody, Terence F., 'John Millington Synge: A Study of the Intruder in His Wicklow Plays', M.Litt. thesis, Trinity College Dublin, 1963.

Carr, Brigid, 'Native Symbolism of Synge', M.A. thesis, University College Dublin.

Christensen, V., 'The Women in Synge's Plays' [in Danish], M.A. thesis, University of Copenhagen, 1968.

Cole, A. S., 'Stagecraft in the Modern Dublin Theatre', Ph.D. dissertation, Trinity College Dublin, 1953.

Coleman, Sr. Anne G., 'Social and Political Satire in Irish Drama', Ph.D. dissertation, University of Fordham, 1954.

Colin-Merchier, Christiane, 'Tradition and Originality in J. M. Synge's Plays', Ph.D. dissertation, Université de Lille, 1970.

Cooper, Mabel, 'The Irish Theatre: Its History and Its Dramatists', M.A. thesis, University of Manitoba, 1931.

Cotter, Eileen Mary, 'The Deirdre Theme in Anglo-Irish Literature', Ph.D. dissertation, University of California at Los Angeles, 1966.

Devemy, Jacques, 'The Theme of Talk in Synge's Drama', Ph.D. dissertation, Université de Lille, 1968.

Doyle, Catherine, 'A Study of John M. Synge and His Relation to Irish Tradition and Character', M.A. thesis, Marquette University.

Estill, Adelaide Duncan, 'The Sources of Synge', Ph.D. dissertation, University of Pennsylvania, 1937 [published].

Flood, Jeanne Agnes, 'John Millington Synge: A Study of His Aesthetic Development', Ph.D. dissertation, University of Michigan, 1967.

Frenzel, Herbert, 'John Millington Synge's Work as Contribution to Irish Folklore and to the Psychology of Primitive Tribes', Ph.D. dissertation, University of Bonn, 1932 [published].

Frese, J. J., 'The Coalescence of Theme and Language in the Comedies of J. M. Synge', M.Litt. thesis, Trinity College Dublin, 1961.

Fulbeck, John Frederick, 'A Comparative Study of Poetic Elements in Selected Plays by John Millington Synge and by Frederico Carcia Lorca', Ph.D. dissertation, University of Southern California, 1960.

Greene, David Herbert, 'The Drama of J. M. Synge; A Critical Study', Ph.D. dissertation, Harvard University, 1944.

Harsch, J. H. H., 'The Curtain of Words', Ph.D. dissertation, University of Dublin, 1970.

Hart, William, 'The Dramatic Work of J. M. Synge', Ph.D. dissertation, University College Dublin, 1968.

Hausvater, Alexander, 'Universality and Irishness in Synge', M.A. thesis, Tel Aviv University.

Heflin, Jacqueline, 'The Poetry of Alienation: An Investigation of the Tramp as a Dramatic Symbol', M.A. thesis, University of Puerto Rico, 1971.

Heger, Sr. M. Rosanne, 'John Millington Synge: His Reception as a Dramatist', M.A. thesis, Marquette University.

Henderson, William A., 'The Irish National Theatre Movement', told in press cuttings, a collection in National Library of Ireland, Dublin, 1899 *et seq.*

Hillery, J., 'John Millington Synge: A Study of the Dramatic Structure of His Tragedies', M.Litt. dissertation, Trinity College Dublin, 1960.

Holloway, Joseph, 'Impressions of a Dublin Playgoer', MSS. at the National Library of Ireland, Dublin.

Holzapfel, R. P., 'A Survey of Irish Literary Periodicals from 1900 to the Present Day', M.Litt. thesis, Trinity College Dublin, 1963.

Hoskot, K. S., 'J. M. Synge, Man and Playwright', Ph.D. dissertation, K. C. College Bombay, 1966.

Jacquin, Bernard, 'Le Thème de l'amour dans le théâtre de Synge', Ph.D. dissertation, Université de Lille, 1964.

Jennings, M., 'John Millington Synge', M.A. thesis, Ohio Wesleyan University, 1969.

Kelson, John Hofstad, 'Nationalism in the Theater: The Ole Bull Theater in Norway and the Abbey Theater in Ireland: A Comparative Study', Ph.D. dissertation, University of Kansas, 1964.

Kilroy, James Francis, 'Dominant Themes and Ironic Techniques in the Works of J. M. Synge', Ph.D. dissertation, University of Wisconsin, 1965.

Kornelius, Joachim, 'Linguistisch-Stilistische Untersuchungen Zum Dramenwerk J. M. Synges', M.A. thesis, Justus Liebig University of Giessen, 1971.

Kostandi, F. M. G., 'A Reconsideration of H. A. Jones, Pinero, Wilde, Synge, with Special Reference to the Influence of Ibsen', Ph.D. dissertation, University of Manchester, 1964.

Krieger, Hans, 'John Millington Synge, ein dichter der "keltischen renaissance"', Ph.D. dissertation, Marburg University, 1916. [published]

Le Touze, Helene, 'Religion and Religious Satire in Synge, Bridie, and Dylan Thomas', Ph.D. dissertation, Université de Lille, 1970.

Lyman, Kenneth C., 'Critical Reaction to Irish Drama on the New York Stage, 1900–1958', Ph.D. dissertation, University of Wisconsin, 1960.

McGuire, James Brady, 'Realism in Irish Drama', Ph.D. dissertation, Trinity College Dublin, 1954.

McKinley, C. F., 'John Millington Synge', Ph.D. dissertation, Trinity College Dublin, 1951.

McLaughlin, Sr. Malachy, 'The Work of J. M. Synge', M.A. thesis, University of Cape Town, 1970.

Martin, Riley T., III, 'The Religious Thought of J. M. Synge', M.A. thesis, University of Puerto Rico, 1966.

Matthews, Arnold, 'A Study of Imaginative Speech in Modern Prose Drama', M.A. thesis, University of Leeds, 1959.

Miller, Marcia S. K., 'The Deirdre Legend in English Literature', Ph.D. dissertation, University of Pennsylvania, 1950.

Milligan, S. E., 'A Dramatic Conflict: Youth and Age in the Plays of J. M. Synge', M.A. thesis, University of Saskatchewan, Saskatoon, 1972.

Mooney, Mary G., 'A Local Habitation', M.A. thesis, University College Dublin, 1967.

Newlin, Nicholas, 'The Language of Synge's Plays; The Irish Element', Ph.D. dissertation, University of Pennsylvania, 1949.

Oliver, Carol H., 'The Art of J. M. Synge: A Developmental Study', Ph.D. dissertation, University of Illinois, 1971.

O'Neill, Michael J., 'The Diaries of a Dublin Playgoer as a Mirror of the Irish Literary Revival', Ph.D. dissertation, National University, Dublin, 1952.

Oppren, Genevieve L., 'The Irish Players in America', M.A. thesis, University of Washington, 1943.

Osborn, Margaret Elizabeth, 'The Concept of Imagination in Edwardian Drama', Ph.D. dissertation, Pennsylvania State University, 1967.

Paterson, Gary James, 'The Sense of Solitude – A Study of the Writings of J. M. Synge', M.A. thesis, Queen's University at Kingston, Ontario, 1971.

Peteler, Patricia M., 'The Social and Symbolic Drama of the English-Language Theatre, 1929–1949', Ph.D. dissertation, University of Utah, 1961.

Price, Alan F., 'The Art of John M. Synge', M.A. thesis, University of Liverpool, 1951.

Quillard, Genevieve, 'Synge's Characters and Nature', Ph.D. dissertation, Université de Lille, 1968.

Randall, Ethel Claire, 'The Celtic Movement: The Awakening of the Fires', M.A. thesis, University of Chicago, 1906.

Robinson, Paul N., 'Medieval Aspects in the Plays of John M. Synge', Ph.D. dissertation, University of Wisconsin, Madison, 1971.

Saddlemyer, E. A. [nn], 'A Study of the Dramatic Theory Developed by the Founders of the Irish Literary Theatre and the Attempt to Apply This Theory in the Abbey Theatre, with Particular Reference to the Achievement of the Major Figures during the First Two Decades of the Movement', Ph.D. dissertation, Bedford College London, 1961.

Smoot, Amelia Jean Johannessen, 'A Comparison of Plays by John Millington Synge and Frederico Garcia Lorca: The Poets and Time', Ph.D. dissertation, University of North Carolina, 1967.

Smyth, Dorothy Pearl, 'The Playwrights of the Irish Literary Renaissance', M.A. thesis, Acadia University, 1936.

Suss, Irving David, 'The Decline and Fall of Irish Drama', Ph.D. dissertation, Columbia University, 1951.

Turner, David Michael, 'Word Patterns in the Drama of J. M. Synge', M.A. thesis, University of Manitoba, 1967.

Walsh, M. W., 'The Lyric and Symbolic Strains of Yeats's and Synge's Work', Ph.D. dissertation, Trinity College Dublin, 1969.

Wickstrom, Gordon M., 'The Deirdre Plays of AE, Yeats, and Synge: Patterns of Irish Exile', Ph.D. dissertation, Stanford University, 1969.

Worth, Katharine J., 'Symbolism in Modern English Drama', Ph.D. dissertation, University of London, 1953.

(e) RECORDINGS

Riders to the Sea and In the Shadow of the Glen, Spoken Arts recording, 743. A Radio Eireann Players Production presented by Arthur Luce Klein (New Rochelle, N.Y.).

The Playboy of the Western World, Angel Recordings 35357 and 35358, with Siobhan McKenna and Cyril Cusack (Dublin, 1955).

The Playboy of the Western World has been recorded on two 33 rpm discs, Columbia ccx4 and 5, with Cyril Cusack as Christy and Siobhan McKenna as Pegeen.

'The Songs of Aran' has been recorded by S. R. Cowell, Monograph Series, Folkways Ethnic Library (New York).

(f) BACKGROUND

Arensberg, Conrad, *The Irish Countryman; An Anthropological Study* (New York: Peter Smith, 1950).

Hedderman, B. N., *Glimpses of My Life in Aran* (Bristol, 1917).

Inglis, Brian, *The Story of Ireland* (London: Faber & Faber, 1956).

Kent, Kay, 'Inishmaan (1898) Revisited', *Ireland of the Welcomes*, XIX, no. 6 (Dublin, Mar–Apr 1971) 28–30.

O'Brien, J. A. (ed.), *The Vanishing Irish; The Enigma of the Modern World* (London: W. H. Allen, 1954).

Ó Crohan, Tomás, *The Islandman*, translated from the Irish by Robin Flower (Dublin & Cork: The Talbot Press; London: Chatto & Windus, 1937; Penguin Books, 1943; Oxford: Clarendon Press, 1951). [a vivid impression of life on the Blasket Islands, roughly contemporary with Synge's visit to Aran].

O'Síocháin, P. A., *Aran: Islands of Legend* (Dublin: Foilsiúchain Éireann; N.Y.: Devin-Adair, 1962). [Detailed account of the geography and history of the Aran Islands; several chapters discuss Synge's visit to the islands].

O'Sullivan, Maurice, *Twenty Years A-Growing*, rendered from the original Irish by Moya Llewelyn Davies and George Thomson (Harmondsworth, Middx.: Penguin Books, 1938).

Somerville, Oenone and Martin Ross, *Further Experiences of an Irish R.M.* (London: Longmans, 1908).

Somerville, Oenone and Martin Ross, *Experiences of an Irish R.M.*, Everyman's Library No. 978 (London: J. M. Dent; New York: E. P. Dutton, 1944).

Tracy, Honor, *Mind You, I've Said Nothing! Forays in the Irish Republic* (London: Methuen, 1953).

Warren, Maude Radford, 'The Aran Islands', *Harper's Monthly Magazine*, CXX, no. 720 (May 1910) 887–99.

White, T. H., *The Godstone and the Blackymor* (London: Jonathan Cape, 1959). [Much of this is set in the country which we may suppose to be the scene of *The Playboy of the Western World*].

Index of Works

Index of Authors

A., J.E., 126. 151
A., L.F., 109, 117
A., M., 69
A., W., 118, 146
Abood, Edward F., 191
Adams, J. Donald, 69
Adelman, Irving, 1
A.E. (George Russell), 41
Agate, James, 15, 131, 171
Alcalay, Esther, 73
Alexander, Jean, 15
Allen, Beverly S., 69
Allen, Ralph G., 31
Allison, Alexander, 15
Allt, G.D.P., 191
Alspach, R.K., 69
Altenbernd, Lynn, 15
Altick, Richard D., 22
Anderson, P., 12
Andrews, Charlton, 16
Angus, W., 12
Archer, William, 16, 69, 112, 120, 127, 150, 188
Arensberg, Conrad, 199
Arms, George, 42
Armstrong, W.A., 16
Arnold, Sidney, 69–70
Atkinson, Brooks, 115, 116, 124, 130, 132, 171, 172, 173, 174, 178, 184, 190
Atkinson, F.M., 70
Auberg, Arild, 191
Aufhauser, Annemarie, 16, 191
Aughtry, Charles Edward, 16

Avis, 139
Ayling, Ronald, 50, 70, 93

B., E.A., 123, 169, 170
B., E.W., 170
B., M.P., 140
Babler, O.F., 1, 70
Baker, Blanch M., 1
Ball, John, 16
Barber, John, 177
Barker, Felix, 116, 179, 182, 185
Barnes, Howard, 175
Barnes, John R., 16
Barnes, T.R., 70
Barnet, Sylvan, 16
Barnett, Pat, 70
Bateman, Reginald, 17
Bates, M.E., 3
Bateson, F.W., 1
Baughan, E.A., 70, 145, 183
Bauman, Richard, 70
Beach, Joseph Warren, 17
Beaty, John O., 37
Beckerman, Bernard, 17
Beeching, H.C., 47
Beerbohm, Max, 17, 109, 112, 118, 120
Bellinger, Martha Fletcher, 17
Benet, William Rose, 17
Benjamin, M.W., 158
Bennet, C.R., 17
Bennett, Charles A., 70
Bennett, James O'Donnell, 112, 122, 147, 148, 164

202

Index of Authors

Index of Authors

Harrison, Austin, 84, 112, 120, 127, 150
Harsch, J.H.H., 193
Hart, Francis R., 34
Hart, William E., 12, 23, 34, 84, 193
Hartnoll, Phyllis, 28
Hatcher, Harlan, 34
Hatton, Frederic, 115, 129, 164, 166
Hausvater, Alexander, 193
Havighurst, Walter, 34
Hawkes, Terence, 84
Hawkins, William, 175
Haycraft, Howard, 41
Hayes, Richard, 178
Hedderman, B.N., 199
Heflin, Jacqueline, 193
Heger, Sr. M. Rosanne, 193
Heilman, Robert B., 20, 34
Henderson, W.A., 34, 84, 193
Hengist, Philip, 58
Henn, T.R., 11, 12, 34-5, 84
Henry, P.L., 84
Hensel, Georg, 35
Hewes, Henry, 183
Hewitt, John, 33
Hillebrand, Harold Newcomb, 35
Hillery, J., 193
Hind, C. Lewis, 35
Hinkson, Katherine Tynan, 35
Hoare, Dorothy Mackenzie, 35
Hoare, John Edward, 84
Hobson, Harold, 116, 132, 177, 179, 182, 185
Hodgson, Geraldine E., 10
Hogan, J.J., 57
Hogan, Robert, 36
Holloway, Joseph, 36, 84, 167, 194
Holt, Edgar, 180
Holzapfel, R.P., 194
Hone, Joseph, 15, 84-5
Hope-Wallace, Philip, 115, 132

Hornimann, E.E.F., 144
Hornstein, Lillian Herlands, 36
Hortmann, Wilhelm, 36
Hoskot, K.S., 194
Houghton, C.H., 83
Howarth, Herbert, 36
Howe, P.P., 36-7, 85
Hubbell, Jay B., 37
Hudson, Lynton, 37
Hughes, Herbert, 11, 85
Hughes, Leo, 37
Huneker, James, 37
Hurtik, Emil, 31
Huscher, Herbert, 53

Ide, S., 85
Inglis, Brian, 199
Inglis, Rewey Belle, 37
Inkster, Leonard, 154
Irish Playgoer, An, 104

J., M., 152
J., P. (John Palmer), 86, 142, 154, 155
Jackson, Holbrook, 9, 38
Jacobs, Willis D., 86
Jacques, 133, 148
Jacquin, Bernard, 194
Jacquot, Jean, 38
James, Thelma G., 38
Jameson, Storm, 38
Jeffares, A. Norman, 20, 57
Jennings, M., 194
Jingle, 147
Jochum, K.P.S., 86
Johns, Eric, 182
Johnson, Wallace H., 87
Johnston, Denis, 38
Jordan, John, 38
Joyce, James, 38

K., 178
K., T.M., 108
Kain, Richard M., 39, 87

207

Index of Authors

Peake, Dorothy Margaret, 6
Pearce, Howard D., 96
Peattie, Elia W., 11, 96
Pellizzi, Camillo, 52
Perry, Henry Ten Eyck, 52
Peteler, Patricia M., 196
Phelan, Kappo, 175
Phelps, William Lyon, 52, 96
Pierce, Lorne, 17
Pinto, Vivian de Sola, 52
Pittock, Malcolm, 96
Pittwood, Ernest H., 11, 17, 96-7
Plunkett, Grace, 52
Pocock, P. J., 11, 52
Podhoretz, Norman, 97
Point, Jack, 115, 148
Pollard, M., 6
Pope, T. Michael, 97
Popkin, Henry, 52
Portyanskaya, N. A., 97
Power, Ambrose, 139
Power, Patrick C., 52
Pressey, Benfield, 64
Price, Alan, 6, 11, 12, 52, 53, 97, 196
Pritchett, V. S., 53, 54, 97
Prior, Moody E., 53
Purser, Philip, 180

Quillard, Genevieve, 196
Quine, Sean, 141
Quinn, Edward, 40
Quinn, John, 97
Quinn, Owen, 97

R., 97
R., G., 173
R., T. B., 152
R.-S., N. G., 169
Rabuse, Georg, 97
Rahilly, Sean O'Mahony, 98
Rajan, Balchandra, 98
Randall, Ethel Claire, 196
Rathbun, Stephen, 131

Ray, R. J., 152
Reade, Arthur Robert, 53
Redfern, James, 131
Reeves, Geoffrey, 58
Reeves, John A., 30
Reid, Alec, 98
Reid, Benjamin L., 53
Reinert, Otto, 53
Reiter, Seymour, 32
Renwick, W. L., 98
Reynolds, Ernest, 54
Reynolds, Lorna, 98
Rhodes, Raymond Crompton, 98
Rhys, Ernest, 53
Richards, Dick, 181
Richardson, Kenneth, 25
Richardson, Maurice, 180
Rickert, Edith, 47
Rischbieter, Henning, 46
Riva, S., 53
Rivoallan, Anatole, 53, 98
Roberts, George, 98
Roberts, Peter, 182
Robertson, A. R., 35
Robinson, Lennox, 50, 54, 98
Robinson, Norman L., 98
Robinson, Paul N., 196
Robinson, Robert, 179
Rodger, Ian, 181
Rodgers, W. R., 35, 54
Rolleston, Thomas William, 19
Rollins, Ronald G., 98-9
Ronsley, Joseph, 54
Roosevelt, Theodore, 57
Rosenberg, James L., 24
Ross, George, 131
Ross, Martin, 199
Rowe, Kenneth Thorpe, 54
Roy, Emil, 18, 54
Roy, James A., 11, 37, 99
Ruberti, Guido, 55
Rubinstein, H. F., 55
Ruhl, Arthur A., 164
Rust, Adolph, 55

211

Index of Authors